NO OFFENCE INTENDED
WHY 18C IS WRONG

JOSHUA FORRESTER

LORRAINE FINLAY

AUGUSTO ZIMMERMANN

Published in 2016 by Connor Court Publishing Pty Ltd

Copyright © Joshua Forrester, Lorraine Finlay and Augusto Zimmermann

All rights reserved. No part of this book may be reproduced or transmitted in any form or by any means, electronic or mechanical, including photocopying, recording or by any information storage and retrieval system, without prior permission in writing from the publisher.

Connor Court Publishing Pty Ltd.
PO Box 7257
Redland Bay QLD 4165
sales@connorcourt.com
www.connorcourt.com
Phone 0497 900 685

ISBN: 978-1-925138-98-6

Front and back cover photos: istockphoto

Cover design, Maria Giordano

Printed in Australia

Notes on Format

1. Readers without a legal background will note that we follow the surnames of judges with "J", "CJ" or "P". These abbreviations refer to the title of the judge. Hence, "J" means "Justice", for example "McHugh J" is read as "Justice McHugh"; "CJ" means "Chief Justice", for example "Mason CJ" is read as "Chief Justice Mason"; and "P" means "President", for example "Allsop P" is read as "President Allsop".
2. Where we refer to other parts of this book, we give the part and section number followed by the page number in brackets. For example, Part IV.E.2 (page 52) refers to page 52 and Part IV.E.2 of this book.
3. Some references have hyperlinks. The hyperlinks are not found in the footnotes, but can be found in the corresponding reference in the bibliography.

CONTENTS

I	INTRODUCTION	7
II	THE AUTHORS' POSITION	13
III	A PRELIMINARY QUESTION OF INTERPRETATION	15
IV	THE EXTERNAL AFFAIRS POWER	23
V	THE IMPLIED FREEDOM OF POLITICAL COMMUNICATION	117
VI	A PROPOSAL FOR LEGISLATIVE REFORM	213
VII	CONCLUSION	241
	BIBLIOGRAPHY	243
	INDEX	259

I

INTRODUCTION

For who knows not that Truth is strong next to the Almighty; she needs no policies, nor stratagems, nor licencings to make her victorious, those are the shifts and the defences that error uses against her power...[1]

From its inception, s 18C of the *Racial Discrimination Act 1975* (Cth) ('RDA')[2] has been controversial. Before the 2013 federal election, the Liberal Party (then in opposition) promised to repeal s 18C. However, in August 2014, then Prime Minister Tony Abbott announced that the Liberal Party (now in government) would not be proceeding with the repeal.[3]

As its title suggests, our book is a treatise about why s 18C is wrong. We mean "wrong" in two senses. The first sense we mean is "wrong in law". Hence, this treatise examines the constitutional validity of s 18C. Because of this, we have written this treatise primarily for an audience with a legal background. (That said, we hope that we have written it in a way that the informed reader without such a background will enjoy reading it.) The second sense we mean is that s 18C is "wrong philosophically", being contrary to Australia's common law legal tradition and liberal democratic heritage. We will touch on these issues

---
1 John Milton, *Areopagitica* (The Legal Classics Library, 1992) 169-70.
2 Subsequent references to s 18C of the RDA will be to just 's 18C' or 'section 18C' as the case requires.
3 Tony Abbott, George Brandis and Julie Bishop, 'Joint Press Conference' (Press Statement, 5 August 2014). See also Jared Owens 'Tony Abbott Dumps Planned Changes to Section 18C of Racial Discrimination Act', *The Australian* (online), 5 August 2014; Emma Griffiths, 'Government Backtracks on Racial Discrimination Act 18C Changes; Pushes Ahead with Tough Security Laws', *ABC News* (online), 6 August 2014.

during the course of our legal analysis.

As to s 18C's constitutional validity, we find s 18C unconstitutional on two grounds. First, s 18C is not supported by the external affairs power of the *Commonwealth Constitution*. Second, s 18C impermissibly infringes the freedom of communication about government and political matters implied from the *Commonwealth Constitution*.

We also argue that the Commonwealth Parliament should enact legislation making incitement to violence based on race, colour, national or ethnic origin a crime. Specifically, we argue that s 18C should be replaced with legislation modeled on clause 28 of the Racial Discrimination Bill 1974 (Cth) ('RDB').[4] Clause 28 better reflects the spirit and letter of the Convention on the Elimination of All Forms of Racial Discrimination ('the Convention'). Further, legislation modeled on cl 28 would not impermissibly impinge the implied freedom of political communication.

Our treatise is split into the following parts: in Part II we state our position regarding the importance of combating racism. We believe that racist speech not advocating racial enmity or racial violence is better fought by civil society using freedoms of expression and association than by state restrictions on speech.

In Part III, we address some important preliminary issues when interpreting s 18C. In particular, we consider whether the High Court of Australia would interpret terms found in s 18C, namely 'offence', 'insult', 'humiliation' and 'intimidation' broadly or narrowly. We conclude that these terms would likely be interpreted narrowly. However, we also conclude that, if these terms were interpreted broadly, then our arguments in Parts IV and V would apply with greater force.

In Part IV, we find that s 18C is not supported by s 51(xxix) of the *Commonwealth Constitution*, known as the external affairs power.[5] The key issue is whether s 18C validly translates Australia's obligations under the Convention into domestic legislation. To validly translate the Convention, s 18C must meet certain requirements, including what are called the specificity and conformity requirements. We find that there are significant issues concerning whether s 18C has met these requirements.

Under the specificity requirement, treaty provisions must impose reasonably

---

4 Subsequent references to cl 28 of the RDB will be to just 'cl 28' or 'clause 28' as the case requires.
5 We will refer to s 51(xxix) of the *Commonwealth Constitution* as the 'external affairs power' from this point onwards.

specific legal obligations on Australia. Treaty provisions containing overly vague language do not meet the specificity requirement. Articles 2, 4 and 6 of the Convention[6] impose reasonably specific obligations on Australia to enact legislation. However, the primarily aspirational nature of Article 7 does not, and therefore fails to meet the specificity requirement.

Under the conformity requirement, Commonwealth legislation must be reasonably capable of being considered appropriate and adapted to implementing the relevant treaty provision. We find that s 18C is not reasonably capable of being considered appropriate and adapted to implementing the Convention. This is because s 18C's prohibition of offensive, insulting and humiliating acts greatly overreaches the obligations under Article 4, and fails to balance freedom of expression, which is expressly guaranteed under Article 5. Further, the more general obligations under Articles 2, 6 and 7 do not provide the necessary support for s 18C. Finally, we find that the exemptions under s 18D of the RDA do not redress the overreach of s 18C's terms. In addition, we find that Article 20(2) of the International Covenant on Civil and Political Rights ('ICCPR') does not support s 18C. As with the Convention, s 18C overreaches the obligations under Article 20(2) of the ICCPR.

In Part V, we find that s 18C impermissibly infringes the freedom of communication about government and political matters implied from the *Commonwealth Constitution*.[7] In finding this, we apply the test that the High Court developed in *Lange v Australian Broadcasting Corporation*,[8] as modified by *Coleman v Power*,[9] *Unions NSW v New South Wales*[10] and *McCloy v New South Wales*.[11] In this treatise, we refer to the *Lange* test as modified by *Coleman*, *Unions NSW* and *McCloy* as 'the modified *Lange* test'.

We find that s 18C is fundamentally incompatible with Australia's system of representative and responsible government. Section 18C fails every stage of the modified *Lange* test. Section 18C burdens the implied freedom of political

---

6 Please note that, in this treatise, when we refer to an Article by itself we mean 'an Article of the Convention'. For example, a reference to Article 4 should be taken to mean 'Article 4 of the Convention'. We refer to articles of other treaties in this treatise. However, when we do this, we will refer to the relevant treaty, for example 'Article 20(2) of the ICCPR'.
7 We will refer to the 'freedom of communication about government and political matters implied from the *Commonwealth Constitution*' as the 'implied freedom of political communication' from this point onwards.
8 [1997] HCA 25; (1997) 189 CLR 520 ('*Lange*').
9 [2004] HCA 25; (2004) 220 CLR 1 ('*Coleman*').
10 [2013] HCA 58; (2013) 252 CLR 530 ('*Unions NSW*').
11 [2015] HCA 34 ('*McCloy*').

communication as it affects speech that Australian electors would employ to discuss Commonwealth and State legislative and executive actions.

Further, s 18C does not serve a legitimate end per the modified *Lange* test. Prohibiting offence is not an end compatible with the constitutionally prescribed system of representative and responsible government. This is so even if the prohibition is aimed at eliminating racial hatred, promoting racial tolerance, or a similar purpose. This is because Australians, who under the *Commonwealth Constitution* are the people in which sovereignty ultimately resides and from whom Australian Parliaments derive their authority, must be able to fully, frankly and robustly discuss controversial government and political matters, including those involving race, colour, ethnicity or nationality. Such discussion may involve employing language that some (or even most) find offensive, insulting or even humiliating.

Finally, we find that s 18C is not reasonably capable of being appropriate and adapted to serve a legitimate end (however conceived) in a manner compatible with a constitutionally prescribed system of representative and responsible government per the modified *Lange* test. This is because:

1. Section 18C imposes a direct, sweeping and heavy burden on the implied freedom of political communication. Hence, any impingement on such speech is difficult to justify, and is not justified in the case of s 18C.
2. Section 18C employs definitions of race and ethnicity that are broad, covering not only biology but also the religion, culture and history of certain groups. It is not appropriate to prohibit language that offends, insults or humiliates when discussing these matters. This is because ideas about religion, culture and history influence politics and government, and therefore must be open to robust public scrutiny. Further, nationality concerns ideas about the history and identity of a people and must be open to the same kind of critique. Finally, race itself is a contested concept, and attempts to define race by government bodies must be open to robust public scrutiny.
3. Many terms used in s 18C and s 18D of the RDA[12] are not defined in the legislation itself, and their scope is uncertain despite having been judicially considered. Hence, ss 18C and 18D are too vague,

---

12 Subsequent references to s 18D of the RDA will be to just 's 18D' or 'section 18D' as the case requires.

especially given the ease by which someone can breach s 18C (all they need to do is speak in public) and that these sections restrict a fundamental freedom (freedom of expression).
4. A breach of s 18C does not require anyone to be actually offended, insulted or humiliated. All that is required is that an act be 'reasonably likely' to offend, insult or humiliate.
5. Truth is not a defence. This impedes the ability to robustly discuss government and political matters, and holding people, policies and ideas to account.
6. Section 18C is a more sweeping intrusion into the implied freedom of political communication than the defamation law considered in *Lange*. Further, the exemptions provided in s 18D are more limited in scope than the defamation defences considered in *Lange*.
7. There are other, reasonably practical means to achieve s 18C's purpose that are less restrictive of the implied freedom of political communication.

Ultimately, we find that s 18C is too broad and too vague to be constitutional.

In Part VI, we argue in favour of legislation modeled on cl 28. Such legislation would better reflect the Convention. Further, it would not impermissibly infringe the implied freedom of political communication. In a representative democracy, the best solution for speech that offends, insults or humiliates is not court-ordered silence but more speech. However, there should be a remedy in extreme cases, such as inciting enmity or violence on the basis of race, ethnicity, colour or nationality. In addition, we explore other means by which racism can be combatted, including enforcing existing laws and more specific targeting of legislative and executive action.

As a final matter, we should note that in this treatise we also explore concepts that are not necessary to finding s 18C unconstitutional, but which may assist in the analysis. These concepts (and the pages on which they are found, in case interested readers wish to go straight to them) are:

1. The body/idea distinction (found on page 136);
2. The realm of freedom (found on page 152); and
3. The implied equality of political communication (found on page 163).

We hope this treatise assists with defending freedom of expression: a fundamental freedom critical to (amongst many things) human dignity and representative and responsible government.

II

THE AUTHORS' POSITION

Given racism is a sensitive subject, we must make our views clear.

We believe racism must be combatted. Further, we think that, save for Part IIA of the RDA,[13] the RDA is constitutional and provides important protections to Australians. No Australian should be denied work, education, accommodation or goods or services because of their race, colour, ethnicity or national origin; nor should anyone be harassed on these grounds in their work or education, or when obtaining accommodation, goods or services.

However, we have serious concerns about the constitutional validity of Part IIA generally, and s 18C in particular. Our opinion is that the Convention does not support s 18C, and that s 18C impermissibly infringes the implied freedom of political communication.

The fact that we believe in protecting freedom of expression does *not* mean that we endorse all that is expressed, or that we tolerate racism. People have used, and will continue to use, freedom of expression to say things we find outrageous. However, we also believe that a fundamental freedom like freedom of expression should not be compromised because some will use it in ways that others don't like. More is required to justify restrictions on freedom of expression. Our view is that, save for limited exceptions, the best cure for speech that offends, insults or humiliates is not court order but more speech.[14]

Australia, as a nation with a common law legal tradition, does not need s 18C. By using the common law freedoms of speech and association, Australians can effectively counter speech that offends, insults or humiliates, or respond on behalf of those who cannot do so themselves. Using these means increases the strength and vitality of Australian civil society. The recent record of Australia's civil society in fighting racism, while not perfect, should be a source

---

13 Subsequent reference to Part IIA of the RDA will be to just 'Part IIA'.
14 We are recalling Brandeis J's comments in *Whitney v California* 274 US 357, 377 (Brandeis J, Holmes J concurring) (1927) ('*Whitney*').

of confidence in its ability to fight racism without state intervention.

However, s 18C substantially fetters the ability of Australians to discuss political matters. Its operation is far more sweeping than other protective legislation. It treats Australians as unequal in its terms if not in its effect. It is state intervention that ultimately enervates civil society.

In our view, Part IIA must be replaced with legislation that is more narrowly focused, and better reflects Australia's obligations under the Convention.

Please note that our book is concerned with state-imposed limitations on freedom of expression. This book is not concerned with private limitations on freedom of expression, such as contractual prohibitions on offensive language that may be found in contracts of employment, the ability of property owners to eject people behaving inappropriately, rules prohibiting racism adopted by organisations, and the like. We think that people should be able to agree to such prohibitions privately.[15] However, there is a material difference between privately agreed prohibitions on the one hand, and compulsion by the state on the other.

---

15 We would note, however, that there is something to be said for the principle that individuals should respect the right of others to hold opinions, even ones that many individuals would find repugnant. There is great merit in Mill's observation that his 'harm principle' should guide not only state action, but those in society: see J S Mill, *On Liberty* (Penguin Classics, first published 1859, 1985 ed) 68-74. That said, it is up to the individual to decide what is best for them in matters concerning their contracts and property.

III

A PRELIMINARY QUESTION OF INTERPRETATION

In this Part, we examine whether the High Court would interpret certain terms found in s 18C broadly or narrowly. We conclude that the terms 'offence', 'insult', 'humiliation' and 'intimidation' are likely to be given a narrow interpretation. Those who are more interested in getting to grips with our main arguments may skip this Part and go to Parts IV and V. However, if this is done, then please note that should 'offence', 'insult', 'humiliation' and 'intimidation' be interpreted broadly then our arguments in Parts IV and V have greater force.

A The text of s 18C and s 18D

Before considering the constitutional validity of s 18C it is useful to set out both s 18C and s 18D in full. These sections read as follows:

18C Offensive behaviour because of race, colour or national or ethnic origin

(1) It is unlawful for a person to do an act, otherwise than in private, if:
   (a) the act is reasonably likely, in all the circumstances, to offend, insult, humiliate or intimidate another person or a group of people; and
   (b) the act is done because of the race, colour or national or ethnic origin of the other person or of some or all of the people in the group.
(2) For the purposes of subsection (1), an act is taken not to be done in private if it:
   (a) causes words, sounds, images or writing to be communicated to the public; or
   (b) is done in a public place; or

(c) is done in the sight or hearing of people who are in a public place.

(3) In this section:

public place includes any place to which the pubic have access as of right or by invitation, whether express or implied and whether or not a charge is made for admission to the place.

18D Exemptions

Section 18C does not render unlawful anything said or done reasonably and in good faith:

(a) In the performance, exhibition or distribution or an artistic work; or

(b) In the course of any statement publication, discussion or debate made or held for any genuine academic, artistic or scientific purpose or any other genuine purpose in the public interest; or

(c) In making or publishing:

(i) A fair and accurate report or any event or matter of public interest; or

(ii) A fair comment on any event or matter of public interest if the comment is an expression of a genuine belief held by the person making the comment.

B Interpreting the terms of s 18C

A preliminary question informing any constitutional analysis of s 18C is this: how broadly should terms 'offence', 'insult', 'humiliation' and 'intimidation' be interpreted?[16] To answer this, we will first examine how case law has interpreted s 18C. We will then examine s 18C's text and purpose, applying the principles of statutory interpretation. On balance, it appears that principles of statutory

---

16 Commentators have noted the incongruity between s 18C's intended purpose and its actual wording: see, for example, Augusto Zimmermann and Lorraine Finlay, 'A Forgotten Freedom: Protecting Freedom of Speech in an Age of Political Correctness' (2014) 14 *Macquarie Law Journal* 185, 193; Dilan Thampapillai, 'Inconsistent at Best?: An Analysis of Australia's Federal Racial Vilification Laws' (2010) 1 *Canberra Law Review* 1, 4; Dilan Thampapillai, 'Managing Dissent under Part IIA of the *Racial Discrimination Act*' (2010) 17(1) *Murdoch University Electronic Journal of Law* 52, 56; Dan Meagher, 'So Far So Good?: A Critical Evaluation of Racial Vilification Laws in Australia' (2004) 32(2) *Federal Law Review* 225, 231. No definition of 'offend', 'insult' or 'humiliate' is provided in the RDA: see the discussion in Part III.B.2.(b) (page 19). Attempts to define words such as 'offend' and 'insult' with any degree of precision 'becomes a circular and question-begging exercise': Dan Meagher, 'So Far So Good?: A Critical Evaluation of Racial Vilification Laws in Australia' (2004) 32(2) *Federal Law Review* 225. The use of 'offend' and 'insult' in particular have been said to be 'so open-ended as to make any practical assessment by judges and administrators as to when conduct crosses this harm threshold little more than an intuitive and necessarily subjective value judgment': ibid 231.

interpretation favour interpreting s 18C narrowly: that is, it is confined to serious, severe or extreme instances of offence, insult, humiliation or intimidation.

Ultimately, our analysis of whether s 18C is constitutional proceeds on this narrow interpretation. This is because, should the High Court interpret s 18C's terms broadly, then our arguments concerning the narrow interpretation apply with even greater force to a broad interpretation.

1   *Case law*

Case law differs concerning how broadly 'offence', 'insult', 'humiliation' and 'intimidation' is interpreted. A number of cases have interpreted these terms very narrowly, requiring that the act that offends, insults, humiliates or intimidates evidence hatred to breach s 18C.[17] If s 18C required that the relevant act evidence 'racial hatred' then s 18C's conformity to, for example, Article 4 would be much easier to establish.

However other, more authoritative cases have not limited s 18C to acts evidencing hatred. In *Creek v Cairns Post Pty Ltd*,[18] Kiefel J stated that: 'To *"offend, insult, humiliate or intimidate"* are profound and serious effects, not to be likened to mere slights'.[19] French J in *Bropho v Human Rights and Equal Opportunity Commission* endorsed this view.[20] While not requiring racial hatred, these cases nevertheless appear to use a narrow interpretation.

Other cases, however, appear to use a much broader interpretation. In *Jones v Scully*,[21] Hely J appeared to endorse Kiefel J's approach in *Creek*, but then went on to state that '[i]n the absence of any statutory definition of the words, it is appropriate that the words be given their ordinary English meanings.'[22] In *Jones v Toben*,[23] Branson J also endorsed Kiefel J's approach in *Creek*, but went on to state:

> I do not understand her Honour to have intended... that a gloss should be placed on the ordinary meaning of the words that Parliament chose to include in s 18C of the RDA. Rather, I understand her Honour to have

---

17 See, for example, *Bryant v Queensland Newspapers Pty Ltd* [1997] HREOCA 23; *Combined Housing Organisation Limited v Hanson* [1997] HREOCA 58; *Shron v Telstra Corporation* [1998] HREOCA 24; *De La Mare v Special Broadcasting Service* [1998] HREOCA 26. See also Luke McNamara, *Regulating Racism: Racial Vilification Laws in Australia* (Sydney Institute of Criminology, 2002) 82.
18 [2001] FCA 1007; (2001) 112 FCR 352 ('*Creek*').
19 *Creek* [2001] FCA 1007; (2001) 112 FCR 352, 356 [16] (Kiefel J).
20 [2004] FCAFC 16; (2004) 135 FCR 105, 124 [69]-[70] (French J) ('*Bropho*').
21 *Jones v Scully* [2002] FCA 1080; (2002) 120 FCR 243 ('*Scully*').
22 *Scully* [2002] FCA 1080; (2002) 120 FCR 243, 269 [102] (Hely J).
23 [2002] FCA 1150; (2002) 71 ALD 629.

found in the context provided by s 18C of the RDA a legislative intent to render unlawful only acts which fall squarely within the terms of the section and not to reach to *'mere slights'* in the sense of acts which, for example, are reasonably likely to cause technical, but not real, offence or insult (see also *Jones v Scully* per Hely J at [102]). It would be wrong, in my view, to place a gloss on the words used in s 18C of the RDA.[24]

In *Toben v Jones*,[25] Carr J appeared to endorse a broader view:

> ...In my view, the Convention can be seen to be directed not only at acts of racial discrimination and hatred, but also to deterring public expressions of offensive racial prejudice which might lead to acts of racial hatred and discrimination.
>
> In my opinion it is clearly consistent with the provisions of the Convention and the [ICCPR] that a State Party should legislate to 'nip in the bud' the doing of offensive, insulting, humiliating or intimidating public acts which are done because of race, colour or national or ethnic origin before such acts can grow into incitement or promotion of racial hatred or discrimination...[26]

Justice Carr's comments concerned whether the Convention confined legislation based on it to racial hatred. However, his comments are relevant to the scope of s 18C. That is, 'nipping [racial hatred] in the bud'[27] suggests a broad approach to s 18C.

2   Section 18C's text and purpose

Were s 18C's constitutional validity challenged in the High Court, the cases we have noted would be persuasive but not binding. Ultimately, it would be for the High Court to interpret s 18C using ordinary principles of statutory interpretation. On balance, these principles suggest that the terms 'offence', 'insult', 'humiliation' or 'intimidation' should be interpreted narrowly.

(a)   Relevant principles of statutory interpretation

While ascertaining a statute's purpose is important, the starting point is the

---

24 *Jones v Toben* [2002] FCA 1150; (2002) 71 ALD 629, 651-2 [92] (Branson J).
25 [2003] FCAFC 137; (2003) 129 FCR 505 ('*Toben*').
26 *Toben* [2003] FCAFC 137; (2003) 129 FCR 505, 524-5 [19]-[20] (Carr J).
27 Ibid.

statute itself and the statutory context in which the provision is found.²⁸ In *Saeed v Minister for Immigration & Citizenship*,²⁹ members of the High Court noted that:

> Statements as to legislative intention made in explanatory memoranda or by Ministers, however clear or emphatic, cannot overcome the need to carefully consider the words of the statute to ascertain its meaning.³⁰

(b)   Relevant terms

We will start with the conduct that s 18C makes unlawful, namely acts that are reasonably likely in all the circumstances to 'offend, insult, humiliate or intimidate'.³¹ The *Macquarie Dictionary*³² defines 'offend' as, relevantly:

> 1. to irritate in mind or feeling; cause resentful displeasure in. 2 to affect (the sense, taste, etc.) disagreeably... 5. to give offence or cause displeasure.³³

It defines 'insult' as, relevantly:

> 1. to treat insolently or with contemptuous rudeness; affront. 2. an insolent or contemptuously rude action or speech; affront. 3. something having the effect of an affront.³⁴

And 'humiliate' as:

> To lower the pride or self respect of; cause a painful loss of dignity to; mortify.³⁵

The *Macquarie Dictionary* defines 'intimidate' as:

> 1. to make timid, or inspire with fear; overawe; cow.
>
> 2. to force into or deter from some action by inducing fear: *to intimidate a voter*.³⁶

---

28 *Project Blue Sky Inc v Australian Broadcasting Authority* [1998] HCA 28; (1998) 194 CLR 355, 381 [69] (McHugh, Gummow, Kirby and Hayne JJ) ('*Project Blue Sky*').
29 [2010] HCA 23; (2010) 241 CLR 252 ('*Saeed*').
30 *Saeed* [2010] HCA 23; (2010) 241 CLR 252, 264-5 [31] (French CJ, Gummow, Hayne, Crennan and Kiefel JJ).
31 RDA s 18C(1).
32 Susan Butler (ed), *Macquarie Concise Dictionary* (Macquarie Dictionary Publishers, 6ᵗʰ ed, 2013) ('*Macquarie Dictionary*').
33 *Macquarie Dictionary* 1020.
34 Ibid 769.
35 Ibid 725.
36 Ibid 777 (emphasis in original).

We will separately consider the constitutional validity of s 18C making unlawful acts that intimidate.[37] Our principal focus in this treatise is on acts that offend, insult or humiliate. However, before going further, we need to explain why we have included in our analysis acts that humiliate along with acts that offend or insult.

Acts that humiliate appear to be more serious that acts that offend or insult. Following the definition given above, humiliation may involve mortification, a painful loss of dignity, or a lowering of self-respect or pride. Conceptually, humiliation may involve serious harm to a person who is subjected to acts that degrade or dehumanise them.

However, humiliation may fall well short of degradation or dehumanisation. In government or political matters, people commonly "stake their pride" in an idea, issue, cause, or position in which they believe. They may not like having their beliefs challenged, let alone mocked or shown to be problematic or false. Further, if the challenge succeeds in demonstrating a belief risible or wrong, then the person holding that belief may well feel humiliated. Hence, it is not uncommon for humiliation, even serious humiliation, to result from contentious discussion about government or political matters. However, it is a type of humiliation that s 18C appears to cover, given that serious humiliation can result from contentious discussion about government or political matters concerning race, colour, ethnicity or nationality. It is this aspect of humiliation to which we refer when we mention humiliation below.

(c) The width of the relevant terms

Given the text and purpose of the RDA, there is no cause for confining s 18C to profound or serious instances of offence, insult or humiliation. There is no ambiguity concerning the ordinary meaning of these terms.

Section 18C is contained within Part IIA which is entitled 'Prohibition of offensive behaviour based on racial hatred'. No further qualification is given to 'offensive behaviour' other than it be based on racial hatred. That is, it appears that relatively minor offensive acts are covered if they are based on racial hatred. Put another way, 'racial hatred' does not qualify 'offence' in the sense of prohibiting only serious instances of offensive conduct.

Under s 15AA of the *Acts Interpretation Act 1901* (Cth),[38] statutes should

---

37 See Part IV.J (page 115) and Part V.E (page 211).
38 The Act ordinarily governing the interpretation of Commonwealth statutes, including the RDA.

be interpreted to best achieve the purpose or object of the statute, whether or not that purpose is expressly stated in the statute.[39] Extrinsic material like explanatory memoranda[40] and second reading speeches[41] may be used to determine the meaning of terms and the purpose or object of a statute.[42]

For reasons detailed below,[43] it appears that s 18C's purpose is to either reduce racial hatred or promote racial tolerance by making unlawful offensive, insulting, humiliating or intimidating acts. Either aim would be best achieved by prohibiting all instances of offence, insult or humiliation as such instances could generate ill-will between groups.

There are several other principles concerning statutory interpretation that we should note. First, there is the principle that protective legislation should be construed broadly and beneficially.[44] Given that the RDA is protective legislation, the principle supports interpreting s 18C's terms broadly.

The second principle is known as the principle of legality. This principle provides that legislation should not be construed to infringe fundamental rights or freedoms unless Parliament clearly legislates.[45] This principle would support a narrow interpretation of s 18C given the chilling effect that a broad interpretation has on freedom of expression. However, it is clear that Parliament had turned its mind to the freedom it was impinging. Hence, the principle of legality is of limited assistance.

The third principle is that legislation should be construed as much as possible to conform to the *Commonwealth Constitution*. This principle is reflected in s 15A of the Interpretation Act, which provides that statutes be construed as valid to the extent that they are constitutional.[46] It is this principle which,

---

39 *Acts Interpretation Act 1901* (Cth) s 15AA ('Interpretation Act').
40 Interpretation Act s 15AB(2)(e).
41 Ibid s 15AB(2)(f).
42 Ibid s 15AB(1)(a).
43 See Part V.C.1 (page 124).
44 *Purvis v New South Wales* [2003] HCA 62; (2003) 217 CLR 92, 111 [45] (McHugh and Kirby JJ). McHugh and Kirby JJ's comments concerned interpreting provisions of the *Disability Discrimination Act 1992* (Cth) ('DDA'). However, this reasoning is applicable to the RDA. See also *IW v City of Perth* [1997] HCA 30; 191 CLR 1, 12 (Brennan CJ, McHugh J).
45 *Bropho v Western Australia* [1990] HCA 24; (1990) 171 CLR 1, 17-8 (Mason CJ, Deane, Dawson, Toohey, Gaudron and McHugh JJ); *Coco v The Queen* [1994] HCA 15; (1994) 179 CLR 427, 436-7 (Mason CJ, Brennan, Gaudron and McHugh JJ); *Electrolux Home Products Pty Ltd v Australian Workers' Union* [2004] HCA 40; (2004) 221 CLR 309, 329 [21] (Gleeson CJ); *K-Generation Pty Ltd v Liquor Licensing Court* [2009] HCA 4; (2009) 237 CLR 501, 520 [47] (French CJ); *South Australia v Totani* [2010] HCA 39 [31] (French CJ); *Harrison v Melham* [2008] NSWCA 67 [7] (Spigelman J).
46 Interpretation Act s 15A. See also *Monis v The Queen* [2013] HCA 4; (2013) 249 CLR 92, 208-10 [327]-[332] (Crennan, Kiefel and Bell JJ) ('*Monis*').

in our view, determines how broadly s 18C's terms should be interpreted. A broad interpretation of 'offence', 'insult' or 'humiliation' would cover all such instances, including any non-trivial instance. It is highly likely that such an approach would lead to the conclusion that s 18C is incapable of being reasonably considered appropriate and adapted to the Convention, and that it impermissibly infringes the implied freedom of political communication. In light of this, these terms should be interpreted narrowly, in order to conform as much as possible with the *Commonwealth Constitution*.

Hence, it is likely that s 18C's terms would be interpreted narrowly. That is, s 18C would be confined to serious, severe or extreme instances of offence, insult or humiliation. However, even if these terms were so confined, s 18C would *still* be incapable of being reasonably considered appropriate and adapted to the Convention, and impermissibly infringe the implied freedom of political communication. It is to these issues that we now turn.

IV

THE EXTERNAL AFFAIRS POWER

For a Commonwealth law to be constitutionally valid, a constitutional head of power must support it. The Commonwealth government has relied upon the external affairs power to support the RDA. In particular, the Commonwealth government enacted the RDA pursuant to Australia's entry into the Convention, thereby giving effect to a treaty.[47] This is evident from the Preamble to the RDA,[48] the fact that the commencement of the RDA is linked to the Convention entering into force,[49] the numerous cross-references to the

---

[47] The external affairs power, of course, encompasses more than simply the power to legislate domestically to incorporate the terms of international treaties. It also provides the Commonwealth government with the constitutional power to introduce legislation dealing with Australia's relations with other countries: *R v Sharkey* [1949] HCA 46; (1949) 79 CLR 121; *Kirmani v Captain Cook Cruises Pty Ltd (No 1)* [1985] HCA 8; (1985) 159 CLR 351, and relating to matters or things geographically situated outside Australia: *Polyukhovich v Commonwealth* [1991] HCA 32; (1991) 172 CLR 501; *XYZ v Commonwealth* [2006] HCA 25; (2006) 227 CLR 532). Section 18C is not a law with regards to the subject of relations between Australia and other governments and does not fall within the scope of the geographic externality principle. The final possible basis for the operation of the external affairs power is in relation to laws with respect to 'a matter of international concern': *Polyukhovich v Commonwealth* [1991] HCA 32; (1991) 172 CLR 501, 560-561 (Brennan J); *Koowarta v Bjelke-Petersen* [1982] HCA 27; (1982) 153 CLR 168, 220 (Stephen J) ('*Koowarta*'). This doctrine has not, however, been definitively accepted by the High Court as providing a valid constitutional basis for domestic legislation, being instead referred to as 'an undeveloped concept': *XYZ v Commonwealth* [2006] HCA 25; (2006) 227 CLR 532, 575 [127] (Kirby J) that gives rise to 'immense difficulties': *XYZ v Commonwealth* [2006] HCA 25; (2006) 227 CLR 532, 612 [225] (Callinan and Heydon JJ).

[48] Which relevantly provides that: 'And whereas it is desirable, in pursuance of all relevant powers of the Parliament, including, but not limited to, its power to make laws with respect to external affairs, with respect to the people of any race for whom it is deemed necessary to make special laws and with respect to immigration, to make the provisions contained in this Act for the prohibition of racial discrimination and certain other forms of discrimination and, in particular, to make provision for giving effect to the Convention.'

[49] RDA s 2.

Convention contained in the RDA[50] and the setting out of the Convention in the Schedule to the RDA.[51]

Further, implementing the Convention through the external affairs power was the basis on which the Commonwealth government defended the constitutional validity of the RDA when it was challenged in *Koowarta*.[52] In this case, a majority of the High Court held that ss 9 and 12 of the RDA were valid laws with respect to the external affairs power.

However, the decision in *Koowarta* pre-dated the introduction of s 18C through the *Racial Hatred Bill 1994* (Cth) ('RHB'). As such, the question of whether the external affairs power supports s 18C is one that the High Court has not directly considered.

In fact, concerns were raised about the constitutionality of s 18C when the provision was first introduced through the RHB. In particular, there was concern whether the external affairs power could validly support the proposed s 18C. For example, the *Bills Digest* produced by the Parliamentary Research Service noted that s 18C was more vulnerable to constitutional challenge than other sections of the RHB, primarily due to its scope extending beyond the Convention. It observed that:

> There is no requirement in proposed s. 18C that the act include ideas based on racial superiority or hatred, or incite racial discrimination or violence, nor is there a requirement that it involve the advocacy of racial hatred or incite hostility. There appears to be quite a wide chasm between racial hatred and 'offending' a person by an act, where one of the reasons for the act was the race of a person.[53]

Members of Parliament also raised similar doubts in debates about the RHB.[54]

In *Toben*,[55] the Full Court of the Federal Court considered the question of s 18C's constitutional validity under the external affairs power. In this case, the Court held that the external affairs power through the Convention supported

---

50 See, for example, RDA ss 8(1), 9(2), 10(2), and 20(c)(iii).
51 See also Committee on the Elimination of Racial Discrimination, *Reports submitted by States parties under article 9 of the Convention (Combined fifteenth, sixteenth and seventeenth periodic reports of States parties due in 2008, Australia)*, 7 January 2010, [25].
52 [1982] HCA 27; (1982) 153 CLR 168.
53 Parliamentary Research Service (Department of the Parliamentary Library), *Bills Digest: Racial Hatred Bill 1994*, 14 November 1994, 12.
54 See, for example, Commonwealth of Australia, *Parliamentary Debates*, House of Representatives, 15 November 1994, 3362 (Daryl Williams).
55 [2003] FCAFC 137; (2003) 129 FCR 515.

s 18C. However, for the reasons stated below,[56] our view is that *Toben* was in error on this point.

Ratifying an international treaty allows the Commonwealth government to legislate domestically to incorporate those treaty terms under the external affairs power. However, the Commonwealth government must meet a number of requirements. These are that the treaty is a *bona fide* treaty, the subject matter of the treaty is a matter of international concern or character,[57] and the legislation meets the specificity and conformity requirements. In this Part, we will examine each of these requirements. However, it is first necessary to say something about how treaties are interpreted, as well as the text and structure of the Convention.

A *Interpreting Treaties, and the Structure of the Convention*

The Convention, like many treaties since the end of the Second World War, is the product of negotiation between many states (which we refer to below as 'States Parties' with respect to the Convention). Given this, particular considerations apply when interpreting the Convention.[58] In *A v Minister for Immigration and Ethnic Affairs*,[59] Brennan CJ noted the following regarding interpreting treaties:

> In interpreting a treaty, it is erroneous to adopt a rigid priority in the application of interpretative rules. The political processes by which a treaty is negotiated to a conclusion preclude such an approach. Rather... it is necessary to adopt an holistic but ordered approach. The holistic approach to interpretation may require a consideration of both the text and the object and purpose of the treaty in order to ascertain its true meaning. Although the text of a treaty may itself reveal its object and purpose or at least assist in ascertaining its object and purpose, assistance may also be obtained from extrinsic sources. The form in which a treaty is drafted, the subject to which it relates, the mischief that it addresses, the history of its negotiation and comparison with earlier or amending instruments relating to the same subject may warrant consideration in

---

56 See Part IV.I (page 99).
57 Although we note, following the *Tasmanian Dam Case*, that this requirement has become largely superfluous in terms of the mere fact of an international treaty being ratified now being sufficient to establish that the subject matter of the treaty is a matter of international concern or character.
58 In particular, there are specific rules of interpretation outlined in the *Vienna Convention on the Law of Treaties* (opened for signature 23 May 1969, 1155 UNTS 331, entered into force 27 January 1980).
59 [1997] HCA 4; (1997) 190 CLR 225.

arriving at the true interpretation of its text.⁶⁰

To summarise, when interpreting treaties the text, object and purpose of a treaty is important, along with the form the treaty takes, the history of its negotiation, the subject to which it relates and the mischief it addresses. Extrinsic sources may assist with determining these things.

Egon Schwelb, writing shortly after the Convention's creation, noted the following about the Convention's structure:

> Part I of the Convention consists of a definition article (Art. 1), followed by a statement of 'the fundamental obligations' of States Parties (Art. 2). These 'fundamental obligations' are elaborated in some detail in Articles 3 to 5 as far as substantive law is concerned, and in Article 6 in regard to procedural safeguards and remedies to be provided in the internal law of the States Parties. Article 7 deals with measures to be adopted in the fields of teaching, education, culture and information.⁶¹

Natan Lerner adopted a similar view of the Convention's structure.⁶² Relevantly, Lerner noted:

- Article 1 provides for definitions;⁶³
- Article 2 provides for the obligation of states;⁶⁴
- Article 3 condemns and prohibits apartheid;⁶⁵
- Article 4 provides for measures to prohibit incitement to racial hatred and discrimination and to prohibit racist organisations;⁶⁶
- Article 5 provides for rights guaranteed by the Convention;⁶⁷

---

60 Ibid 231 (Brennan CJ). See also ibid 251-6 (McHugh J), 240 (Dawson J) and 294 (Kirby J). In short, these approaches embody how Articles 31 and 32 of the *Vienna Convention on the Law of Treaties* are applied to interpreting treaties enacted into Australian law. See also *Povey v Qantas Airways Ltd* [2005] HCA 33; (2005) 216 ALR 427, 433 (Gleeson CJ, Gummow, Hayne and Heydon JJ).
61 Egon Schwelb, 'The International Convention on the Elimination of All Forms of Racial Discrimination' (1966) 15 *International and Comparative Law Quarterly* 996, 1000. Schwelb has been cited favourably in Australian case law concerning the Convention: see *Koowarta* [1982] HCA 27; (1982) 153 CLR 168, 219 (Stephen J), 248 (Wilson J); see also *Toben* [2003] FCAFC 137; (2003) 129 FCR 505, 536-7 [92]-[98], 539-40 [102]-[111] (Allsop J).
62 Like Schwelb, Lerner has been cited favourably in Australian case law concerning the Convention: see *Toben* [2003] FCAFC 137; (2003) 129 FCR 505, 536-7 [92]-[98], 539-40 [105]-[111] (Allsop J).
63 Natan Lerner, *The UN Convention on the Elimination of all Forms of Racial Discrimination* (Sijthoff & Noordhoff, 2nd ed, 1980) 25-33.
64 Ibid 33-9.
65 Ibid 40-3.
66 Ibid 43-53.
67 Ibid 54-60.

- Article 6 provides for remedies against racial discrimination;⁶⁸ and
- Article 7 provides for steps in the fields of education and information.⁶⁹

We agree with Schwelb's and Lerner's observations concerning the Convention's structure. We now turn to analysing the requirements for legislating to implement a treaty under the external affairs power.

B *A Bona Fide Treaty*

The first requirement is that there must be a *bona fide* treaty. If a treaty is entered into as 'merely a device to procure for the Commonwealth an additional domestic jurisdiction' then it will not enliven the external affairs power.⁷⁰ That said, this doctrine of *bona fides* is '… a frail shield, and available in rare cases', because it is extremely difficult to prove that the Commonwealth might have entered into a treaty in bad faith.⁷¹

It cannot be sensibly suggested that the Convention is anything but a *bona fide* treaty entered into in good faith. The Convention was adopted by the United Nations General Assembly in 1965⁷² and, as at November 2014, had 177 State parties. The Convention also establishes a reporting mechanism for States Parties, and an individual complaints mechanism through the Committee on the Elimination of Racial Discrimination,⁷³ providing further evidence of its status as a *bona fide* international agreement that has been entered into in good faith.

C *A Matter of International Character*

A second requirement that was proposed in early cases such as *R v Burgess; Ex parte Henry*⁷⁴ was that domestic laws will only be valid under the external affairs power if the subject matter of the treaty is 'of sufficient international significance to make it a legitimate subject for international cooperation and agreement'.⁷⁵ The more expansive approach to the external affairs power

---

68 Ibid 60-2.
69 Ibid 63-4.
70 *R v Burgess; Ex parte Henry* [1936] HCA 52; (1936) 55 CLR 608, 687 (Evatt and McTiernan JJ).
71 *Koowarta* [1982] HCA 27; (1982) 153 CLR 168, 200 (Gibbs CJ).
72 UNGA Res 2106 (XX) (21 December 1965).
73 Convention Arts 8-15.
74 [1936] HCA 52; (1936) 55 CLR 608.
75 Ibid 658 (Starke J), 669 (Dixon J). See also *Koowarta* [1982] HCA 27; (1982) 153 CLR 168, 216-217 (Stephen J).

adopted by the High Court in the *Tasmanian Dam Case*[76] and subsequent cases has relaxed this requirement to the point where '[t]he existence of international character or international concern is established by entry by Australia into the Convention or treaty'.[77] Australia entering a treaty is thus all that is necessary to meet this requirement. It is highly unlikely now that the High Court would revert to the earlier, narrower view of the external affairs power on this point. Hence, the very fact that Australia has ratified the Convention will be sufficient to satisfy any requirement of 'international character'.

D *The Specificity Requirement*

In *Victoria v Commonwealth*,[78] members of the High Court noted that there may be some treaties 'which do not enliven the legislative power conferred by the external affairs power even though their subject matter is of international concern'.[79] They stated:

> When a treaty is relied on under s. 51(xxix) to support a law, it is not sufficient that the law prescribes one of a variety of means that might be thought appropriate and adapted to the achievement of an ideal. The law must prescribe a regime that the treaty has itself defined with sufficient specificity to direct the general course to be taken by the signatory states.[80]

This statement of principle informs whether or not the specific requirement is met. When a treaty is primarily aspirational and fails to impose reasonably specific legal obligations on Australia, it will not provide a constitutionally sound basis for domestic legislation under the external affairs power.

The focus must be on establishing an agreement by nations to take 'common action' such that 'a broad objective with little precise content and permitting widely divergent policies by parties does not meet the description'.[81] This general principle was expanded upon by Heydon J in *Pape v Federal Commissioner of Taxation* observing that '[t]he treaty or commitment need not have the precision necessary to establish a legally enforceable agreement at common

---

[76] *Commonwealth v Tasmania* [1983] HCA 21; (1983) 158 CLR 1 (*'Tasmanian Dam Case'*).
[77] Ibid 125 (Mason J).
[78] *Victoria v Commonwealth* [1996] HCA 56; (1996) 187 CLR 416 (*'Industrial Relations Act Case'*).
[79] Ibid 486 (Brennan CJ, Toohey, Gaudron, McHugh and Gummow JJ).
[80] Ibid.
[81] *Industrial Relations Act Case* [1996] HCA 56; (1996) 187 CLR 416, 486 (Brennan CJ, Toohey, Gaudron, McHugh and Gummow JJ), quoting Leslie Zines, *The High Court and the Constitution* (Butterworths, 3rd ed 1992) 250.

law, but it must avoid excessive generality'.[82]

The key Articles of the Convention in relation to s 18C and the external affairs power appear to be Articles 2, 4, 6 and 7, being the treaty provisions most often referred in this context.[83] The terms of each of these treaty provisions need to be considered to determine whether they establish a sufficiently specific legal obligation. In this section, we will be examining Article 4, as it is the most relevant to hate speech laws. We will then examine Articles 2, 6 and 7 respectively.

1   Article 4

The opening words of Article 4 appear to be primarily aspirational and to lack specific content.[84] It is admirable for States Parties to agree to '... undertake to adopt immediate and positive measures designed to eradicate all incitement to, or acts of, such discrimination'. However, such an open-ended statement leaves it entirely to the discretion of each State Party as to what measures should be implemented and, in itself, does not commit a State Party to taking any specific form of action.

That said, the three specific actions under Articles 4(a)-(c) adds content to these opening words. They are sufficiently specific as to what States Parties are required to do. In the context of s 18C, the most relevant of these obligations is Article 4(a) which provides that States Parties:

> [s]hall declare an offence punishable by law all dissemination of ideas based on racial superiority or hatred, incitement to racial discrimination, as well as all acts of violence or incitement to such acts against any race or group of persons of another colour or ethnic origin, and also the provision of any assistance to racist activities, including the financing thereof.[85]

Hence, Article 4(a) appears to satisfy the specificity requirement by prescribing the general course to be taken by States Parties, namely making laws.

2   Article 2

Similarly, Article 2(1) begins by stating that States Parties 'condemn racial discrimination and undertake to pursue by all appropriate means and without delay a policy of eliminating racial discrimination in all its forms and promoting

---

82 [2009] HCA 23; (2009) 238 CLR 1, 162 (Heydon J) ('*Pape*').
83 See *Toben* [2003] FCAFC 137; (2003) 129 FCR 515, 524 [19] (Carr J), 551 [144] (Allsop J).
84 For the full text of Article 4 please see Part IV.E.1(a) (page 36).
85 Convention Art 4(a).

understanding among all races'.[86] If this were the extent of the treaty obligation under Article 2(1) then it is strongly arguable that the specificity requirement is not met. The opening words of Article 2(1) are primarily aspirational, with the requirement that States Parties 'pursue by all appropriate means' a policy of 'promoting understanding among all races' providing little guidance as to what common action States Parties are actually expected to take.

Article 2(1) does, however, go on to provide specificity through the narrower obligations outlined at (a)-(e). In particular, the word 'undertakes' – which was considered in the *Tasmanian Dam Case* as being 'apt to create such an obligation'[87] – appears in Articles 2(1)(a), (b) and (e). Of course, as was noted by Heydon J in *Pape*, given this:

> [t]he appropriate process would be to read what was said in [the *Tasmanian Dams Case*], a case in which the Court was sharply and closely divided on many questions, in the light of the detailed treatment of specificity by five Justices in the later decision of *Victoria v The Commonwealth*.[88]

Even doing so, the aspirational language at the beginning of Article 2(1) is qualified by the more specific obligations imposed in the later subsections. Notably, Articles 2(1)(c) and (d) require specific action through legislation. The language remains broad with, for example, phrases such as 'by all appropriate means' and 'as required by circumstances' qualifying the obligation imposed by Article 2(1)(d). However, the references to using legislative means to prohibit racial discrimination avoid excessive generality, and sufficiently specify what is expected of States Parties.

Thus it appears that Article 2(1)(d) would support a wide variety of legislation prohibiting racial discrimination. Schwelb noted that Article 2(1)(d) was the 'the most important and far reaching of all substantive provisions of the Convention'.[89] However, it is important to note the structure of the Convention and, in particular, the relationship between Article 2(1)(d) and Article 4. Lerner noted the following with respect to this relationship:

> [Article 2(1)(d)] is a crucial one, and is closely connected with Article 4

---

86 Noting that Article 5 of the Convention provides that the obligations laid down in Article 2 are 'the fundamental obligations'. For the full text of Article 2 see Park IV.E.3 (page 58).
87 *Tasmanian Dam Case* [1983] HCA 21; (1983) 158 CLR 1, 132 (Mason J).
88 *Pape* [2009] HCA 23; (2009) 238 CLR 1, 164 (Heydon J).
89 Egon Schwelb, 'The International Convention on the Elimination of All Forms of Racial Discrimination' (1966) 15 *International and Comparative Law Quarterly* 996, 1017. See also Natan Lerner, *The UN Convention on the Elimination of all Forms of Racial Discrimination* (Sijthoff & Noordhoff, 2nd ed, 1980) 38.

of the Convention, which penalizes the dissemination of ideas based on racial superiority or hatred...

[Article 2(1)(d)] gave rise to many difficulties. The whole matter of the use of legislation in order to stop racial discrimination came under scrutiny during the discussion of this sub-paragraph, particularly with regard to the problem arising for States with a common law legal system, where racial discrimination was dealt with, not by making it an offence, but by the protection given under the law to all without distinction. The possibility of jeopardizing freedom of thought and of expression, and of invading the private life of individuals, was raised in discussion, as well as the general controversy on the use of legislation or education in the fight against racial discrimination.[90]

Hence, it appears that Article 2(1)(d) is directed at legislation that prohibits racial discrimination in all areas except when it impinged certain rights, notably freedom of expression. In those cases, Article 4 directed States Parties as to the appropriate course of action.

This brings us to Article 2(1)(e). This Article appears to direct States Parties to encourage certain activities that fight racial discrimination, and discourage activities that promote it.

Schwelb noted that the Convention contained "promotional conventions", that is, Articles that promoted a defined objective. Schwelb contrasted these "promotional conventions" to Articles that 'are not merely hopes to future enjoyment, but "warrants for the here and now"'.[91] Schwelb identified the "promotional conventions" as Article 7, the introduction to Article 2, and Article 2(1)(e).[92] Those Articles that were 'more than merely promotional' were Articles 2(1)(a)-(d).[93]

Lerner noted the following with respect to Article 2(1)(e):

[Article 2(1)(e)] is broadly and vaguely worded. It imposes upon States the duty to use their moral influence in order to strengthen those organizations and movements that advocate racial integration, as well as

---

90 Natan Lerner, *The UN Convention on the Elimination of all Forms of Racial Discrimination* (Sijthoff & Noordhoff, 2nd ed, 1980) 37-8. See also Part IV.E.2 (pages 51-2) and Part IV.E.3 (pages 58-9).
91 Egon Schwelb, 'The International Convention on the Elimination of All Forms of Racial Discrimination' (1966) 15 *International and Comparative Law Quarterly* 996, 1016.
92 Ibid.
93 Ibid 1016-7.

to discourage *anything* which strengthens racial division.[94]

Schwelb's description of a "promotional convention" and Lerner's description of "moral influence" correctly identify Article 2(1)(e)'s purpose. It appears Article 2(1)(e) is directing States Parties to have an official stance opposing racism, including adopting appropriate policies to fight it, rather than implementing legislation (which appears to be the work of Articles 2(1)(c) and 2(1)(d)).

3 Article 6

Article 6 is a provision of sufficient specificity to create obligations on State Parties.[95] However, it is important to keep in mind the obligations that Article 6 creates. As further discussed below, Article 6 of the Convention is directed at *remedies* for racial discrimination. Article 6 not only obliges States Parties to undertake the general task of assuring 'to everyone within their jurisdiction effective protection and remedies' against acts of racial discrimination but provides for the specific mechanism to be used to achieve this general aim, namely 'competent national tribunals and other State institutions'.[96] The Article also provides for the specific right to seek 'just and adequate reparation or satisfaction for any damage suffered as a result of such discrimination'.[97] Thus, Article 6 meets the specificity requirement, but only with respect to remedies.

4 Article 7

The open-ended obligations and primarily aspirational language of Article 7 create significant doubts about whether it satisfies the specificity requirement. Article 7 provides that:

> States Parties undertake to adopt immediate and effective measures, particularly in the fields of teaching, education, culture and information, with a view to combating prejudices which lead to racial discrimination and to promoting understanding, tolerance and friendship among nations and racial or ethnic groups, as well as to propagating the purposes and principles of the Charter of the United Nations, the Universal Declaration of Human Rights, the United Nations Declaration on the Elimination of

---

[94] Natan Lerner, *The UN Convention on the Elimination of all Forms of Racial Discrimination* (Sijthoff & Noordhoff, 2nd ed, 1980) 38 (emphasis in original).
[95] For the full text of Article 6 see Part IV.E.4 (page 87).
[96] Article 6.
[97] Ibid.

All Forms of Racial Discrimination, and this Convention.

Article 7 provides no guidance concerning the measures that might be considered effective in combating prejudices and promoting understanding, tolerance and friendship amongst nations. It would certainly be open to States Parties to take significantly divergent views about these measures. For example, laws prohibiting hate speech may be seen by some States Parties as a measure combating racial prejudice. However, other States Parties may see such a measure as doing the opposite by preventing the types of public discussions that ultimately help eliminate racial discrimination in the longer-term.

Further, the States Parties have not committed to any tangible common action under Article 7 but rather to a symbolic statement that provides 'a broad objective with little precise content'.[98] The lack of an imperative obligation is reinforced by the softer language adopted in Article 7. For example, whereas both Articles 2 and 4 use the mandatory term 'shall' when referring to the obligations to be undertaken by States Parties, this is missing from Article 7, which instead outlines an undertaking to adopt measures 'with a view to' combating prejudices.

This analysis is supported by Schwelb's and Lerner's observations. As noted above, Schwelb identified "promotional conventions" in the Convention, which included the introduction to Article 2, Article 2(1)(e) and Article 7.[99] Lerner noted the following about Article 7:

> During debate in the Commission it was pointed out that the wording of [Article 7] should follow closely that of Article 8 of the Declaration [on the Elimination of All Forms of Racial Discrimination]. The attention of the Commission was called to the fact that in another article reference was made not only to racial discrimination but also to racial hatred. However, since [Article 7] dealt with measures connected with teaching, education and information, it was decided to refer only to discrimination.[100]

And later:

> Article 7 is inspired by Article 8 of the Declaration [on the Elimination

---

98 Leslie Zines, *The High Court and the Constitution* (Butterworths, 3rd ed, 1992) 250 cited in *Industrial Relations Act Case* [1996] HCA 56; (1996) 187 CLR 416, 486 (Brennan CJ, Toohey, Gaudron, McHugh and Gummow JJ).
99 Egon Schwelb, 'The International Convention on the Elimination of All Forms of Racial Discrimination' (1966) 15 *International and Comparative Law Quarterly* 996, 1016.
100 Natan Lerner, *The UN Convention on the Elimination of all Forms of Racial Discrimination* (Sijthoff & Noordhoff, 2nd ed, 1980) 63.

of All Forms of Racial Discrimination]. It has a similar intention to that of Article 26(2) of the Universal Declaration [of Human Rights], which refers to the purposes of education.[101]

Given the foregoing, Article 7's text and purpose is directed towards encouraging efforts in teaching, education, culture and information to address racial discrimination. It is not directed to laws imposing sanctions on racial discrimination or racial hatred.

Thus, s 18C is a significant step beyond '[adopting] immediate and effective measures particularly in the fields of teaching, education, culture and information …'. Further, it is significant that Article 7, unlike Articles 2 and 4, fails to specifically refer to legislative measures. Hence, it appears that Article 7 does not meet the specificity requirement as regards supporting s 18C.

5   Concluding thoughts on the Specificity Requirement

For the reasons outlined above, Article 2 (except Article 2(1)(e)), Article 4 and Article 6 appear to satisfy the specificity requirement. These Articles direct States Parties to enact legislation to prohibit racial discrimination, or provide remedies in the event of racial discrimination. However, Article 7 does not satisfy the specificity requirement as it does not direct States Parties to legislate to prohibit or remedy racial discrimination. Rather, Article 7 directs States Parties to pursue policies that combat racial discrimination in the fields of teaching, education, culture and information.

Consequently, Article 2(1)(e) and Article 7 cannot provide constitutionally valid support for s 18C. Article 2, Article 4 and Article 6 may provide constitutionally valid support for s 18C, as long as the conformity requirement is satisfied. It is to this issue we now turn.

---

[101] Ibid 64. Article 8 of the *United Nations Declaration on the Elimination of All Form of Racial Discrimination* provides: 'All effective steps shall be taken immediately in the fields of teaching, education and information, with a view to eliminating racial discrimination and prejudice and promoting understanding, tolerance and friendship among nations and racial groups, as well as to propagating the purposes and principles of the *Charter of the United Nations*, of the *Universal Declaration of Human Rights*, and of the *Declaration on the Granting of Independence to Colonial Countries and Peoples*.' (Emphasis in original). Article 26(2) of the *Universal Declaration of Human Rights* provides: 'Education shall be directed to the full development of the human personality and to the strengthening of respect for human rights and fundamental freedoms. It shall promote understanding, tolerance and friendship among all nations, racial or religious groups, and shall further the activities of the United Nations for the maintenance of peace'.

E *The Conformity Requirement*

> 'I hate him.'
> 'Hate's a strong word, Betty. I hate Nazis. I have an ex-wife. She bothers me. I don't like seeing her. I don't hate her.'
> 'You're a saint.'
> 'I'm an adult.'[102]

The final requirement is conformity: domestic legislation must conform to the treaty being implemented. In our view, the conformity requirement is the key issue regarding the constitutional validity of s 18C under the external affairs power. It requires a close examination of the specific wording used in both the domestic legislation and the Convention.

As to the relevant principle, to meet the conformity requirement 'the law must be reasonably capable of being considered appropriate and adapted to implementing the treaty'.[103] It is for the Commonwealth Parliament to choose the legislative means by which it gives effect to treaty obligations, 'provided that the means chosen are reasonably capable of being considered appropriate and adapted to that end'.[104]

It is important to keep in mind what "appropriate" and "adapted" mean.[105] The *Macquarie Dictionary* defines 'appropriate' as, relevantly:

---

102 Dialogue spoken between the characters of Betty Francis and Henry Francis in *Mad Men* (Directed by Phil Abraham, AMC, 2010) episode 4.8 'The Summer Man' 18:44.
103 *Industrial Relations Act Case* [1996] HCA 56; (1996) 187 CLR 416, 487 (Brennan CJ, Toohey, Gaudron, McHugh & Gummow JJ).
104 Ibid. "Reasonable proportionality" may also assist resolving issues concerning whether a law is reasonably capable of being appropriate and adapted to a particular end. In the *Industrial Relations Act Case*, a majority of the High Court stated the test thus: 'a law will not be capable of being seen as appropriate and adapted... unless it appears that there is "reasonable proportionality" between the purpose or object and the means adapted by the law to pursue it.': ibid. However, the majority noted that 'the notion of "reasonable proportionality" will not always be particularly helpful': ibid 488 and that: '...to ask of the legislation whether it may reasonably be seen as bearing a relationship of reasonable proportionality to the provisions of the treaty in question appears to restate the basic question. This is whether the law selects means which are reasonably capable of being considered appropriate and adapted to achieving the purpose or object of giving effect to the treaty...': ibid. That is, the majority did not rule out the "reasonable proportionality" test, but thought that such a test did the same thing as asking whether a law was reasonably capable of being appropriate and adapted to achieving the purpose or object of the treaty. Our view is that the test of reasonable proportionality assists to demonstrate whether or not a law is adapted to (that is, a fitting means of achieving) a purpose.
105 We note that terms used in statements of legal principle in cases should not be treated the same as words used in statutes. However, given that "appropriate" and "adapted" are often used in constitutional law cases, and the degree of similarity between these two words on their face, some further elaboration is warranted.

> 1. suitable or fitting for a particular purpose, person occasion, etc.[106]

It defines 'adapt' as, relevantly:

> 1. to make suitable to requirements; adjust or modify fittingly.[107]

As noted above, a number of Articles have been variously cited in support of s 18C. These are Articles 2, 4, 6 and 7. Each of these will be considered in terms of the conformity requirement. We will examine Article 4 first as it is the most relevant to hate speech laws. We will also examine Article 5 along with Article 4. After this, we will examine Articles 2, 6 and 7. We will then consider the approach that has been taken in various reports and in *Toben*.

1   Article 4

As noted above,[108] Article 4 appears to be the Article that most directly supports s 18C. The real issue is whether s 18C's use of the terms 'offend', 'insult' and 'humiliate' is reasonably capable of being considered appropriate and adapted to implementing Article 4.[109]

(a)   The text of Article 4

Given its importance to our analysis of the conformity requirement, Article 4 should be stated in full:

> States Parties condemn all propaganda and all organizations which are based on ideas or theories of superiority of one race or group of persons of one colour or ethnic origin, or which attempt to justify or promote racial hatred and discrimination in any form, and undertake to adopt immediate and positive measures designed to eradicate all incitement to, or acts of, such discrimination and, to this end, with due regard to the principles embodied in the Universal Declaration of Human Rights and the rights expressly set forth in article 5 of this Convention, *inter alia*:
>
> > (a) Shall declare an offence punishable by law all dissemination of ideas based on racial superiority or hatred, incitement to racial discrimination, as well as all acts of violence or incitement to such acts against any race or group of persons of another colour or ethnic origin, and also the provision of any assistance to racist

---

106 *Macquarie Dictionary* 60.
107 Ibid 16.
108 See Part IV.D.1 (page 29).
109 RDA s 18C(1).

activities, including the financing thereof;

(b) Shall declare illegal and prohibit organizations, and also organized and all other propaganda activities, which promote and incite racial discrimination, and shall recognize participation in such organizations or activities as an offence punishable by law;

(c) Shall not permit public authorities or public institutions, national or local, to promote or incite racial discrimination.

Articles 4(b) and 4(c) are not relevant to the issue as to whether s 18C meets the conformity requirement. This is because they are directed against organisations and public authorities promoting racial discrimination.[110]

It is Article 4(a) and the paragraph that precedes it that is most relevant to s 18C. Of particular relevance are the following types of conduct that States Parties are obliged to prohibit under Article 4(a):

- The dissemination of ideas based on racial superiority or hatred; and
- The incitement to racial discrimination or violence.

We will now examine each of these types of conduct.

(b) Dissemination of ideas based on racial superiority or hatred

In our view, this is the phrase most relevant to the issue as to whether the external affairs power supports s 18C. We will examine what 'dissemination' means, before turning to what 'based on racial superiority or hatred' means.

(i) Dissemination

The phrase 'all dissemination of ideas based on racial superiority or hatred'[111] contains a number of key terms. The first such term is 'dissemination'. The *Macquarie Dictionary* defines 'disseminate' as:

1. to scatter, as seed in sowing; spread abroad; diffuse; promulgate.[112]

In the context of Article 4, the term 'disseminate' could have a broad application. This is supported by the fact that '*all* dissemination' is prohibited.[113] Someone who mentions an idea to others could be said to disseminate that idea.

---

110 Although Article 4(b) as well as the opening sentence of Article 4 affect freedom of association.
111 Convention Art 4(a).
112 *Macquarie Dictionary* 430.
113 Convention Art 4(a) (emphasis ours).

However, the word 'dissemination' appears to have a purposive element, which narrows its scope. That is, dissemination involves spreading ideas *on purpose*, as someone sows seeds with the purpose of spreading them. The requirement of a purposive element is supported by the opening sentence of Article 4, which condemns (among other things) 'propaganda'[114] and attempts to 'justify or promote racial hatred'.[115] This suggests the prohibition is directed not at lively or heated argument, but proselytising: that is, the intentional and sustained spreading of ideas based on racial superiority or hatred.

(ii) Based on racial superiority or hatred

As to ideas 'based on racial superiority or hatred'.[116] The *Macquarie Dictionary* defines 'hate' as:

> 1. to regard with a strong or passionate dislike; detest... 3. to feel hatred.[117]

It defines 'superiority' as, relevantly:

> 2. above the average in excellence, merit, intelligence, etc. 3. of higher grade or quality. ... 5. showing a consciousness or feeling of being above others in such respects...[118]

And defines 'base' as, relevantly:

> 1. the bottom of anything, considered as its support; that on which a thing stands or rests. 2. A fundamental principle or groundwork; foundation; basis. ... 5. The principal element or ingredient of anything, considered as its fundamental part.[119]

We note here that Article 4 directs States Parties to do a Herculean task: to

---

114 Which the *Macquarie Dictionary* defines as: '1. the systematic propagation of a given doctrine. 2. the particular doctrines or principles propagated by an organisation or movement. 3. dissemination of ideas, information or rumour for the purpose of injuring or helping an institution, a cause or a person. 4. doctrines, arguments, facts spread by deliberate effort through any medium in order to further one's cause or to damage an opposing cause. 5. A public action or display aimed at furthering or hindering a cause.': ibid 1175.
115 Convention Art 4. The *Macquarie Dictionary* defines 'justify' as, relevantly '1. To show (an act claim, statement, etc.) to be just, right or warranted: *the ends justify the means.*': ibid 805 (emphasis in original). It defines 'promote' as, relevantly: '2. to further the growth, development, progress, etc., of; encourage. 3. To help to found; originate; organise; launch (a financial undertaking, publicity campaign, etc.).': ibid 1174.
116 Convention Art 4(a).
117 *Macquarie Dictionary* 683.
118 Ibid 1472.
119 Ibid 116.

enact laws prohibiting expression based on an *emotion*, namely hatred. We say "Herculean" because while the task is not impossible, it is difficult. Laws rarely prohibit conduct embodying or creating emotions, for good reason. Laws can and do concern themselves with states of consciousness, with *mens rea* (or "the guilty mind") and intent being the classic examples. However, these states of mind pertain to *knowledge* or *volition* and not *feelings*.

It is one thing to attach legal liability on a state of mind that the accused has consciously created, like knowledge or volition. It is another to attach legal liability to an emotion: a state of mind whose origins may not be conscious but visceral. Of course, individuals are responsible for controlling their own emotions.[120] Hence, a law could (but not necessarily *should*) impose liability for expression *manifesting* an emotion. However, it is legitimate to ask whether the law should impose liability on expression that *creates* an emotional response in *other* people. Given that an emotional response is visceral, another's emotional response to an individual's expression may vary widely.

Despite these conceptual difficulties, laws can and do attach legal liability to manifesting or creating an emotion.[121] However, such laws may encounter further difficulties defining the emotion, and hence the actual scope of the law. There may also be difficulties proving that certain conduct manifested or created the prohibited emotion. Confining the prohibited emotion to that created against certain groups creates additional problems with defining who is or is not a member of the group.

This all said, it is possible to draft enforceable laws based on Article 4 provided attention is paid to its text, purpose and limits.

As noted, the text of Article 4 directs States Parties to prohibit expression based on racial hatred, or based on racial superiority. We suggest States Parties may do this a number of ways.

First, by targeting hateful expression that is *motivated* by racial hatred or superiority. That is, when the speaker feels racial hatred or superiority, *and proceeds to express that racial hatred or superiority*. We say that the hatred or superiority must be expressed, as it is unlikely that a law could target the feeling of hatred or superiority alone. Putting aside the practical difficulties of proving

---

120 Hence, the limited operation of the laws concerning provocation: see, for example, *Criminal Code 1913* (WA) s 246.
121 See, for example, ibid s 44. This section prohibits 'seditious intention'. It provides (amongst other things) that it is seditious intention to 'bring the Sovereign into hatred or contempt': see ibid s 44(a).

someone felt a certain way if they did not express that particular feeling, Article 4 must pay due regard to the guarantees of rights in Article 5. These rights include freedom of opinion and freedom of conscience. The Human Rights Committee ('HRC')[122] regards freedom of opinion as an absolute freedom, permitting no exception or restriction.[123] It holds similar views about freedom of conscience.[124] Hence, it appears to be necessary for expression to *manifest* hatred or superiority. This way, there is an act that breaches the law.[125] We cover Article 5 in more detail below.

Second, laws could target expression that promotes a *policy* or *system* based on racial hatred or superiority. That is, the speaker may not feel racial hatred or superiority, but *knowingly* promotes policies or systems manifesting racial hatred or superiority. Note that by "policy" or "system" we do not mean, "expression that might be considered a criticism of a particular race, or an unfavourable comparison of one race with another". Rather, the expression is based on a systematic or programmatic set of beliefs that embodies racial hatred or superiority.[126] This interpretation appears to be supported by the opening sentence of Article 4, which condemns 'all propaganda and all organizations which are based on ideas or theories of superiority… or which attempt to justify or promote racial hatred and discrimination in any form'. This interpretation is also supported by the use of the term 'dissemination' which, as noted above, has a purposive aspect and, in the context of Article 4, connotes proselytising ideas based on racial hatred or superiority.

Hence, laws based on Article 4 may require proof that a person *subjectively felt* hatred or superiority towards other races, and proceeded to express that hatred or superiority. Such laws may also require proof that a person *subjectively knew* they were promoting a programmatic or systematic set of beliefs based on racial hatred or superiority.

That said, laws based on Article 4 may also prohibit expression a third way, by targeting the *expression itself.* That is, the speaker may not be motivated by racial hatred or superiority, or knowingly promote a set of beliefs based on racial hatred or

---

122 The United Nations committee that monitors the implementation of the ICCPR. While we are dealing with the Convention and the UDHR, similar considerations apply to the freedoms of conscience and expression mentioned in these documents.
123 Human Rights Committee, *General Comment 34, Article 19: Freedom of opinion and expression* (12 September 2011) [9]-[10].
124 Human Rights Committee, *General Comment 22 (art 18)* (27 November 1993) [3].
125 This is similar to the requirement for an *actus reus*, or "guilty act", in criminal law.
126 As was found, for example, in the Nazi regime in Germany and the apartheid regime in South Africa.

superiority. However, they will be found to be expressing racial hatred or superiority if they cross a legal threshold. This threshold is objectively determined using some form of test, usually a "reasonable person test" or the like.

Many States Parties have enacted laws prohibiting expressions of racial hatred or superiority that are determined objectively. However, extreme caution must be exercised when enacting such laws. This is because reasonable minds can and do differ about whether a particular statement manifests or creates hate. One person's harmless opinion is another person's hate speech. That a law may deem a person's comment as racial hatred in matters where reasonable minds may differ (and differ greatly) creates a real risk of chilling expression, and alienating people who feel they are being deprived of their say in matters.[127]

Hence, the objective tests used to determine whether expression constitutes racial hatred or superiority must be carefully drafted. As noted above, a reasonable person standard is commonly employed. But reasonable minds may differ about what a reasonable person would think. One person may conclude that the reasonable person in particular circumstances would view a statement as a frank opinion. However, another may conclude that the reasonable person in the same circumstances would view the same statement as hateful. That reasonable minds are likely to come different conclusions using the same test in the same circumstances is a major concern, especially when someone's legal liability depends on the conclusion.

For example, consider during a heated online argument between numerous participants about whether Timor-Leste should have remained part of Indonesia, the sole contribution of one of the participants is this comment: "The people of Timor-Leste can't run their country!" (We hasten to add that this is not our view in any way.) Is this a comment on the inherent ability of the people of Timor-Leste to govern themselves? Or is it a comment about circumstances being so difficult for the people of Timor-Leste that they cannot succeed no matter how hard they try? The former interpretation could be considered hateful; the latter interpretation would not. However, reasonable minds may differ concerning what the comment meant. Further, such minds using a reasonable person test may come to opposite conclusions concerning whether or not the comment was an expression of hatred.

Laws prohibiting expressions of racial hatred or superiority create another

---

127 In Part VI.A (page 216) we provide some examples of the operation of hate speech laws in other jurisdictions that encounter the problems we identify here.

risk: that of legally-enforced "argument stoppers" being employed in debates involving race, colour, ethnicity or nationality. Allegations that a person's opinion or position is racist have been and are employed to stop or forestall debate. Such allegations are often little more than *ad hominem* attacks. That such attacks are used to stop debate when robust debate is needed is bad enough. It is much worse if the attack is backed by a threat of an official finding of racial hatred, with the considerable stigma this entails. Hence, States Parties should be slow to put legal force behind what are, in essence, fallacious methods of argument.

For these reasons, imposing any kind of objective standard about what constitutes hate will create problems.[128] However, it is worth noting that Article 4(a) requires laws prohibiting the dissemination of racial hatred to pay due regard to the guaranteed rights in Article 5, which include freedom of opinion and expression. This suggests that any threshold for what constitutes hate speech should be high, thereby accommodating a wide range of opinion and expression. Using a high threshold for hate speech would also minimise (though not negate completely) the risk of encountering the problems noted above. Again, we consider the effect of Article 5 in more detail below.

As a final point, we note that Article 4 not only concerns an emotion, but a *strong* emotion. Article 4 targets hate. Not dislike. Not disdain. Hate. The use of the word, along with paying due regard to the guarantee of freedom of expression, reinforces the view that Article 4 sets a high threshold for hate speech.

(c) Incitement to racial discrimination or violence

Article 4(a) also prohibits incitement to racial discrimination, and incitement to violence against 'any race or group of persons of another colour or ethnic origin'. The *Macquarie Dictionary* defines 'incite' as:

> '[T]o urge on; stimulate or prompt to action.'[129]

Like dissemination, the prohibited conduct appears to involve a purposive element. That is, the conscious urging of racial discrimination, or violence against people of a different race, colour or ethnicity. Like dissemination, laws may target the subjective motivation to urge racial discrimination or violence, which then manifests in acts that urge these things. Alternatively, laws may determine objectively whether a person crossed a legal threshold for inciting

---

128 However, this is not a problem for expression that promotes a policy or system of racial superiority or hatred in the manner we have described it above. This is because it is possible to objectively prove that a person has based their expression on such a policy or system.
129 *Macquarie Dictionary* 750.

racial discrimination or racial violence.

(d) Overview

Article 4(a) therefore appears to be considerably narrower in scope than s 18C. It is directed to certain conduct based on racial hatred or superiority, or that incites racial discrimination or racial violence, rather than conduct that creates offence, insult or humiliation.

We will return to s 18C's conformity with Article 4 shortly. However, before doing so, it is worth considering how others have interpreted Article 4.

(e) How others have interpreted Article 4

It could be said that our interpretation of Article 4 is too narrow. However, the Committee on the Elimination of Racial Discrimination ('the Committee'), the United Nations committee that monitors the implementation of the Convention, as well as relevant commentary, appear to support an interpretation of Article 4 which, if not narrow, is at least limited.

In General Recommendation No. 15, the Committee noted that Article 4(a) creates an obligation upon States Parties to declare four types of conduct as offences:[130]

1. Dissemination of ideas based upon racial superiority or hatred;
2. Incitement to racial discrimination;
3. Acts of violence against any race or group of persons of another colour or ethnic origin; and
4. Incitement to such acts.

Lerner noted:

> The reference in the opening sentence [of Article 4] to the Universal Declaration [of Human Rights] and to the rights set forth in Article 5 should… help to interpret [Article 4(a)]. It is not the free discussion of ideas which should be punished, but the dissemination of ideas based on 'racial superiority or hatred,' and this always in accordance with the constitutional framework of each country in order not to violate fundamental rights.[131]

---

[130] Committee on the Elimination of Racial Discrimination, *General Recommendation 15: Measures to eradicate incitement to or acts of discrimination* (Forty-second session, 1993), UN Doc A/48/18 (1994) [3].

[131] Natan Lerner, *The UN Convention on the Elimination of all Forms of Racial Discrimination* (Sijthoff & Noordhoff, 2nd ed, 1980) 49.

In General Recommendation No. 35, when considering the obligation imposed under Article 4, the Committee recommended:[132]

> [T]hat the States parties declare and effectively sanction as offences punishable by law:
> (a) All dissemination of ideas *based on* racial or ethnic superiority or hatred, by whatever means;
> (b) Incitement to hatred, contempt or discrimination against members of a group on grounds of their race, colour, descent, or national or ethnic origin;
> (c) Threats or incitement to violence against persons or groups on the grounds in (b) above;
> (d) Expression of insults, ridicule or slander of persons or groups or justification of hatred, contempt or discrimination on the grounds in (b) above, *when it clearly amounts to incitement to hatred or discrimination*;
> (e) Participation in organizations and activities which promote and incite racial discrimination.

When applied to laws restricting freedom of expression, it appears that Article 4 directs States Parties to confine such laws to expression that:

- Either manifests or creates racial hatred or superiority;[133]
- Incites others to racial hatred, contempt, discrimination or violence.

Hence, under Article 4, the *minimum* requirement for prohibiting expression is that it manifests or creates a particular emotion: hatred.[134]

(f) *The conduct that s 18C makes unlawful*

To repeat the conformity requirement in the context of Article 4: to be valid, s 18C must be reasonably capable of being considered appropriate and adapted to implementing Article 4. As we noted above, under Article 4, the minimum

---

132 Committee on the Elimination of Racial Discrimination, *General recommendation No. 35: Combating racist hate speech* (26 September 2013) [13] (emphasis ours).
133 As the Committee notes with respect to insults, ridicule or slander, these things must clearly amount to incitement to racial hatred or superiority.
134 It appears that "superiority" can be either an emotion (that is, one feels superior to another) or knowledge (that is, one thinks that they are superior to another). Our analysis below assumes superiority is an emotion. However, the difficulties that s 18C encounters in conforming to Article 4 do not change if superiority is regarded as knowledge.

requirement for prohibiting expression is that it manifest or create hatred.

Section 18C makes unlawful acts that offend, insult or humiliate. In our view, it is worth looking beyond how these terms are *defined* to what these terms describe.[135] Put simply, like hatred, offence, insult and humiliation describe *emotions*. However, offence, insult and humiliation are each emotions *substantially different from hatred*.[136] They are substantially different in degree if not in kind.[137]

Before going further, we should note that, of course, the emotions that Article 4 and s 18C describe concern race, colour, ethnicity and nationality. However, in our view, it is worthwhile focusing for now on the emotions themselves. We will return to the issue of race, colour, ethnicity and nationality further below.

As to the emotions described, the question in the conformity analysis becomes this: is making unlawful acts that offend, insult or humiliate reasonably capable of being considered appropriate and adapted to Article 4's direction to prohibit conduct manifesting or creating hatred? The answer is no, for the following reasons.

To summarise and reiterate our analysis, it appears laws based on Article 4 can target the following conduct:

- Expression motivated by hate – although laws targeting this alone would be unsustainable for the reasons stated above.[138] Laws targeting this would also need to target one of the following. (Further, neither of the following requires an element that expression be motivated by hate.)
- Expression manifesting hate. That is, the expression's tone, content, or both, is hateful.
- Expression creating hate. That is, the expression inspires or incites

---

135 On a semantic analysis of the terms 'offend', 'insult', 'humiliate' and 'hate' as we have defined them above, there appears to be a heavy overlap between 'offend' and 'insult'. There also appears to be an overlap between 'insult' and 'humiliate'. However, there appears to be minimal overlap between 'offend', 'insult' and 'humiliate' on the one hand and 'hate' on the other. Our concern is that a semantic analysis of these terms may miss issues that an analysis based on the actual emotions described would identify.
136 We are using the basic emotions listed in David L Robinson, 'Brain function, emotional experience and personality' (2008) 64(4) *Netherlands Journal of Psychology* 152, 155. There are other schema for classification: see, for example Paul Ekman and Daniel Cordaro, 'What is Meant by Calling Emotions Basic' (2011) 3(4) *Emotion Review* 364, 365-6.
137 Using Robinson's list, hate is an emotion separate from those on which offence, insult or humiliation are based. It appears offence and insult are based on aversion, anger or embarrassment. Humiliation appears to be based on embarrassment. See David L Robinson, 'Brain function, emotional experience and personality' (2008) 64(4) *Netherlands Journal of Psychology* 152, 155.
138 See Part IV.E.1.(b).(ii) (pages 39-40).

hate in others.[139]

However, section 18C does not do any of these things. Rather, it targets expression creating offence, insult or humiliation. We will focus on the disparity between s 18C and Article 4's direction to enact laws targeting expression that either manifests hate or creates hate. This is because these are the types of conduct most closely related to the conduct that s 18C targets. However, it is first worth noting the disparity between s 18C and laws targeting expression motivated by hate. Doing so will help illustrate how far removed the conduct that s 18C targets is from the conduct that laws drafted pursuant to Article 4 should target.

As to expression motivated by hate, acts that offend, insult or humiliate may be motivated by feelings far removed from hatred. Such feelings include (but are not limited to) the following:

- Concern:[140] for example, where one notes appalling conditions in remote Aboriginal communities and the possible causes.
- Sorrow: for example, when one recounts the details of atrocities committed by a group of people of a particular race, colour, ethnicity or nationality.
- Amusement:[141] for example, when someone makes jokes or otherwise attempts humour on the basis of race, colour, ethnicity or nationality.

As noted above, motivation may be an element for laws drafted pursuant to Article 4. However, it is not necessary for such laws. Section 18C does not require an element of motivation. That said, the foregoing illustrates that the emotions motivating the acts that s 18C targets may vary widely.

As to expression manifesting hatred, acts that offend, insult or humiliate do not always manifest hatred. In fact, such acts may manifest hatred only some of the time. As with the motivation for acts that s 18C targets, the emotion

---

[139] We should note here that our analysis does not change if the laws are directed not against hatred, but to contempt or superiority. This is because contempt and superiority are strong emotions that appear to be based on pride. (It may be contended that the laws are directed against racial discrimination. However, there are substantial logical difficulties with the contention that if someone happens to offend a person of a certain race, colour, ethnicity or nationality then this constitutes racial discrimination. We cover this point in Part IV.E.3 (page 60).)

[140] By "concern" we mean low intensity interest or alarm resulting from caring about a situation or outcome: see David L Robinson, 'Brain function, emotional experience and personality' (2008) 64(4) *Netherlands Journal of Psychology* 152, 155.

[141] By "amusement" we mean "making light" of something. It is an emotion employed to deal with a wide range of matters, including (especially?) serious matters.

that such acts manifest vary widely. To take the examples cited above, the tone and content of an act that s 18C targets may manifest concern, sorrow or amusement. The tone and content may be far removed from manifesting hatred, and will not lead to hatred.[142] Yet, s 18C will hold a person liable for the act if it causes offence, insult or humiliation to a reasonable representative of a group or sub-group.[143]

We make three further points here. First, there is even an issue as to whether acts that offend, insult or humiliate and that manifest stronger emotions like anger or fear *necessarily* manifest hate. For example, suppose in the above example concerning recounting an atrocity, the tone and content manifests not sorrow but anger. Would the account necessarily be hateful, or lead to hate? We suggest no, because anger and hate are two distinct emotions.[144] Obviously, when it comes to a particular matter a person may be both angry and hateful, or start out angry and become hateful. However, the presence of anger regarding a matter does not mean that hate is *also* present, or that anger *must* result in hate.

Second, and related to the last point, it *is* possible that acts manifesting a certain emotion will also manifest hate. For example, the tone and content of an account of an atrocity may manifest both sorrow and hate. However, this occurs in some instances; it will not occur in all, most, or even many instances.

Third, at the other end of the spectrum from strong emotions, are acts creating offence, insult or intimidation that do not manifest *any* discernable emotion. These range from deliberately dispassionate observations to "offhand" or extemporaneous comments entailing little or no feeling.

This brings us to acts creating hatred. We should note that here our focus

---

142 The same reasoning applies to emotions less intense than hatred, like disdain and dislike.
143 We cover the reasonable representative test in more detail below.
144 Robinson categorises anger as an 'event related emotion' and hate as a 'cathecated emotion' and remarks with respect to the latter that 'there are marked differences in the extent to which [it] is experienced by different people': see David L Robinson, 'Brain function, emotional experience and personality' (2008) 64(4) *Netherlands Journal of Psychology* 152, 155. Ekman and Cordaro categorise hate as a 'mental state' separate from the emotion of anger, stating that hate 'is an enduring state marked by anger towards a person, but not the acts of that person. Unlike anger, fury or rage, it does not subside. Rather, hate persists over time and is easily called forth by any stimulus.': see Paul Ekman and Daniel Cordaro, 'What is Meant by Calling Emotions Basic' (2011) 3(4) *Emotion Review* 364, 366. Hence, to Ekman and Cordaro, anger at a person or event subsides, whereas with hate the anger endures. Relating this to the example given, recounting the atrocity may provoke anger in an audience, but this anger subsides. It does *not* mean that hate automatically results, or that the anger will 'feed' a mental state where hate results. This may happen in some cases, but does not happen in many others. Hence, a law that acted against nonthreatening expressions of anger would be a disproportionate response to combatting hate.

shifts from the person making the expression to those whom the expression affects. With motivation, the thoughts and feelings of the speaker is relevant. With manifestation, the tone and content of the speaker's expression is relevant. With acts creating hatred, the effect of the speaker's expression on others[145] is relevant.[146]

We have already noted s 18C meets a serious difficulty in that acts that offend, insult or humiliate will, in many instances, not manifest hatred. However, the shift of focus to those the expression affects creates further difficulties for s 18C.

First, the emotions created in an audience may vary widely. Continuing the examples given above, an account of an atrocity may create sorrow in a large part of the audience, but offend, insult or humiliate a small part. Note that nowhere in this example is hate a serious risk. However, under s 18C, the expression risks being unlawful. If a person wanting to speak about the atrocity declines from doing so because of the risk of it being unlawful,[147] then the majority of the audience is deprived of the account of the atrocity.

That part of the audience is offended, insulted or humiliated about expression concerning them is *not* an indication of the emotional reaction of the remainder of the audience. However, it is the emotional reaction of the remainder that should be the proper subject of laws against creating hate drafted pursuant to Article 4. That is, the question is whether the expression created hatred in the audience towards a group characterised by race, colour, ethnicity or nationality. Given this, it cannot be said that acts offending, insulting or humiliating a group or sub-group *necessarily* create hate in others towards that group or sub-group. Certainly, *some* acts that offend, insult or humiliate will do this. However, *many* such acts will not.

Second, even if offence, insult or humiliation lead to hate, then s 18C is targeting the wrong people. Under s 18C, offence, insult or humiliation is determined by the reasonable representative test. That is, whether a reasonable representative of the group or sub-group subject to the remark would be offended, insulted or humiliated.[148] The relevant group or sub-group may well be offended, insulted or humiliated. However, these are the people *least* likely to end up hating the group or sub-group, that is, end up *hating themselves*. (This raises an issue as to whether s 18C is suited at all to implementing Article 4.) Once again, the proper focus of a law drafted pursuant to Article 4 should

---

145 Which we refer to below as "the audience".
146 Although an analysis of the effect of an expression on others will often involve assessing its tone and content.
147 The "chilling effect" which we cover in more detail below.
148 Once again, we cover the reasonable representative test in more detail below.

be whether the expression created hate in the audience towards a group characterised by race, colour, ethnicity or nationality.

Third, s 18C does not require anyone to be *actually* offended, insulted or humiliated. All that is required is that the act be 'reasonably likely' to offend, insult or humiliate.[149] Section 18C's scope extends beyond actual harm to "theoretical harm", thereby widening its application.

Fourth, by requiring an expression to create hate (or manifest hate, for that matter), it appears that a law drafted pursuant to Article 4 would ask far less of people than s 18C. Under a law based on Article 4, people need to avoid conduct that manifests or creates hate towards people of a certain race, colour or ethnicity. By contrast, under s 18C, people need to avoid conduct that creates offence, insult or humiliation in certain groups or sub-groups. This is asking far more of people than what Article 4 requires, especially when the guarantee of freedom of expression in Article 5 is considered.

Given the foregoing, s 18C is too broad for a law purporting to target hate. It targets the wrong feelings, in the wrong people. In making unlawful offence, insult or humiliation of a group or sub-group, s 18C targets a wide range of expression manifesting or creating emotions substantially different from hate. These problems are not remedied by making unlawful acts based on the race, colour, ethnicity or nationality of any given group. This is because Article 4 is *specifically* directed to this particular form of hatred. Even here, Article 4's prohibitions on freedom of expression are limited. We cover the reasons why Article 4's drafters took this approach when discussing Article 5 below.

The difficulties with s 18C that we have outlined have been remarked upon by others. As Dan Meagher noted, 'it is clear enough that one can racially insult or offend another without ever expressing or intending hatred for that person's race or ethnicity'.[150] However, s 18C extends well beyond speech based on racial hatred, or incitement to racial discrimination or violence. Indeed, the words of s 18C are 'broad enough to encompass all manner of racist speech from the hateful to even that which is somewhat trivial'.[151] It was observed in *Bropho* that the words of s 18C are 'a long way removed from the mischief to

---

149 RDA s 18C(1)(a).
150 Dan Meagher, 'So Far So Good?: A Critical Evaluation of Racial Vilification Laws in Australia' (2004) 32(2) *Federal Law Review* 225, 232. See also Senator Ellison (Minister for Justice and Customs), *Hansard (Senate)*, 19 August 2003, 14046.
151 Dilan Thampapillai, 'Managing Dissent under Part IIA of the *Racial Discrimination Act*' (2010) 17(1) *Murdoch University Electronic Journal of Law* 52, 53.

which Article 4 of Convention is directed.'¹⁵²

Section 18C therefore appears to greatly overreach the boundaries that Article 4 sets for prohibited expression. Indeed, it is no exaggeration to say that s 18C's approach to implementing Article 4 is not just legislative overreach, but legislative overkill. However, even if it were only a case of legislative overreach, then this is sufficient to say that s 18C is not reasonably capable of being a suitable or fitting way of implementing Article 4.¹⁵³ Hence, s 18C fails the conformity requirement.

Section 18C's overreach is not remedied by s 18D. This is because s 18D provides that acts are not unlawful so long as they are (amongst other things) made 'reasonably and in good faith'.¹⁵⁴ However, speech that offends, insults and even humiliates will fall short of the harm threshold Article 4 requires even if that speech is made *unreasonably* and in *bad faith*. Speech that offends, insults or humiliates is often unfair, tendentious, gratuitous, hyperbolic or disingenuous. "Cheap shots" and "hits below the belt" abound.¹⁵⁵ This is especially so when it comes to discussing contentious political or social issues. However, many (if

---

152 *Bropho* [2004] FCAFC 16; (2004) 135 FCR 105, 123-4 [68] (French J).
153 The disparity between means and end is illustrated strikingly when a proportionality test is employed. Making unlawful offence, insult and even humiliation is plainly disproportionate to the purpose of Article 4, which prohibits incitement to racial hatred.
154 RDA s 18D. We note the observation by French J in *Bropho* [2004] FCAFC 16; (2004) 135 FCR 105, 125-6 [72]-[73] that s 18D is not strictly speaking a free speech exception to s 18C but instead should be seen as 'defining the limits of the proscription in s 18C'.
155 The classic example is humour in all its manifestations. Chris Rock no longer plays US colleges because of (amongst other things) 'their willingness not to offend someone': see Frank Rich, 'In Conversation with Chris Rock', *Vulture* (online) 30 November 2014. Jerry Seinfeld commented in a radio interview that he was warned by fellow comics '"don't go near colleges, they're so PC"': Caitlin Flanagan, 'That's Not Funny! Today's college students can't seem to take a joke', *The Atlantic* (online), September 2015. Seinfeld's comment prompted a college student to write a letter to *The Huffington Post* giving Seinfeld advice about appropriate types of provocative comedy (no, we are not making this up): Anthony Berteaux, 'An Open Letter to Jerry Seinfeld from a "Politically Correct" College Student', *The Huffington Post* (online), 10 June 2015. This prompted a spirited rejoinder from Bill Maher: Lydia O'Conner, 'Bill Maher Calls College Student A "Little Sh*t" for Criticizing Jerry Seinfeld', *The Huffington Post* (online), 21 June 2015. For an analysis of the underlying politics of the student's criticism of Seinfeld, see Scott Greer, 'The Left's Outrage At Jerry Seinfeld Proves His Point', *Daily Caller* (online), 13 June 2015. While the focus on US college campuses may appear far removed from contemporary Australia, it bears remembering that university graduates go on to influence prevailing thought in society. Battles over freedom of expression on US campuses are relevant to battles over freedom of expression elsewhere. Remarking on the importance of humour, John Cleese said 'There are some people who one would wish to offend', and later: 'All humour is critical. If you start to say "Ooh! We mustn't criticise or offend them, then humour's gone, [and] with humour goes a sense of proportion, and as far as I'm concerned you're living in *1984*"': John Cleese, 'Political Correctness Can Lead to an Orwellian Nightmare', Big Think, 31 January 2016.

not most) instances of such speech will also *not* be based on racial hatred, or amount to threats or incitement to racial hatred.

Thus, there is significant disparity between the type of activity Article 4 prohibits, and the language s 18C makes unlawful. This indicates that the means s 18C uses to regulate speech are, if not appropriate to Article 4's purpose, are plainly not adapted to it. As we have demonstrated, making unlawful offence, insult and humiliation is not a suitable or fitting way to prohibit racial hatred, or the incitement to racial hatred or violence.[156] Hence, s 18C it is not reasonably capable of being considered appropriate and adapted to implementing the obligation contained under Article 4 of the Convention.

2 Article 5

Our conformity analysis cannot focus on just Article 4. This is because Article 4 itself requires that due regard be given to the rights in the *Universal Declaration of Human Rights* ('UDHR') and in Article 5. It is important to note both the text and purpose of Article 5. As to its text, Article 5 provides, relevantly:

> In compliance with the fundamental obligations laid down in article 2 of this Convention, States Parties undertake to prohibit and to eliminate racial discrimination in all its forms and to guarantee the right of everyone, without distinction as to race, colour, or national or ethnic origin, to equality before the law, notably in the enjoyment of the following rights:
>
> ...
>
> (b) The right to security of person and protection by the State against violence or bodily harm, whether inflicted by government officials or by any individual, group or institution...
> (d) Other civil rights, in particular: ...
>   (vii) The right to freedom of thought, conscience and religion;
>   (viii) The right to freedom of opinion and expression...

As to the purpose of Article 5, Schwelb noted the origin of Article 4's reference to Article 5:

> The requirement of due regard to 'the rights set forth in Article 5 of this Convention' has its origin in an amendment by the Nordic delegations which was intended to arrive at 'the most constructive possible text'

---

156 This is so even if a more expansive view is taken of 'dissemination'. As noted above, in many instances acts that offend, insult or humiliate will not be motivated by, manifest or create hate. Section 18C would remain ill-suited and maladapted to Article 4.

under which the objective of Article 4, designed to safeguard certain human rights and fundamental freedoms, *should not be achieved at the expense of other equally fundamental human rights*.[157]

Lerner noted:

> In the second part of the opening paragraph [of Article 4], States Parties undertake to adopt *immediate* and *positive* measures to eradicate incitement to, or acts of, racial discrimination. To this end, States Parties will have to adopt, *inter alia*, three kinds of measures [Articles 4(a)-(c)], always *with due regard to the principles embodied in the Universal Declaration of Human Rights and the rights expressly set forth in Article 5* of the Convention.
>
> The phrase beginning with 'with due regard' was introduced... in order to meet objections of those who maintained that Article 4 would violate the principles of freedom of speech and freedom of association. The incorporated phrase was interpreted in the sense of giving State Parties the right to understand Article 4 'as imposing no obligation on any party to take measures which are not fully consistent with constitutional guarantees of freedom including freedom of speech and association.'[158]

The Committee has noted that Article 4 'requires that measures to eliminate incitement and discrimination must be made with *due regard* to the principles of the Universal Declaration of Human Rights and the rights expressly set forth in Article 5 of the Convention'.[159] It has also noted that freedom of opinion and expression should be 'borne in mind as the most pertinent reference principle when calibrating the legitimacy of speech restrictions'.[160] The Committee has expressed concern about 'broad or vague restrictions',[161] stating that 'States parties should formulate restrictions on speech with sufficient precision, according to the standards in the Convention as elaborated in the present recommendation'.[162] We would argue that this has not been done in the case of s 18C, which reaches considerably farther than the measures outlined in General Recommendation No. 35.

---

157 Egon Schwelb, 'The International Convention on the Elimination of All Forms of Racial Discrimination' (1966) 15 *International and Comparative Law Quarterly* 996, 1024 (emphasis ours).
158 Natan Lerner, *The UN Convention on the Elimination of all Forms of Racial Discrimination* (Sijthoff & Noordhoff, 2nd ed, 1980) 48 (emphasis in the original, citations omitted).
159 Committee on the Elimination of Racial Discrimination, *General recommendation No. 35: Combating racist hate speech* (26 September 2013) [19] (emphasis ours).
160 Ibid.
161 Ibid [20].
162 Ibid.

Article 5 *guarantees* the right of everyone, without distinction as to race, colour, or national or ethnic origin, to (amongst other rights) freedom of expression.[163] This freedom extends to expression that offends, insults or even humiliates. Consequently, the problems we noted above concerning s 18C's compliance with Article 4 are only worsened when Article 5 is taken into account (as it must). This is because making unlawful 'offence', 'insult' and even 'humiliation' are measures that are plainly ill-suited and maladapted to prohibiting racial hatred *while paying due regard to the guarantee of freedom of expression*.[164] Hence, s 18C cannot be said to be reasonably capable of being appropriate and adapted to the purpose of Article 4.

Compounding this, it appears that s 18C does not give due regard to Article 5's guarantee of equality before the law. The test used to determine offence, insult, humiliation or intimidation is the 'reasonable representative' test.[165] Section 18C(1)(a) requires that offence, insult or humiliation be determined 'in all the circumstances'. Hence, attributes of a person's race, colour, ethnicity or nationality should be considered. The reasonable representative may be of a group or sub-group bound by race, colour, ethnicity or nationality.[166] As Bromberg J noted in *Eatock*:

> The assessment as to the likelihood of people within a group being offended by an act directed at them in a general sense, is to be made by reference to a *representative member or members of the group*. For that purpose the 'ordinary' or 'reasonable' member or members of the group are to be isolated... In that

---

163 Convention Art 5(d)(viii).
164 Once again, the "reasonable proportionality" test provides a striking illustration of the disparity between the means s 18C uses to achieve Article 4's purpose. Making unlawful offence, insult and even humiliation is plainly disproportionate to the purpose of Article 4, which prohibits incitement to racial hatred while paying due regard to the guarantee of freedom of opinion and expression.
165 *Creek* [2001] FCA 1007; (2001) 112 FCR 352, 356-7 [16] (Kiefel J); *Scully* [2002] FCA 1080; (2002) 120 FCR 243, 272 [108] (Hely J); *Eatock v Bolt* [2011] FCA 1103; (2011) 197 FCR 261, 321 [253] (Bromberg J) ('*Eatock*'). Barker J used the perspective of the "reasonable victim" in *Clarke v Nationwide News Pty Ltd trading as The Sunday Times* [2012] FCA 307; (2012) 201 FCR 389, 401-3 [50]-[59] (Barker J). In doing so, Barker J did not apply principles different from the "reasonable representative test". However, in our view, the phrase "reasonable victim" should be avoided when describing the relevant test. The phrase "reasonable victim" implies that those subject to the alleged offensive, insulting or humiliating conduct are *already* victims. The only issue is whether a "reasonable victim" would have been offended, insulted or humiliated, thereby meeting the threshold for legal liability. Descriptions of legal tests should avoid language that suggests an outcome. Hence, the description "reasonable representative test" should be preferred, and is the description we use in this treatise.
166 *Eatock* [2011] FCA 1103; (2011) 197 FCR 261, 321 [252] (Bromberg J) (emphasis ours).

way, reactions which are extreme or atypical will be disregarded.[167]

Bromberg J noted that the reasonable representative test may apply to subgroups within a particular group:

> [I]t is necessary to bear in mind that conduct may be directed at a diverse group of people. A diverse group will likely comprise discernible subgroups. Reactions to the same conduct may vary as between sub-groups. That may be because of an extra attribute common to the sub-group. An example from the decided cases is 'young and impressionable Jews' who were regarded as a vulnerable sub-group of Australian Jewry by Branson J in *Jones*. Additionally, it may be appropriate in some cases of alleged group offence to assess the reaction of those within a group to whom the conduct is particularly targeted and thus most likely to have been offended. Finkelstein J in *.au Domain* expressed that approach when… he said:
>
>> Logic demands that if one is dealing with a diverse group then, for the purpose of determining whether particular conduct has the capacity to mislead, it is necessary to select a hypothetical individual from that section of the group which is most likely to be misled. If the court is satisfied that this hypothetical individual is likely to have been misled by that conduct, that would be sufficient.[168]

Elaborating on what the phrase 'in all the circumstances' entailed for the reasonable representative of a group or sub-group, Bromberg J noted that:

> It is the values, standards and other circumstances of the person or group of people to whom s 18C(1)(a) refers that will bear upon the likely reaction of those persons to the act in question.[169]

And later:

> It requires that the social, cultural, historical and other circumstances attending the person or the people in the group be considered when assessing whether offence was reasonably likely.[170]

However, there are significant problems with the reasonable representative

---

167 Ibid 320 [251] (Bromberg J) (citations omitted, emphasis ours).
168 Ibid 321 [252] (Bromberg J) (citations omitted).
169 Ibid 321 [253] (Bromberg J). See also Adrienne Stone, 'The Ironic Aftermath of *Eatock v Bolt*' (2015) 38 *Melbourne University Law Review* 926, 931.
170 *Eatock* [2011] FCA 1103; (2011) 197 FCR 261, 322 [257] (Bromberg J). See also Adrienne Stone, 'The Ironic Aftermath of *Eatock v Bolt*' (2015) 38 *Melbourne University Law Review* 926, 931.

test. First, attributes or beliefs (or both) of the race, colour, ethnicity or nationality of the group or sub-group are assigned to the reasonable representative. How is this to be determined? Are such attributes or beliefs those thought commonly held by that group? This would make sense in the context of the test so described. However, if so, it is not that far from (and, in some cases, the same as) *stereotypical* attributes or beliefs being assigned to the reasonable representative. This is a curious result for legislation whose aim is to eliminate racial discrimination. Rather, racial discrimination appears to be entrenched in the tests to be used to determine complaints.

Further, given the breadth of the phrase 'in all the circumstances',[171] we submit that the circumstances of the *speaker* are also relevant. Such circumstances include the speaker's race, colour, national or ethnic origin. This means that a speaker may have a wider or narrower range of language in relation to an issue depending on (i) the speaker's race, colour or national or ethnic origin; and (ii) the race, colour or national origin of the group or sub-group to which the speaker refers. Hence, a person's legal liability depends on:

- The race, colour, ethnicity or nationality of the reasonable representative of the group or sub-group; and
- The person's own race, colour, ethnicity or nationality.

To take a controversial but relevant example, suppose someone said at a social gathering[172] "it is moronic for Palestinians to claim that they are a nation". (We hasten to add that this is not our view. The issues concerning Palestine are complex and vexed, and beyond the scope of this treatise. We are only using a topical example to illustrate a problem with s 18C.) Under s 18C, someone's legal liability would depend on the following:

- Whether the statement was made to a group of Palestinian expatriates,[173] who are reasonably likely to be offended or insulted.
- Whether the statement was made to a group of people who are not Palestinian expatriates, who may find the statement controversial but would not be reasonably likely to be offended or insulted.
- Whether the speaker was Palestinian, in which case their statement may be "given a pass" by Palestinian expatriates and thus not be

---

171 RDA s 18C(1)(a).
172 Which we will assume is a public place for the purposes of s 18C.
173 We assume that the Palestinian expatriates referred to here are also Australian citizens.

considered reasonably likely to offend or insult.
- Whether the speaker was an Israeli expatriate,[174] in which case a group of Palestinian expatriates would be reasonably likely to not only be offended or insulted, but outraged.

To have someone's legal liability depend on the race, colour, ethnicity or nationality of their audience or themselves is the antithesis of equality before the law. That someone may be legally liable in circumstances where another may not, and the *only* point of difference is the race, colour, ethnicity or nationality of the speaker or audience, suggests that s 18C's text or operation (or both) perpetuates racial discrimination. To be clear, racial equality – and notably equality before the law[175] – is one of the Convention's major objectives.[176] Section 18C appears to not pay due regard to this objective when both Article 4 and Article 5 require otherwise. Consequently, s 18C's legislative means are plainly inappropriate to serving the end of prohibiting incitement to racial discrimination or disseminating racial hatred while paying due regard to equality before the law.[177]

Once again, s 18D does not remedy s 18C's problems. Indeed, s 18D itself compounds s 18C's problems by not paying due regard to equality before the law. Section 18D appears to provide a broader range of expression to certain classes of people, in particular those engaged in academic, artistic, scientific or journalistic pursuits. As we note below concerning the implied equality of political communication,[178] there is no reason why people routinely engaged in academic, artistic, scientific or journalistic pursuits are better able to speak about matters of race, culture or ethnicity than people not engaged in such pursuits. If anything, history suggests that great damage can be done to race relations through academic, scientific, artistic or journalistic works.[179] Ultimately, however, an individual's legal liability should not depend on whether they

---

174 Likewise, we assume that the Israeli expatriate is an Australian citizen.
175 Egon Schwelb, 'The International Convention on the Elimination of All Forms of Racial Discrimination' (1966) 15 *International and Comparative Law Quarterly* 996, 1025-6.
176 Ibid 1057; see also *Koowarta* [1982] HCA 27; (1982) 153 CLR 168, 220 (Stephen J), 248 (Wilson J), 265 (Brennan J).
177 We note that the reasonable representative test also appears to breach RDA s 10(1), which provides for equality before the law in the enjoyment of rights. RDA s 10(2) specifically refers to Article 5.
178 Please see Part V.D.4.(b).(ii) (page 163).
179 Lerner noted that 'It should not be forgotten... that in the past many books and papers aimed at disseminating racial hatred adopted the form of 'scientific' books or studies. The Nazi regime was specially prolific in the production of such studies': see Natan Lerner, *The UN Convention on the Elimination of all Forms of Racial Discrimination* (Sijthoff & Noordhoff, 2nd ed, 1980) 49.

are engaged in an academic, scientific, artistic or journalistic pursuit. This is especially so considering that such criteria favour classes of people who are routinely engaged in such work over classes of people who are not.

Further, the reasonable representative test appears to violate Articles 2(1)(c) and 4(c) of the Convention. As stated above, Article 2(1)(c) provides that State Parties to the Convention must amend or rescind laws that have the effect of creating or perpetuating racial discrimination.[180] Article 4(c) provides that State Parties '[s]hall not permit public authorities or public institutions, national or local, to promote or incite racial discrimination'.[181]

We note in closing that Article 1(4) and Article 2(2) do not remedy the inequitable operation of s 18C. Both Articles concern affirmative action. Article 1(4) provides:

> Special measures taken for the sole purpose of securing adequate advancement of certain racial or ethnic groups or individuals requiring such protection as may be necessary in order to ensure such groups or individuals equal enjoyment or exercise of human rights and fundamental freedoms shall not be deemed racial discrimination, provided, however, that such measures do not, as a consequence, lead to the maintenance of separate rights for different racial groups and that they shall not be continued after the objectives for which they were taken have been achieved.[182]

Article 2(2) provides:

> States Parties shall, when the circumstances so warrant, take, in the social, economic, cultural and other fields, special and concrete measures to ensure the adequate development and protection of certain racial groups or individuals belonging to them, for the purpose of guaranteeing them the full and equal enjoyment of human rights and fundamental freedoms. These measures shall in no case entail as a consequence the maintenance of unequal or separate rights for different racial groups after the objectives for which they were taken have been achieved.[183]

In General Recommendation No. 32, the Committee commented on the operation of these Articles as follows:

---

180 Convention Art 2(1)(c).
181 Convention Art 4(c).
182 Convention Art 1(4).
183 Convention Art 2(2).

Special measures should be appropriate to the situation to be remedied, be legitimate, necessary in a democratic society, respect the principles of fairness and proportionality, and be temporary. The measures should be designed and implemented on the basis of need, grounded in a realistic appraisal of the current situation of the individuals and communities concerned.

Appraisals of the need for special measures should be carried out on the basis of accurate data, disaggregated by race, colour, descent and ethnic or national origin and incorporating a gender perspective, on the socio-economic and cultural status and conditions of the various groups in the population and their participation in the social and economic development of the country.

States parties should ensure that special measures are designed and implemented on the basis of prior consultation with affected communities and the active participation of such communities.[184]

That is, Articles 1(4) and 2(2) are limited in nature. They allow specific, targeted measures to help certain racial or ethnic groups. These measures must have a limited duration, and should be carefully calibrated based on available data. Section 18C appears to be a permanent law whose terms and effect discriminate on grounds of race, colour, ethnicity and nationality.[185]

3   *Article 2*

Like Article 4, Article 2 is important to our analysis and should be cited in full. Article 2 provides:

> 1. States Parties condemn racial discrimination and undertake to pursue by all appropriate means and without delay a policy of eliminating racial discrimination in all its forms and promoting understanding among all races, and, to this end:
> (a) Each State Party undertakes to engage in no act or practice of racial discrimination against persons, groups of persons or institutions and to ensure that all public authorities and public institutions, national and local, shall act in conformity with this obligation;

---

184 Committee on the Elimination of Racial Discrimination, *General recommendation No. 32: The meaning and scope of special measures in the International Convention on the Elimination of All Forms of Racial Discrimination* (24 September 2009) [16]-[18] (citations omitted).
185 Section 18C's effect has the potential to *worsen* over time, as a body of precedent builds up that reinforces the inequality inherent in s 18C itself.

(b) Each State Party undertakes not to sponsor, defend or support racial discrimination by any persons or organizations;
(c) Each State Party shall take effective measures to review governmental, national and local policies, and to amend, rescind or nullify any laws and regulations which have the effect of creating or perpetuating racial discrimination wherever it exists;
(d) Each State Party shall prohibit and bring to an end, by all appropriate means, including legislation as required by circumstances, racial discrimination by any persons, group or organization;
(e) Each State Party undertakes to encourage, where appropriate, integrationist multi-racial organizations and movements and other means of eliminating barriers between races, and to discourage anything which tends to strengthen racial division.

Articles 2(1)(a)-(c) are directed to government activities. Article 2(1)(e) is directed to eliminating racial barriers. It is Article 2(1)(d) that appears to most directly support s 18C.

Article 2(1)(d) appears 'one step removed' from the specific issue that Article 4 addresses. Put another way, Article 4 directly addresses the problem of hate speech and incitement to racial hatred. There is good reason for this. As noted above,[186] when the Convention was being drafted, the fact that anti-discrimination law may adversely affect freedom of speech and freedom of association was the subject of much controversy.[187] Article 4 was designed to specifically deal with this issue. Even then, the wording of Article 4 was the subject of much discussion and deliberation.[188] While Article 2 has a significant role to play in combatting discrimination, its more general wording should not be taken to sweep aside Article 4 (and the specific concerns it addresses) by a side-wind. Consequently, laws regulating speech are more likely not to be reasonably considered to be appropriate and adapted to the language that Article 2 (and in particular Article 2(1)(d)) employs.

Article 2(1)(d) is directed towards the elimination of racial discrimination, with racial discrimination defined in Article 1 as a distinction, exclusion, restriction or preference based on race, colour, descent or national or ethnic origin. This language is too vague to justify restricting speech that offends,

---
186 See Part IV.D.2 (pages 30-1) and Part IV.E.2 (pages 51-2).
187 Natan Lerner, *The UN Convention on the Elimination of all Forms of Racial Discrimination* (Sijthoff & Noordhoff, 2nd ed, 1980) 11-2, 37-8.
188 Ibid 11-2, 43, 47.

insults or humiliates. It brings into sharp focus the concerns that the Committee expressed about 'broad or vague restrictions' and the need to carefully formulate restrictions so that they give due regard to freedom of expression.[189]

Further, Article 5 expressly states that it applies to Article 2.[190] That is, eliminating racial discrimination requires the guarantee of the right (amongst others) to freedom of opinion and expression. The same considerations that apply to Article 4 with respect to Article 5 also apply to Article 2.

We now turn to some further issues concerning Article 2.

(a)   Is there a right not to be offended, insulted or humiliated?

A difficulty that Article 2(1)(d) encounters in supporting s 18C is identifying the specific right referred to in Article 2(1)(d) that would overcome the guarantee of freedom of expression in Article 5. As noted above, Article 2(1)(d) supports legislation to eliminate racial discrimination. This invites consideration of what 'racial discrimination' means in the Convention.

The definition of 'racial discrimination' is found in Article 1. This definition is essential to understand the way that Article 5 interacts with the other Articles of the Convention. Article 1 states that for the purposes of the Convention 'racial discrimination' means:

> [A]ny distinction, exclusion, restriction or preference based on race, colour, descent, or national or ethnic origin which has the purpose or effect of nullifying or impairing the recognition, enjoyment or exercise, on an equal footing, of human rights and fundamental freedoms in the political, economic, social, cultural or any other field of public life.[191]

This is substantially the same definition that is adopted in s 9(1) of the RDA. As was noted by Frédéric Mégret this definition of 'racial discrimination' means that:

> [r]acial discrimination occurs not simply when differences are made between certain racial groups, *but when this differentiation adversely affects the enjoyment of rights otherwise protected by international human rights treaties by members of one group.*[192]

This requirement was also confirmed by the Committee, with specific

---
189 See Part IV.E.2 (page 52).
190 Convention Art 5.
191 Convention Art 1(1).
192 Frédéric Mégret, *The Relevance of international instruments on racial discrimination to racial discrimination policy in Ontario* (Ontario Human Rights Commission, December 2004) (emphasis added).

reference to the obligations under Article 2.[193] The central rights referred to are expressly outlined in Article 5 of the Convention, and include 'the right to freedom of opinion and expression'.[194]

This limitation is central when reconciling rights. When, for example, speech reaches a level that constitutes an incitement to violence, it adversely affects the enjoyment of 'the right to security of person and protection by the State against violence or bodily harm, whether inflicted by government officials or by any individual group or institution' by individuals or groups targeted by that speech.[195] The right of security of person is an express right recognised in international law.

However, in international law there is no express right protecting people from being offended, insulted or even humiliated.[196] At best, the right not to be offended, insulted or humiliated may be an aspect of other rights, in particular the rights to security of person, to dignity and to equality.

(b) Security of person

In addition to Article 5's guarantee of security of person, Article 3 of the UDHR and Article 9(1) of the ICCPR provides that everyone 'has the right to life, liberty and security of person'. However, the right to security of person does not extend to protection against offence, insult or even humiliation. The HRC noted the following about the right to security of person in General Comment No. 35:

> The right to security of person protects individuals against intentional infliction of bodily or mental injury, regardless of whether the victim is detained or non-detained. ... The right to personal security also obliges States parties to take appropriate measures... to protect individuals from foreseeable threats to life or bodily integrity proceeding from any governmental or private actors.[197]

The HRC went on to note:

---

193 Committee on the Elimination of Racial Discrimination, *General Recommendation 14* (16 March 1993). See also Human Rights Committee, *General Comment 18: Non-discrimination* (10 November 1989).
194 Convention Art 5(viii).
195 Convention Art 5(b).
196 See James Spigelman, 'Free Speech Tripped up by Offensive Line', *The Australian*, 11 December 2002, 12, quoting Jeremy Waldron, *The Harm in Hate Speech* (Harvard University Press, 2012) 106.
197 Human Rights Committee, *General Comment 35: Article 9 (Liberty and security of person)* (13 February 2014) [9].

The right to security of person does not address all risks to physical or mental health and is not implicated in the indirect health impact of being the target of civil or criminal proceedings.[198]

The HRC's comments need to be read in light of what it said in General Comment No. 34 regarding freedom of expression:

> [Article 19(2) of the ICCPR] requires States parties to guarantee the right to freedom of expression, including the right to seek, receive and impart information and ideas *of all kinds* regardless of frontiers. This right includes the expression and receipt of communications of *every form of idea and opinion* capable of transmission to others, subject to the provisions in [Articles 19(3) and 20 of the ICCPR]. It includes political discourse, commentary on one's own and on public affairs, canvassing, discussion of human rights, journalism, cultural and artistic expression, teaching, and religious discourse. It may also include commercial advertising. The scope of [Article 19(2) of the ICCPR] embraces *even expression that may be regarded as deeply offensive*, although such expression may be restricted in accordance with the provisions of [Articles 19(3) and 20].[199]

As we demonstrate below, Article 20 of the ICCPR sets a high harm threshold for prohibitions on expression promoting racial hatred.[200]

Hence, the right to security of person is not concerned with all risks to a person either physically or mentally. Rather, the right appears directed to protection from physical harm or serious mental injury. It is not directed to expression that is, without more, deeply offensive. By extension, it does not apply to expression that is, without more, insulting or humiliating.

(c) Dignity and equality

This brings us to the rights to dignity and to equality. These are rights have been held in case law to justify prohibiting speech that offends, insults or humiliates. For example, in *Eatock*, Bromberg J held that equality and dignity were the underlying rationale for protecting both individuals and society from the ills of

---

198 Ibid. The HRC's comments concerning the indirect health impact of being the target of civil or criminal proceedings also apply analogously to other processes necessary to democratic governance and the rule of law, such as being exposed to controversial ideas discussed publicly.
199 Human Rights Committee, *General Comment 34, Article 19: Freedom of opinion and expression* (12 September 2011) [11] (emphasis ours).
200 See Part IV.G (page 91).

dissemination of racial prejudice.[201]

However, there are fundamental problems with finding a right not to be offended, insulted or even humiliated within the rights to dignity or equality. What follows is an exploration of these problems.

(i)   Vague notions of dignity, or equality, confining the express, fundamental, freedom of expression

> You keep using that word. I do not think it means what you think it means.[202]

What do "dignity" and "equality" mean? This question is important because it is claimed that rights to dignity, equality, or both, restrict freedom of expression. Freedom of expression itself is a freedom both expressly stated in the UDHR, and expressly guaranteed under the Convention. In addition, the constitutional validity of s 18C under the external affairs power ultimately depends on whether it can be reasonably considered to be appropriate and adapted to the Convention. A fundamental freedom like freedom of expression should not be at risk of being compromised to promote vague notions of dignity or equality.

We will first consider dignity. For our analysis, we assume that the right to dignity is that provided in Article 1 of the UDHR, which provides:

> All human beings are born free and equal in dignity and rights. They are endowed with reason and conscience and should act towards one another in a spirit of brotherhood.

The Convention's preamble, recites:

> *Considering* that the Charter of the United Nations is based on the principles of the dignity and equality inherent in all human beings…
> *Considering* that the Universal Declaration of Human Rights proclaims that all human beings are born free and equal in dignity and rights and that everyone is entitled to all the rights and freedoms set out therein, without distinction of any kind, in particular as to race, colour or national origin…

There is no definition as to what 'dignity' means in the UDHR or the Convention. However, whatever dignity means in these instruments, it *cannot*

---

201 *Eatock* [2011] FCA 1103; (2011) 197 FCR 261, 314-5 [226] (Bromberg J).
202 A classic quote from the character of Inigo Montoya in the *The Princess Bride* (Directed by Rob Reiner, Act III Communications, 1987) 15:47.

mean freedom from offence, insult or humiliation. This is because, first, the term 'dignity' was used in the UDHR *precisely* because it was vague, thereby permitting a wide range of interpretations about its nature.[203] That is, people of different ideological, cultural or philosophical backgrounds would interpret dignity their own way. As Jacques Maritain, who was influential in the drafting of the UDHR[204] and who advocated using dignity as an underlying concept for human rights, later noted:

> Conceivably the advocates of the liberal-individualist; of the Communist and of the co-operative type of society might draw up similar, even identical, lists of Human Rights. But their exercise of these rights will differ. All depends on the *ultimate value* whereon those rights depend and in terms of which they are integrated by mutual limitations. It is in terms of the scale of values which we thus acknowledge that we establish the norms whereby, in our eyes, Human Rights, economic and social, as well as individual, shall impinge on life; it is from these different scales of values that spring mutual accusations of misunderstanding certain essential rights of the human being leveled by those for whom the mark of *human dignity* lies firstly and chiefly in the power to appropriate individually the gifts of nature so that each may be in a position to do freely what pleases him; by those who see it in the power to place those gifts under the collective control of the social body and thus deliver man from the treadmill of labour and gain control of history; or by those who see it in the power of bringing the gifts of nature into service for the joint attainment of an immaterial good and of the free self-determination of the person. *It remains to be decided which has a true and which a distorted vision of Man.*[205]

This concept of dignity necessarily presupposes the freedoms of conscience, opinion and expression in order for people from different ideologies, cultures or philosophies to interpret and express their own concept of dignity. It also meant that *disagreement*, including *vehement disagreement*, over the concept was

---

203 Christopher McCrudden, 'Human Dignity and Judicial Interpretation of Human Rights' (2008) 19(4) *European Journal of International Law* 655, 677-8.
204 Ibid 662, 677-8. See also Andrew Woodcock. 'Jacques Maritain, Natural Law and the Universal Declaration of Human Rights' (2006) 8 *Journal of the History of International Law* 245, 247-8, 260, 264-6.
205 Jacques Maritain, 'Introduction' in United Nations Educational, Social and Cultural Organization (ed), *Human Rights: Comments and Interptretations* (UNESCO, 1948) viii (emphasis ours).

inevitable.[206] Offense, insult and humiliation are, in turn, inevitable incidents of such disagreement.

Second, while allowing for different conceptions of human dignity, Maritain himself favoured a conception based on natural law.[207] This is unsurprising given the prevalence of natural law theory in Western legal thought at the time. Andrew Woodcock, arguing that the UDHR fits firmly into the natural law tradition,[208] summarised the rights Maritain thought fundamental to the preservation of human dignity as follows:

1. The right to life;
2. The right to personal freedom;
3. The right to free enjoyment of family;
4. The right to intellectual, and – perhaps most importantly – religious freedom; and
5. The right to property ownership.[209]

The right to freedom of expression is found in the right to personal and intellectual freedom. Notably absent from the list of rights that Maritain thought fundamental to human dignity was a right not to be offended, insulted or humiliated. Indeed, we can surmise that, given Maritain was a Catholic philosopher, the notion that people had such rights would be contrary to Christian humility.

Third, it is possible to identify unifying themes concerning dignity across cultures and across legal systems. Christopher McCrudden identified the 'minimum core' of human dignity as comprising three elements:

> The first is that every human being possesses an intrinsic worth, merely by being human. The second is that this intrinsic worth should be recognized

---

206 Mary Ann Glendon has noted that, to Maritain, the UDHR needed 'some ultimate value whereon rights depend and in terms of which they are integrated by mutual limitations'. She noted 'that value, explicitly set forth in the Declaration, is human dignity. But as time went on, it has become painfully apparent that human dignity possesses no more immunity to hijacking than any other concept.' She later noted that 'All in all, one may say of "dignity" in the [UDHR] what Abraham Lincoln once said about "equality" in the Declaration of Independence: it is a hard nut to crack.': Mary Ann Glendon, 'Foundations of Human Rights: The Unfinished Business' (1999) 44(1) *American Journal of Jurisprudence* 1, 12-3.
207 Maritain's conception of human dignity appears to accord with the 'fundamental dignity' expressed in Patrick Lee and Robert P George 'The Nature and Basis of Human Dignity' (2008) 21(2) *Ratio Juris* 173.
208 Andrew Woodcock. 'Jacques Maritain, Natural Law and the Universal Declaration of Human Rights' (2006) 8 *Journal of the History of International Law* 245, 262.
209 Ibid 260.

and respected by others... [Third]... recognizing the intrinsic worth the individual requires that the state should be seen to exist for the sake of the individual human being, and not vice versa...[210]

The first two elements McCrudden identified are worth exploring, as they illuminate the apparent tension between freedom of expression and the alleged right not to be offended, insulted or humiliated.[211] According to certain commentators, human dignity entails being accorded a certain level of respect.[212] Being accorded respect precludes an individual being offended, insulted or humiliated.[213] Hence, the right to human dignity entails a right not to be offended, insulted or humiliated. However, there are historical and conceptual difficulties with such an argument.

Historically, given the rationale for using dignity in the UDHR, one should

---

210 Christopher McCrudden, 'Human Dignity and Judicial Interpretation of Human Rights' (2008) 19(4) *European Journal of International Law* 655, 679.
211 We should note that our exploration of the concepts in these elements may not accord with how McCrudden would explore them. We use McCrudden's statement as a framework for our own exploration.
212 For example, Jeremy Waldron has advanced the concept of 'status dignity' when exploring to what extent respect should be accorded human beings. Waldron has described the historical evolution of human rights as being the 'upwards equalisation of rank, so that we now try to accord to every human being something of the dignity, rank and expectation of respect that was formerly accorded to nobility': Jeremy Waldron, 'How Law Protects Dignity' (2012) 71(1) *Cambridge Law Journal* 200, 213. Putting aside the problems we are about to cover, were everyone to be treated as nobility, then in democracies it is better that everyone conducted themselves with the phlegm of English yeomen rather than the touchiness of *ancien régime* courtiers. That said, Waldron has said elsewhere that hate speech laws should not cover offence: see Jeremy Waldron 'Dignity and Defamation: The Visibility of Hate' (2010) 123 *Harvard Law Review* 1596, 1612-3; see also Jeremy Waldron, *The Harm in Hate Speech* (Harvard University Press, 2012) 105-8.
213 For example, Tim Soutphommasane in defending s 18C's prohibition on offence, insult and humiliation has asserted that freedom from racial vilification is linked to dignity. He states: 'If we do not always make the connection between racism and its curtailment of freedom, it is because we are more likely to regard the harm as one involving dignity. Racism reduces the standing of another to that of a second-class citizen. But dignity is also connected to freedom. Where there is an injury to dignity, there is an impact as well on someone's ability to exercise freedom. In the case of racism, the experience undermines the assurance of security to which every member of a good society is entitled. It undermines the sense of confidence that everyone will be treated fairly and justly – that everyone can walk down the street and conduct their business, without fear of abuse and assault.' See Tim Soutphommasane, *I'm Not Racist, But... 40 Years of the Racial Discrimination Act* (University of New South Wales Press, 2015) Kindle Ebook Location 1367. Soutphommasane appears to conflate offence, insult and humiliation on the basis of race with racial abuse, racial vilification and racism. With respect, for reasons we give elsewhere in this treatise, the former does not necessarily entail the latter: see Part IV.E.1 (page 36). Further, laws of equal application already protect people walking down the street from abuse and assault, a point we cover below: see Part VI.B (page 220). We should add that, given that our book was in the closing stages of being written when Soutphommasane's book was published, we do not have the opportunity to address all the points he makes in his book. We address various points he makes elsewhere, usually in footnotes.

hesitate to read into dignity any particular meaning. This is especially so when using dignity to displace the express right to freedom of expression.

Conceptually,[214] and returning to the first element of the 'minimum core' McCrudden identified, Patrick Lee and Robert P George observed the following about the intrinsic worth each human possesses:

> What distinguishes human beings from other animals, what makes human beings persons rather than things, is their rational nature. Human beings are rational creatures by virtue of possessing natural capacities for *conceptual thought*, deliberation and free choice, that is, the natural capacity to shape their own lives.[215]

Lee and George expanded upon the capacity of human beings for conceptual thought as follows:

> The capacity for conceptual thought in human beings *radically* distinguishes them from other animals known to us. The capacity is at the root of most of the other distinguishing features of human beings. Thus, syntactical language, art, architecture, variety in social groupings and in other customs, burying the dead, making tools, religion, fear of death… wearing clothes, true courting of the opposite sex, free choice, and morality – all of these and more, stem from the ability to reason and understand.[216]

Lee and George argued that *variation* in the capacity for conceptual thought was not morally relevant, rather it is the *possession* of the capacity itself:

> The capacity for conceptual thought is a capacity that human beings have in virtue of the kind of the entity they are. That is, from the time they come to be they are developing themselves towards the mature stage at which they will (unless prevented from doing so by disability or circumstances) perform such acts. Moreover, they are structured – genetically and in the non-material aspect of themselves – in such a way that they are oriented to maturing to this stage. So, every human being, including human infants

---

214 Here, we mean "conceptually" in the sense that there is a *concept* of dignity. This is distinct from what we are about to do in our analysis, which is examine the capacity of humans to think *conceptually*, and also the *concepts* they create.
215 Patrick Lee and Robert P George 'The Nature and Basis of Human Dignity' (2008) 21(2) *Ratio Juris* 173, 174 (emphasis ours).
216 Ibid 184-5 (emphasis ours, citations omitted). We should note that Lee and George also add that humans are distinguished by 'the basic natural capacity to deliberate among options and make free choices': see ibid 185-7. We agree with Lee and George. However, the focus of our analysis is the human capacity for conceptual thought.

and unborn human beings, has this basic natural capacity for conceptual thought.[217]

Hence, the capacity for conceptual thought is what makes humanity *unique among species*. However, we would add that the capacity for conceptual thought makes each human *unique among humans*. That is, each human has a capacity[218] for conceptual thought, and also a unique existence in time and space in which this capacity is employed. Even genetically identical humans have separate existences and lead separate lives.[219]

This brings us to the second element McCrudden identified: that the intrinsic worth of each human should be recognised and respected. There is much to commend this element. However, it must be clear what "intrinsic worth" and "respect" means in this context.

As noted above, the "instrinsic worth" of humans as distinct from other animals or things depends upon their capacity for conceptual thought. It follows that the intrinsic worth of *individual* humans also depends upon their capacity for conceptual thought.

Further, humans generally and individuals in particular may *express* their capacity for conceptual thought. Expression is how they *manifest* their capacity for conceptual thought to the outside world. Expression is therefore a critical incident to both the human and individual capacity for conceptual thought.[220]

However, a common outcome of an *individual* exercising their capacity for conceptual thought is a *unique point of view* about a concept or concepts. Consequently, two humans, each exercising their respective capacities for conceptual thought – the capacity that gives *each* intrinsic worth – may arrive at *different points of view about a concept*. Each may then *express* their point of view, as expression is how humans *manifest* their point of view to the outside world.

---

217 Ibid 184 (citations omitted). We would add that someone who lacks the capacity for conceptual thought through infirmity is not to be thought as "less that human" but rather a *human being with an infirmity*. If the infirmity did not exist or was healed then their ability to use their capacity for conceptual thought would be restored.
218 We use "capacity" in the sense that Lee and George use it, that is, a capacity for conceptual thought that will reach a mature stage, unless prevented from doing so by infirmity or circumstances.
219 We will return the concept of human uniqueness when we explore the "body/idea" distinction below: see Part V.C.4 (page 136).
220 Judith Lichtenberg remarked that 'thinking requires language, and language requires communication – because often we do not know what we think or feel until we put our inchoate inner goings-on into words or discuss them with others.': Judith Lichtenberg, 'Foundations and Limits of Freedom of the Press' (1987) 14(4) *Philosophy and Public Affairs* 329, 336.

Disagreement, even heated disagreement, may result.

From the foregoing, it would appear that in order to exercise that which gives a human individual intrinsic worth – that is, their capacity to employ conceptual thought in a unique way – the following is necessary. First, the individual needs to be alive, otherwise there is no capacity at all for conceptual thought. Second, the individual needs the freedom to think conceptually in order to arrive at a unique point of view. Third, the individual needs the freedom to express their unique point of view. These needs establish the fundamental importance to human dignity of the corresponding rights to life, conscience and expression.

This brings us to respect. The first point we note here is that, following Lee and George, respect is a *concept* concerning how humans should treat each other. That is, respect is a *product* of the capacity of humans for conceptual thought. Further, it is a concept over which humans may differ. This is not ordinarily a problem except, when it comes justifying a restriction on freedom of expression, the concept (respect) purports to restrict a freedom (freedom of expression) that is not only logically prior and necessary to the concept's creation, but is fundamental to a human individual's intrinsic worth (that is, their dignity as a human).

The point we wish to make here is this: to accord any respect, an individual must first be alive, be able to exercise their capacity for conceptual thought, and be able express their conceptual thought. One should be slow to use *any* concept (respect included) to restrict freedoms that are logically prior to forming that concept, and further, more fundamental not only to human dignity (that is, what makes *humans human*) but also to individual dignity (that is, what makes *individuals individual*).

Put another way, it is *fundamentally disrespectful* to stop humans from expressing the capacity that *makes them human*, and individuals from expressing the capacity that *makes them individual*.

The second point we note concerns the *object* to which respect is given. There is a material difference between according respect to a *human* capable of conceptual thought, and according respect to the *concepts* they create or adopt. A human is entitled to respect because of their capacity for conceptual thought. A concept itself is entitled to no such respect.

One must be clear whether respect is being claimed for a human being or a concept. For example, if a person claims they ought not to be physically harmed[221] owing to their culture or religion, then this is a claim that other

---
221 We explore mental harm further when discussing the "body/idea" distinction below.

humans should respect. This is because the person is entitled to respect as a human capable of conceptual thought, and the person's life[222] is necessary for their capacity for conceptual thought. However, if a person claims that their culture or religion ought not to be harmed by way of criticism then this is a different matter. Culture and religion are *concepts*.

This is not to say that restrictions on freedom of speech cannot be justified. However, one must be clear as to the type of restriction that can be justified. Hence, restrictions on expression based on protecting others from physical harm[223] are justified on the basis that humans need to be alive, and not subject to threats to their life and body, in order to exercise their capacity for conceptual thought. However, beyond protections from physical harm, restrictions on freedom of expression must be strictly limited in application and effect,[224] as these restrictions impinge on what makes *humans human* and *individuals individual*.[225] Restrictions on freedom of speech to protect concepts will not be justified in all but exceptional cases.[226]

That individuals purport to restrict debate by prohibiting offense, insult or humiliation is bad enough. That states purport to do it by law is far worse.

---

[222] We include here being free from physical violence against the person as well as threats to life and body.

[223] Once again, we explore mental harm further when discussing the body/idea distinction below.

[224] Laws providing for national security are justified on the basis that the first duty of the state is to defend its borders and citizens from external threats. As we have noted elsewhere, the law of defamation is justified on the basis that individuals may protect their own reputation. However, the tension between the right to individual reputation on the one hand, and freedom of expression on the other, is long-standing. See Part V.D.6.(c) (page 186) and Part V.D.7.(a) (page 190).

[225] What about laws pertaining to property? It is worth recalling that our focus is on state action directly affecting freedom of expression. Property laws (for the most part) have an indirect effect on freedom of expression. Further, when property laws are used, they are (again, for the most part) limited in their application to and effect on freedom of expression. In order to commit an actionable wrong or an offence, a person needs to direct a particular form of expression at a particular item of property. A person may sit on their front lawn all day and say bad things about their neighbour's car. It is only when they spray paint these bad things on the car that the law has anything to say about it. The law concerning misleading or deceptive conduct applies only when a person says or does something misleading in relation to a particular good or service in the context of trade or commerce. However, even with these laws, care must be taken to ensure that laws relating to property do not unnecessarily infringe freedom of expression. A good contemporary example from the United States is using the *Digital Millennium Copyright Act*, Pub L No 105-304, 112 Stat 2860 (1998) ('DMCA'), to stifle online criticism through issuing DMCA takedown notices alleging copyright infringement: see, for example Jacqui Cheng, 'Five examples of lame DMCA takedowns', *Ars Technica* (online), 17 May 2010.

[226] The only one that a state could justify is sedition (that is the concept of the state itself). Even then it would only be justified in rare cases, as individuals need to be able to discuss the concept of the state. Laws pertaining to blasphemy are fundamentally unsound for the reasons we have given.

As noted above, disagreement is inevitable where individuals, exercising their capacity for conceptual thought, bring their unique perspectives to bear on concepts. Disagreement commonly results in offence, insult and humiliation. Legal restrictions on offence, insult or humiliation risk impinging the capacity of individuals to bring their unique perspectives to bear to concepts by threat of deprivation of property,[227] liberty,[228] or both.[229]

We will return the subject of concepts when we explore the "body/idea" distinction below.[230]

Fourth, and putting aside for now the rationale for including dignity in them, the text of the UDHR and the Convention themselves suggest that dignity means *intrinsic worth*, and further, *equality* in intrinsic worth. That is, no one, by virtue of their race, colour, ethnic or national origin is *intrinsically better* than anyone else.

That everyone is equal in intrinsic worth is a salutary principle for reasons stated below.[231] However, it does *not* follow from this principle that people are therefore free from being offended, insulted or humiliated. Indeed, the guarantee of freedom of expression in both the UDHR and the Convention – where such expression will in many cases offend, insult or humiliate – runs directly counter to such an assertion.

We now turn to equality. There are two types of equality expressly specified by both the UDHR and the Convention. The first is *equality before the law*. This, in effect, is a right of people against states (which make and execute the law). That this is so should not be surprising. In the modern era, states far surpass any other entity in their capacity to persecute people on the basis of race, colour, or ethnic or national background. It is the state that has the monopoly of legitimate force in given territory. It is the state that can enforce widespread inequality under colour of law. It is the state that can authorise its officers to persecute minorities without fear of punishment.

The second type of equality specified in the UDHR and the Convention is *equality in the range of rights each person may enjoy*. That is, the UDHR and the Convention prescribe certain rights to every person regardless of race, colour, ethnicity or nationality. Under the Convention, such rights include:

---

227 In the case of civil claims.
228 In the case of criminal charges.
229 Such as in civil claims where damages are awarded and an individual is ordered to publish a retraction (thereby compelling them to do something they would not otherwise do).
230 See Part V.C.4 (page 136).
231 See Part V.C.4 (page 136).

- Freedom of movement and residence within the border of a State;
- The right to own property alone or in association with others;
- Freedom of thought, conscience and religion;
- Freedom of opinion and expression;
- Freedom of peaceful assembly and association;
- The right to work, including equal pay for equal work;
- The right to housing;
- The right to public health, medical care, social security and social services;
- The right to education and training; and
- The right to equal participation in cultural activities.[232]

However, there is no right, express or inferred, under either the UDHR or the Convention to *equal treatment by everyone in society in every instance*.[233] While people (following the UDHR) *should* (note: not *must*)[234] act towards everyone in the spirit of brotherhood[235] they are also (following the UDHR) endowed with reason and conscience. It is a regrettable fact, but a fact nonetheless, that an individual's reason or conscience may lead them to *not* act in a spirit of brotherhood towards others. Of course, this is an issue if the person's reason and conscience leads them to engage in acts of physical violence against others. This is because those subject to physical violence have express rights to security of person under the UDHR and the Convention.[236] However, if a person's reason

---

232 Article 5.
233 This type of "Harrison Bergeron" interpretation would be impractical in any event (we refer to Kurt Vonnegut's dystopian short story: see Kurt Vonnegut, 'Harrison Bergeron' (1991) 44 *Arkansas Law Review* 927. For those curious about how a short story found its way into a law journal, Vonnegut's piece was used as a discussion piece in a symposium about affirmative action: see Mark R Killenbeck, 'Introduction: Prologues without Pasts, Answers without Questions' (1991) 44 *Arkansas Law Review* 915).
234 It might appear that we are giving the UDHR a close or narrow reading here. However, it must be remembered that a fundamental freedom is at stake – that of freedom of expression. Consequently, the difference between an aspirational but permissive word ("should") and an imperative word ("must") is important when considering whether the fundamental freedom has been displaced. In our view, the use of the word "should" has not displaced the fundamental freedom of expression.
235 The 'spirit of brotherhood' is a salutary phrase. However, it cannot be said that using such a phrase rules out expression that offends, insults or humiliates. After all (speaking rhetorically, and assuming kinship is an appropriate analogy), who among us has not been critical of a family member in an offensive, insulting or even humiliating way?
236 Similar considerations apply when someone's reason or conscience leads them to discriminate against someone on expressly prohibited grounds, like denying them employment, education, accommodation or goods and services on the basis of another's race, colour, ethnicity or nationality.

and conscience leads the person to act by expressing criticism or disapproval of others then this is a different matter. This is because everyone has a right to freedom of conscience and freedom of expression under the UDHR and the Convention. Further, and as noted above, there is no express right under the UDHR and the Convention not be offended, insulted or humiliated.

In the case of the constitutional validity of laws passed under the Convention, the bottom line is this: freedom of expression should not be compromised on the basis of vague principles that are not clearly expressed in the Convention itself. Under the Convention, there is no express or implied right to equality of treatment by people (as opposed to states) in every instance. There is also no express right not to be offended, insulted or humiliated even on the basis of race, colour, ethnic or national origin. There is, however, a clearly expressed guarantee of freedom of expression.

We now turn to considering other issues concerning the claim that rights to dignity, equality, or both, restrict freedom of expression.

(ii) Freedom of expression is critical to human dignity

The claim that rights to dignity or equality may restrict freedom of expression often treats freedom of expression as antithetical to dignity and equality. However, this is not the case. For example, a critical aspect of human dignity is the ability to speak one's mind. Imposing fetters on freedom of expression such that people fear speaking their mind in fact corrodes dignity.

As we note elsewhere, every person is physically unique.[237] Barring infancy or infirmity, every person is also aware of themselves and the world around them. A person's uniqueness in time and space is perhaps the one thing that they can claim against everyone and everything else. Hence, the ability to express that uniqueness in both form and content is critical to an individual's dignity.

Ronald Dworkin spoke of the importance of free speech to human dignity as follows:

> The original right of free speech must suppose that it is an assault on human personality to stop a man from expressing what he honestly believes, particularly on issues affecting how he is governed. Surely, the assault is greater, and not less, when he is stopped from expressing those principles of political morality that he holds most passionately, in the face

---

237 See Part IV.E.3.(c).(i)(page 68). We explore the concept of human uniqueness further at Part V.C.4 (page 136).

of what he takes to be outrageous violations of these principles.[238]

Dworkin continued:

> A man cannot express himself freely if he cannot match his rhetoric to his outrage, or when he must trim his sails to protect values he counts as nothing next to those he is trying to vindicate. It is true that some political dissenters speak in ways that shock the majority, but it is arrogant for the majority to suppose that the orthodox methods of expression are the proper ways to speak, for this is a denial of equal concern and respect.[239]

Dworkin's statements were not idle speculation. The systematic degradation of entire populations under communist regimes through (amongst other things) restrictions on free speech exemplify how restrictions on speech corrode human dignity. Vaclav Havel, who spent much of his life as a dissident intellectual in communist Czechoslovakia, spoke of this as follows:

> The manager of a fruit-and-vegetable shop places in his window, among the onions and carrots, the slogan: "Workers of the world, unite!" Why does he do it? What is he trying to communicate to the world? Is he genuinely enthusiastic about the idea of unity among the workers of the world? Is his enthusiasm so great that he feels an irrepressible impulse to acquaint the public with his ideals? Has he really given more than a moment's thought to how such a unification might occur and what it would mean?
>
> I think it can safely be assumed that the overwhelming majority of shopkeepers never think about the slogans they put in their windows, nor do they use them to express their real opinions. That poster was delivered to our greengrocer from the enterprise headquarters along with the onions and carrots. He put them all into the window simply because it has been done that way for years, because everyone does it, and because that is the way it has to be. If he were to refuse, there could be trouble. He could be reproached for not having the proper decoration in his window; someone might even accuse him of disloyalty. He does it because these things must be done if one is to get along in life. It is one of the thousands of details that guarantee him a relatively tranquil life "in harmony with society," as they say...
>
> Let us take note: if the greengrocer had been instructed to display the

---

238 Ronald Dworkin, *Taking Rights Seriously* (Duckworth, 1977) 201.
239 Ibid.

slogan "I am afraid and therefore unquestioningly obedient," he would not be nearly as indifferent to its semantics, even though the statement would reflect the truth. The greengrocer would be embarrassed and ashamed to put such an unequivocal statement of his own degradation in the shop window, and quite naturally so, for he is a human being and thus has a sense of his own dignity. To overcome this complication, his expression of loyalty must take the form of a sign which, at least on its textual surface, indicates a level of disinterested conviction. It must allow the greengrocer to say, "What's wrong with the workers of the world uniting?" Thus the sign helps the greengrocer to conceal from himself the low foundations of his obedience, at the same time concealing the low foundations of power...[240]

Indeed, a slave cannot speak his mind but a free person can. As Tim Wilson points out, 'anyone who has studied a skerrick of history knows that protecting free speech is about giving voice to the powerless against the majority and established interests'.[241] Freedom of expression promotes and protects equality. Civil rights struggles in Australia, the United States and elsewhere have demonstrated the value of people using freedom of expression to win and protect equal recognition before the law.

(iii) The rights to dignity and equality are not unqualified

Bromberg J in *Eatock* treated the rights to dignity and equality as unqualified. However, this is not the case. The right to dignity does not protect a person from defamatory allegations (which may be offensive, insulting or humiliating in the extreme) if those allegations are true or fair comment. Further, the right to dignity does not protect a person from the indignity of being physically taken and held in police custody if they are suspected of committing a crime. Similarly, the right to equality before the law does not entitle a member of

---

240 Vaclav Havel, *The Power of the Powerless* (Hutchinson, 1985) 27-8. Robert Conquest wrote of the effect of Stalinist repression as follows: 'In fact, the stage was reached which the writer Isaak Babel summed up, "Today a man only talks freely with his wife – at night, with the blankets pulled over his head". Only the very closest of friends could hint to one another of their disbelief of official views (and often not even then). The ordinary citizen had no means of discovering how far the official lies were accepted. He might be one of a scattered and helpless minority, and Stalin might have won his battle to destroy the idea of truth in the Soviet mind. "Millions led double lives," as the grandson of the executed Army Commander Yakir was to write later. Every man became in one sense what Donne says he is not – "an island."': Robert Conquest, *The Great Terror: A Reassessment* (Oxford University Press, 1990) 256.
241 Tim Wilson, 'Insidious Threats to Free Speech', *The Weekend Australian*, 5-6 April 2014, 17.

one racial group to equal legal resources when engaged in litigation against a member of another racial group in that society.

However, case law has treated rights to dignity and equality as if they were unqualified. In *Eatock*, Bromberg J noted that freedom of expression was not unqualified,[242] but did not note the same for dignity or equality.[243] The effect of this in a balancing exercise is to weigh a qualified right (freedom of expression) against an unqualified right (dignity or equality). With respect, if there is to be a balancing exercise then it should be a qualified right (freedom of expression) against another qualified right (dignity or equality).

(iv) Not all affronts to dignity are grave, and some may in fact be salutary

A problem with the vague definition of dignity is what is considered "undignified" or "an affront to dignity". Not all affronts to dignity are grave.

To be clear, there are indeed affronts to dignity that involve degradation or dehumanisation, for example, treating people as if they were property or animals. Every person should expect protection from these indignities on the basis that they are someone who has inherent worth as a human being.

However, there are other affronts to dignity that are not grave, and may be beneficial overall. Criticising an individual's conduct may involve that individual being offended, insulted or humiliated. However, the criticism may be directed to improving that individual's conduct in the future. Further, the criticism is not (and should not be taken as) treating someone as less than a person. Indeed, if the conduct involves the person degrading themselves, and the criticism prompts them to change, then the offence, insult or humiliation may ultimately protect and promote human dignity.

For example, an alcoholic may be very comfortable with their alcoholism. They may enjoy alcohol even when they know it leads to atrocious behavior on their part. The alcoholic may be abjectly humiliated when those affected by their behaviour explain how the alcoholic's behaviour is a problem. The alcoholic may take extreme offence when others exhort the alcoholic to get help and change their ways. However, it cannot be said that those pointing out the alcoholic's problems are dehumanising or degrading the alcoholic. If anything, they are doing the opposite.

Criticising an individual for an attribute that they cannot control (like their skin colour) is more problematic. We cover this issue below when discussing

---
242 *Eatock* [2011] FCA 1103; (2011) 197 FCR 261, 316-8 [235]-[239] (Bromberg J).
243 Ibid 311-5 [212]-[226] (Bromberg J).

the "body/idea" distinction. However, we note here that criticising someone based on an attribute derived from their race, colour, national or ethnic origin *does not necessarily* involve degradation or dehumanisation in the sense that the critic is treating that person as less than human. There may be other bases for the criticism. This is an important point to keep in mind when determining the constitutional validity of legislation that compromises freedom of expression.

Behaviour that solely offends, insults or even humiliates does not (without more) necessarily adversely affect the enjoyment of other human rights. Therefore, it is not inevitably a form of racial discrimination that comes within the terms of the Convention. The minimal harm threshold adopted by s 18C by making unlawful acts that are reasonably likely to offend, insult or humiliate extends beyond the scope of the Convention, in particular by failing to acknowledge the important role that Article 5 plays in understanding the intended practical operation of the Convention.

(v) Applying R v Keegstra *in an Australian context*

A problem specific to Bromberg J's approach to dignity and equality is his adoption of certain comments in the Canadian case of *R v Keegstra*[244] as part of his philosophical justification for restricting freedom of expression. In *Eatock*, Bromberg J stated:

> In *Keegstra*, the Canadian Supreme Court considered the extent to which the right to freedom of expression could permissibly be qualified by legislation which made racial hatred (as defined) a criminal offence. In that context, the Court examined the qualified nature of freedom of expression by reference to its underlying rationale embodied in the three pillars to which I have already referred. Relevantly, the majority said:
> [(i) In relation to the pursuit of truth:]
> ... the argument from truth does not provide convincing support for the protection of hate propaganda.
> ... the greater the degree of certainty that a statement is erroneous or mendacious, the less its value in the quest for truth. Indeed, expression can be used to the detriment of our search for truth; the state should not be the sole arbiter of truth, but neither should we overplay the view that rationality will overcome all falsehoods in the unregulated marketplace of ideas. There is very little chance that statements intended to promote

---
244 *R v Keegstra* [1990] 3 SCR 697 ('*Keegstra*').

hatred against an identifiable group are true, or that their vision of society will lead to a better world. To portray such statements as crucial to truth and the betterment of the political and social milieu is therefore misguided: at 762-763.

[(ii) In relation to individual self-fulfilment or autonomy:]

...such self-autonomy stems in large part from one's ability to articulate and nurture an identity derived from membership in a cultural or religious group. ... The extent to which the unhindered promotion of this message furthers free expression values must therefore be tempered insofar as it advocates with inordinate vitriol an intolerance and prejudice which view as execrable the process of individual self-development and human flourishing among all members of society: at 763.

[(iii) In relation to participation in democratic governance:]

... expression can work to undermine our commitment to democracy where employed to propagate ideas anathemic to democratic values. Hate propaganda works in just such a way, arguing as it does for a society in which the democratic process is subverted and individuals are denied respect and dignity simply because of racial or religious characteristics. This brand of expressive activity is thus wholly inimical to the democratic aspirations of the free expression guarantee: at 764.[245]

We have the following comments concerning the quoted passage. First, *Keegstra*, was a decision of the Canadian Supreme Court. In this case, the court held 4:3 that s 319(2) of Canada's *Criminal Code*[246] did not violate the guarantee of freedom of expression provided by s 2(b) of Canada's *Charter of Rights and Freedoms* ('the Charter').[247] Of the 11 judges who heard the *Keegstra* case from first instance through to Canada's Supreme Court, six held that s 319(2) *did* violate the guarantee of freedom of expression.[248] However, of the five who held that s 319(2) did not violate this guarantee, four sat on Canada's Supreme Court.[249]

Second, the majority in *Keegstra* was informed by considerations of Canadian law that are relevantly different from Australian law. Dickson CJ, who gave judgment for the majority of Canada's Supreme Court in *Keegstra*, made the

---

245 *Eatock* [2011] FCA 1103; (2011) 197 FCR 261, 317-8 [239] (Bromberg J).
246 Subsequent reference to s 319(2) of Canada's *Criminal Code* will be to just 's 319(2)' or 'section 319(2)' as the case requires.
247 Subsequent reference to s 2(b) of Canada's *Charter of Rights and Freedoms* will be to just 's 2(b)' or 'section 2(b)' as the case requires.
248 These judges were the unanimous bench in the Alberta Court of Appeal (Kerans, Stevenson and Irving JJA) and three judges on the Supreme Court (McLachlin, La Forest and Sopinka JJ).
249 These judges were the judge at first instance (Quigley J) and four judges on the Supreme Court (Dickson CJ, Wilson, L'Heureux-Dubé and Gonthier JJ).

comments quoted by Bromberg J in the context of considering both s 319(2) and s 2(b).

As to s 2(b), previous Canadian Supreme Court decisions held that certain values underpinned this provision. These values were:

> (1) Seeking and attaining truth is an inherently good activity; (2) participating in social and political decision-making is to be fostered and encouraged; and (3) diversity in forms of individual self-fulfillment and human flourishing ought to be cultivated in a tolerant and welcoming environment for the sake of those who convey a meaning and those to whom meaning is conveyed.[250]

However, Dickson CJ noted that these values needed to be considered within the textual framework of the Charter.[251] Dickson CJ noted that equality and multiculturalism had been given a special role in the Canadian Constitution and justified a departure from the US view that suppression of hate propaganda was incompatible with free expression.[252] Canada's entry into the Convention reinforced this view.[253]

There are no provisions in the *Commonwealth Constitution* equivalent to those in the Charter concerning multiculturalism and equality. Hence, there are problems with applying values developed with reference to the Charter to an Australian context. Unlike Canada, there is no need to 'read down' freedom of expression in Australia with reference to constitutionally-prescribed values. Indeed, if anything, the implied freedom of political communication (examined further below) appears directed to ensuring the free and robust exchange of information concerning government and political matters in order to effect Australia's constitutionally-prescribed system representative and responsible government.

If Bromberg J wanted to apply relevant Canadian Supreme Court jurisprudence, he would have done better with cases decided prior to the Charter. In several such cases, Canada's Supreme Court implied a freedom of political communication similar to that later adopted in Australia. Indeed, these Canadian cases were referred with approval in early Australian cases concerning the implied freedom of political communication. Thus, in *Nationwide News Pty Ltd v Wills*,[254] Brennan J referred with approval the following passage from the

---
250 *Keegstra* [1990] 3 SCR 697, 728 (Dickson CJ).
251 Ibid.
252 Ibid 743 (Dickson CJ).
253 Ibid 743, 750 (Dickson CJ).
254 [1992] HCA 46; (1992) 177 CLR 1 ('*Wills*').

Canadian Supreme Court decision of *Re Alberta Statutes*:[255]

> [The British North America Act (Cananda's constitution)] contemplates a parliament working under the influence of public opinion and public discussion. There can be no controversy that such institutions derive their efficacy from the free public discussion of affairs, from criticism and answer and counter-criticism, from attack upon policy and administration and defence and counter-attack; from the freest and fullest analysis and examination from every point of view of political proposals. This is signally true in respect of the discharge by Ministers of the Crown of their responsibility to Parliament, by members of Parliament of their duty to the electors, and by the electors themselves of their responsibilities in the election of their representatives.
> The right of public discussion is, of course, subject to legal restrictions; those based upon considerations of decency and public order, and others conceived for the protection of various private and public interests with which, for example, the laws of defamation and sedition are concerned. In a word, freedom of discussion means, to quote the words of Lord Wright in James v. Commonwealth ((96) (1936) AC 578, at p 627), 'freedom governed by law.'
> Even within its legal limits, it is liable to abuse and grave abuse, and such abuse is constantly exemplified before our eyes; but it is axiomatic that the practice of this right of free public discussion of public affairs, notwithstanding its incidental mischiefs, is the breath of life for parliamentary institutions.[256]

Third, the values to which Dickson CJ referred do not encompass the entirety of justifications for free speech. Free expression is critical to human dignity, being the way that individuals — each unique — choose to "show themselves" to the world. That free expression may challenge ideas held by others is ultimately edifying. Those challenged are prompted to examine, refine or change their ideas, or respond to the challenge with challenges of their own.

There is much to be said for the concept of the "marketplace of ideas". It is the best way to arrive at truth. Note that "best" does not mean "infallible" – and critics usually seize the marketplace concept's lack of infallibility to attack it. But lack of infallibility does not mean this concept should be abandoned. Indeed, the marketplace concept is superior to all alternatives that have been tried. (To continue the marketplace metaphor, critics often advocate state-enforced "monopolies" which, when applied to ideas (as in many other areas), are a far worse alternative.)

---

255 [1938] SCR 100, 133 (Duff CJ).
256 *Wills* [1992] HCA 46; (1992) 177 CLR 1, 49-50 (Brennan J).

An advantage of the marketplace concept that critics (and, alas, some advocates) overlook is the *discipline of competition*. This discipline is critical maintaining the strength of ideas – especially ideas that have merit. The need to respond to challenges keeps ideas alive and vital. This is crucial to transmitting ideas across generations. The problem with closing off debate by "legislating truth" is that it leads to intellectual laziness. Once vital ideas defended by informed advocates become stale dogma enforced by unthinking zealots.[257]

Fourth, there are issues with the values expressed by Dickson CJ. As McLachlin J (writing for the dissenting judges in *Keegstra*) noted:

> Attempts to confine the guarantee of free expression only to content which is judged to possess redeeming value or to accord with accepted values strike at the very essence of the value of freedom, reducing the realm of protected discussion to that which is comfortable and compatible with current conceptions. If the guarantee of free expression is to be meaningful, it must protect expression which challenges even the very basic conceptions about our society. A true commitment to free expression demands nothing less.[258]

Fifth, even if the values Dickson CJ noted were wholly applicable to Australia to the exclusion of any other value, these remarks referred to s 319(2). This provision has far narrower scope than s 18C. Section 319(2) provides that anyone who 'wilfully promotes hatred against any identifiable group' is guilty

---

[257] To give a somewhat pointed example, during the Cold War, Irving Kristol observed with respect to socialism: 'In the case of contemporary socialism, there are no Church Fathers – only heretics, outside the reach of established orthodoxies, developing doctrines for which socialist authority has no use at all. Not a single interesting work on Marxism – not even an authoritative biography of Karl Marx! – has issued from the Soviet Union in its sixty years of existence. If you want to study Marxism, with Marxist intellectuals, you go to Paris, or Rome, or London, or some American campus. There are no intellectual hegiras to Moscow, Peking or Havana. Moreover, the works of Western Marxist thinkers – and some are indeed impressive – are suppressed in socialist lands. Sartre's Marxist writings have never been published in Russia, just as Brecht's plays have never been produced there, and just as Picasso's paintings have never been exhibited there. Socialism, apparently, is one of those ideals which, when breathed upon by reality, suffers immediate petrification. Which is why all those who remain loyal to this ideal will always end up bewailing another "revolution betrayed"': see Irving Kristol, *Neoconservatism: The Autobiography of an Idea* (The Free Press, 1995) 301-2. We suggest that the better Marxist thought in the West resulted from Marxist theorists needing to respond to criticism with reasoned debate, rather than just sending the critic to a gulag. It is ironic (but ultimately unsurprising, when one thinks about it) that totalitarian regimes that routinely criticised liberal democracies for being soft could not tolerate even the slightest criticism.

[258] *Keegstra* [1990] 3 SCR 697, 842 (McLachlin J).

of an indictable offence.[259] This means that intent to promote hatred must be proven beyond reasonable doubt. By contrast, s 18C requires no intent to promote hatred. All that s 18C requires is proof on balance of probabilities that an act be reasonably likely to offend, insult or humiliate a group because of their race, colour or national or ethnic origin. Indeed, Australian courts have rejected the requirement to prove that acts breaching s 18C must be based on racial hatred.[260]

This distinction between s 319(2) and s 18C is important because Dickson CJ prefaced the comments Bromberg J quoted by stating:

> From the outset, I wish to make clear that in my opinion the expression prohibited by s. 319(2) is not closely linked to the rationale underlying s 2(b). Examining... values... fundamental to the protection of free expression, arguments can be made for the proposition that each of these values is diminished by the suppression of hate propaganda. While none of these arguments is spurious, I am of the opinion that *expression intended to promote the hatred of identifiable groups is of limited importance when measured against free speech values*.[261]

That is, in Dickson CJ's view the conduct that s 319(2) prohibited, namely intent to promote racial hatred, was far removed from the values informing s 2(b). The same cannot be said for the conduct that s 18C makes unlawful. Under s 18C, acts that are not intended to, and would not, promote racial hatred are made unlawful. As noted above, s 18C does not require intent to promote hatred. Rather, s 18C's threshold is whether it is reasonably likely that a reasonable representative of the group (or sub-group) would be offended, insulted or humiliated.[262] Conduct that offends, insults or humiliates is far from conduct that promotes hatred (and it was with hatred that Dickson CJ was concerned). Indeed, those who would seek or attain truth, or participate in social and political decision-making, may avoid doing so for fear of being liable for offending, insulting or humiliating someone. Thus, s 18C may undermine the values of which Dickson CJ spoke.

Sixth, Dickson CJ's approach was informed by the effect of hate propaganda on society at large, quoting with approval the comments from the Special Committee on Hate Propaganda in Canada (the 'Cohen Committee'):

---

259 *Criminal Code* (Can) s 319(2).
260 *Toben* [2003] FCAFC 137; (2003) 129 FCR 505, 526 [27]-[28] (Carr J), 549 [133]-[136] (Allsop J).
261 *Keegstra* 762 (Dickson CJ) (emphasis ours).
262 We examine the 'reasonable representative' test in Part IV.E.2 (page 53).

> ... we are less confident in the 20th century that the critical faculties of individuals will be brought to bear on the speech and writing which is directed at them. In the 18th and 19th centuries, there was a widespread belief that man was a rational creature, and that if his mind was trained and liberated from superstition by education, he would always distinguish truth from falsehood, good from evil. So Milton, who said "let truth and falsehood grapple: who ever knew truth put to the worse in a free and open encounter".
>
> We cannot share this faith today in such a simple form. While holding that over the long run, the human mind is repelled by blatant falsehood and seeks the good, it is too often true, in the short run, that emotion displaces reason and individuals perversely reject the demonstrations of truth put before them and forsake the good they know. The successes of modern advertising, the triumphs of impudent propaganda such as Hitler's, have qualified sharply our belief in the rationality of man. We know that under strain and pressure in times of irritation and frustration, the individual is swayed and even swept away by hysterical, emotional appeals. We act irresponsibly if we ignore the way in which emotion can drive reason from the field.[263]

Chief Justice Dickson then noted:

> It is thus not inconceivable that the active dissemination of hate propaganda can attract individuals to its cause, and in the process create serious discord between various cultural groups in society. Moreover, the alteration of views held by the recipients of hate propaganda may occur subtlely, and is not always attendant upon conscious acceptance of the communicated ideas. Even if the message of hate propaganda is outwardly rejected, there is evidence that its premise of racial or religious inferiority may persist in a recipient's mind as an idea that holds some truth, an incipient effect not to be entirely discounted.[264]

We'll be blunt: the remarks of the Cohen Committee and Dickson CJ are astonishingly condescending to Canada's citizenry. They engage in speculation, "slippery slope" reasoning and a *reductio ad Hitlerum*,[265] all of which are historically suspect when applied to Canada. In the lead-up to the Second World

---

263 *Keegstra* [1990] 3 SCR 697, 747 (Dickson CJ) quoting the Special Committee on Hate Propaganda in Canada, Report of the Special Committee on Hate Propaganda in Canada (Queen's Printer, 1966) 8.
264 *Keegstra* [1990] 3 SCR 697, 747-8 (citations omitted).
265 Leo Strauss, *Natural Right and History* (University of Chicago Press, first published 1953, 1965 ed) 42-3.

War, with dire economic circumstances and fascism on the rise in Europe and elsewhere, *Canada did not go fascist*. Indeed, Canada, along with other nations with a common law legal tradition, fought to defeat fascism. In addition, after the Second World War the horrific results of fascism were widely known. With that experience, why was it a sound assumption that Canada (of all places) may well go backwards?

Further, those who wrote about the value of freedom of expression in the 18th and 19th centuries did so at a time when slavery was widely practiced and autocracy wrestled with democracy across the world. Milton wrote at a time when people were still being burned for their religious views. Yet, even in these circumstances, he thought that truth would win when in conflict with error. Dickson CJ continued:

> The threat to the self-dignity of target group members is thus matched by the possibility that prejudiced messages will gain some credence, with the attendant result of discrimination, and perhaps even violence, against minority groups in Canadian society. With these dangers in mind, the Cohen Committee made clear in its conclusions that the presence of hate propaganda existed as a baleful and pernicious element, and hence a serious problem, in Canada (at p. 59):
>
>> The amount of hate propaganda presently being disseminated and its measurable effects probably are not sufficient to justify a description of the problem as one of crisis or near crisis proportions. Nevertheless the problem is a serious one. We believe that, given a certain set of socio-economic circumstances, such as a deepening of the emotional tensions or the setting in of a severe business recession, public susceptibility might well increase significantly. Moreover, the potential psychological and social damage of hate propaganda, both to a desensitized majority and to sensitive minority target groups, is incalculable. As Mr. Justice Jackson of the United States Supreme Court wrote in *Beauharnais v. Illinois*, such 'sinister abuses of our freedom of expression . . . can tear apart a society, brutalize its dominant elements, and persecute even to extermination, its minorities'.[266]

Again we'll be blunt: this is little more than speculation and "slippery slope" reasoning that is, once again, historically suspect when applied to Canada. Given

---

266 *Keegstra* [1990] 3 SCR 697, 748 (Dickson CJ).

the importance of freedom of expression, it should not be compromised on the basis of obvious and easily-disproved rhetorical fallacies.

Indeed, arguments justifying restrictions on freedom of expression on the basis that its exercise creates a "climate" where people feel unsafe must be treated with caution. Restricting freedom of expression requires a clear-eyed risk analysis of the perceived threat. What is the source of the perceived threat? Is it a direct threat against an identified person or group of people? Or (at the other end of the spectrum) does the perceived threat stem from someone hearing comments they simply don't like? A person's emotional reaction can be disproportionate to the conduct about which they complain. Care must be taken to ensure that claimed threats are not vague, speculative, exaggerated, or contrived.

Advocates of restrictions on freedom of expression often cite the "lived experience" of those subject to racist abuse.[267] We do not wish to minimise the real hurt this abuse causes. However, "lived experience" is anecdotal evidence.[268] From a legal standpoint, such evidence may be speculative, conclusory and hearsay. With respect, and as a matter of policy, fundamental freedoms should not be compromised on the basis of such evidence. Further, the Australian Human Rights Commission ('AHRC') has noted that there has been very little qualitative research on the lived experience of racism in Australia.[269] Absent such evidence, claims about lived experience must be treated cautiously. This is especially so when they are used to support assertions about race relations in Australia generally, and to justify laws restricting freedom of expression that apply to all Australians.

In any event, care must be exercised in calibrating the law to address any harm. As noted above, legislative overreach must be avoided so as to not unnecessarily infringe freedom of expression. Mari Matsuda provided a moving account of the harmful effects of racism,[270] noting:

> As much as one may try to resist a piece of hate propaganda, the effect on one's self-esteem and sense of personal security is devastating. To be hated, despised, and alone is the ultimate fear of all human beings.

---

267 See Tim Soutphommasane, *I'm Not Racist, But... 40 Years of the Racial Discrimination Act* (University of New South Wales Press, 2015) Kindle Ebook Location 241; see also Australian Human Rights Commission, *Freedom from Discrimination: Report on the 40th anniversary of the Racial Discrimination Act* (Australian Human Rights Commission, 2015) 50 [10.1.1].
268 A point made (amongst others) in a somewhat unsparing way in Milo Yiannopoulos, 'Coming 2016: All-Out War on So-Called "Social Justice"' *Breitbart* (online), 31 December 2015.
269 40th Anniversary Report 6 [2.1].
270 Mari Matsuda, 'Public Response to Racist Speech: Considering the Victim's Story' (1989) 87 *Michigan Law Review* 2320.

However irrational racist speech may be, it hits right at the emotional place where we feel the most pain. The aloneness comes not only from the hate message itself, but also from the government response of tolerance.[271]

However, even on her own case, Matsuda proposed laws far narrower in scope than s 18C.[272] These laws would have the following elements:

1. The message is one of racial superiority;
2. The message is directed against a historically oppressed group;[273] and
3. The message is persecutorial, hateful, and degrading.[274]

In our view, when assessing the response necessary to address the harm, there is merit in the "clear and present danger" principle developed by the United States Supreme Court. In an early iteration of the principle, Brandeis J stated that:

> ...no danger flowing from speech can be deemed clear and present, unless the incidence of the evil apprehended is so imminent that it may befall before there is opportunity for full discussion. If there be time to expose

---

271 Ibid 2337-8.
272 Matsuda's work has been influential, and she has been cited favourably in Australia: see Tim Soutphommasane, *I'm Not Racist, But... 40 Years of the Racial Discrimination Act* (University of New South Wales Press, 2015) Kindle Ebook Location 1322. However, Matsuda's analysis is not without its faults. Amongst other criticisms, Warren Sandmann noted: '...Matsuda utilizes personal experience, narratives and oral histories as evidence to support a claim. While Matsuda also uses more traditional evidential sources (government reports and statistical findings), the heart of her argument – that hate speech causes real harm to individuals – is bolstered mainly by anecdotal evidence and behavioristic studies showing a relationship between hate speech and psychological and physiological harm. While there is no question that some targets of hate-speech suffer from these symptoms, nor that this suffering is great, there is a question concerning the strength of the relationship between the speech and the harm. ... [Matsuda] offers little evidence that even the majority of recipients will respond to hate speech in the same way.' And further: '... more importantly than the lack of evidence to support her claim is her dependence on the notion of a virtual cause-effect relationship between word and deed. ... Contemporary theorists have strongly questioned the possibility of showing a direct link between word and response. To propose a restriction on certain forms of speech that have been shown only anecdotally and questionably to 'cause' harm is, at best, an overreach on Matsuda's part': See Warren Sandmann, 'Three Ifs and a Maybe: Mari Matsuda's Approach to Restricting Hate Speech Laws' (1994) 45 (3-4) *Communication Studies* 241, 250 (citations omitted) (see 249-254 for Sandmann's other criticisms of Matsuda' approach). We noted above that there has been little qualitative research on the lived experience of racism in Australia. Should such research be conducted, it needs to avoid the type of criticism that Sandmann has made of Matsuda's work.
273 There are considerable difficulties with this element. We explore them in more detail in Part VI.D.2 (page 232).
274 Mari Matsuda, 'Public Response to Racist Speech: Considering the Victim's Story' (1989) 87 *Michigan Law Review* 2320, 2357.

the evil by processes of education, the remedy to be applied is more speech, not an enforced silence. Only an emergency can justify repression.[275]

Ultimately, Canada and Australia (and the United States, for that matter) share a similar common law heritage. They also share a history of valuing freedom of expression and combatting fascism (indeed, these two things are not unrelated).[276] One of the rationales for s 18C – that it combats attitudes that might lead to racial hatred[277] – is problematic for same reasons that the rationale for s 319(2) is problematic.

(d)   An overview of Article 2

To be clear, Article 2 provides the basis for important protections against racial discrimination. However, it has its limits. As regards laws affecting freedom of expression, Article 4 is the Article that governs this important matter. In any event, Article 5 also applies to Article 2. Under the relevant treaties, there is no right not to be offended, insulted or humiliated, and the rights to dignity and equality do not extend to creating such rights. This is an important point to bear in mind when assessing whether s 18C is reasonably capable of being considered appropriate and adapted to implementing Article 2 while paying due regard to the guarantee of freedom of expression in Article 5.

4   *Article 6*

Article 6 of the Convention provides that:

> State Parties shall assure to everyone within their jurisdiction effective protection and remedies, through the competent national tribunals and other State institutions, against any acts of racial discrimination which violate his human rights and fundamental freedoms contrary to this Convention, as well as the right to seek from such tribunals just and adequate reparation or satisfaction for any damage suffered as a result of such discrimination.

The key point to note here is that while Articles 2 and 4 impose general obligations upon States Parties relating to the combating of racial hatred and

---

275 *Whitney* 274 US 357, 377 (Brandeis J, Holmes J concurring) (1927).
276 Tom Wolfe once wrote that 'the dark night of fascism is always descending in the United States and yet lands only in Europe': Tom Wolfe, *Mauve Gloves & Madmen, Clutter & Vine* (Farrar, Straus and Giroux, 1976). We would go a step further by way of paraphrase: the dark night of totalitarianism is forever descending on common law countries yet lands in civil law countries.
277 See Part IV.I.1.(b) (page 102).

discrimination, Article 6 is different in nature. Article 6 is a remedial rather than substantive provision and, as such, cannot itself provide the constitutional justification for the implementation of a substantive prohibition such as that contained within s 18C.

This analysis is supported by Schwelb's and Lerner's observations concerning Article 6. Both Schwelb[278] and Lerner[279] compare Article 6 to Article 8 of the UDHR, which provides that 'everyone has the right to an effective remedy by the competent national tribunals for acts violating the fundamental rights granted to him by the constitution or by law'. Schwelb observed:

> By Article 6 States Parties assure to everyone within their jurisdiction effective protection and remedies against any of the acts of racial discrimination which violate its human and fundamental freedoms contrary to the Convention.[280]

Lerner observed:

> The intention of the drafters of [Article 6] was to ensure that the party responsible for causing the injury as a result of racial discrimination, whether it be the State itself or private individual or organization, should provide an effective remedy to the victim.[281]

When considering the conformity requirement, Article 6 supports Commonwealth legislation providing remedies for racial discrimination. Such legislation includes that providing for the conciliation processes noted below.[282] However, Article 6 does *not* support legislation that makes conduct unlawful, as this is the work of Articles 2 and 4.[283]

5 Article 7

As noted above,[284] the obligation under Article 7 requires States Parties to

---

278 Egon Schwelb, 'The International Convention on the Elimination of All Forms of Racial Discrimination' (1966) 15 *International and Comparative Law Quarterly* 996, 1027-8.
279 Natan Lerner, *The UN Convention on the Elimination of all Forms of Racial Discrimination* (Sijthoff & Noordhoff, 2nd ed, 1980) 62.
280 Egon Schwelb, 'The International Convention on the Elimination of All Forms of Racial Discrimination' (1966) 15 *International and Comparative Law Quarterly* 996, 1027.
281 Natan Lerner, *The UN Convention on the Elimination of all Forms of Racial Discrimination* (Sijthoff & Noordhoff, 2nd ed, 1980) 62.
282 See Part V.D.5 (page 173).
283 Also Article 3 of the Convention, which is not relevant to our analysis.
284 See Part IV.D.4 (page 32).

adopt measures *'with a view to combating prejudices which lead to racial discrimination'*.[285] Article 7 is directed towards eliminating racial discrimination through teaching, education, culture and information.[286] It is not directed towards legislation prohibiting expressions of racial hatred. Because of this, s 18C is plainly inappropriate and maladapted to Article 7's purpose.

Finally, even if Article 7 could be interpreted as directing legislation prohibiting expressions of racial hatred, it would need to account for the rights expressed in Article 5. To hold otherwise would defeat the purpose of including Article 5 in the Convention. Hence, our analysis concerning Article 5's relationship with Articles 2 and 4 also apply here.

F *A summary of whether s 18C conforms to the Convention*

Before going further, it is useful to summarise our arguments concerning whether or not s 18C conforms to the relevant Articles of the Convention:

(a)   Article 4

Section 18C is not reasonably capable of being considered appropriate or adapted to the purpose of Article 4. Article 4 sets a harm threshold far higher than the one s 18C establishes. The relevant purpose of Article 4 is to prohibit speech *based on* racial hatred, and speech that amounts *incitement* to racial hatred. Further, Article 4 requires due regard to the guarantee of freedom of expression in Article 5. This freedom entails a very broad range of expression, including expression that offends, insults or even humiliates. Section 18C does not require acts that offend, insult or humiliate be based on racial hatred or to amount to incitement to racial hatred. Rather, the minimum threshold s 18C sets are acts that are reasonably likely to offend. This suggests s 18C is not suited to the purpose of Article 4, and certainly not a fitting legislative response to the purpose of Article 4.

In addition, s 18C's use of the "reasonable representative test" is not appropriate or adapted to Article 4's requirement to pay due regard to the guarantee of equality before the law in Article 5. This is because legal liability under s 18C may depend on the race, colour, ethnicity or nationality of the audience, the speaker, or both. Further, s 18D's allowance for a broader range of speech for those whose work concerns academic, scientific, artistic or journalistic

---

285 Convention Art 7 (emphasis added).
286 See Part IV.D.4 (pages 32-4).

pursuits also does not pay due regard to Article 5's guarantee of equality before the law.

(b) Article 2

Section 18C is not reasonably capable of being considered appropriate or adapted to the purpose of Article 2. As a preliminary objection, the text, structure and purpose of the Convention suggests that legislation regulating, restricting or prohibiting freedom of expression should be resolved through Article 4 and not Article 2. This is because the risk of legislation prohibiting racial discrimination adversely affecting freedom of expression was of considerable concern to those who drafted and approved the Convention. Hence, Article 4 was intended to specifically address this concern.

Putting that objection aside, and in any event, Article 5's guarantees of freedom of expression and equality before the law apply to Article 2. Hence, the considerations that applied to Article 4 also apply to Article 2. In addition, there is no express right not to be offended, insulted or even humiliated under the Convention or the UDHR. At best, these rights may be found in the rights to security of person, to dignity or equality.

However, there are significant issues concerning whether the right not to be offended, insulted or humiliated can be found in the rights security of person, to dignity or to equality. The right to security of person concerns threats graver than offence, insult or humiliation. The right to equality does not cover the right not to be offended, insulted, or humiliated. The right to dignity is vague such that it should not be taken to displace the express freedom of expression. In any event, the rights to security of person, to dignity and the right to equality are qualified, and must give way to freedom of expression in respect of expression that (without more) offends, insults or humiliates.

(c) Article 6

Article 6 provides for remedies in the event of racial discrimination. Article 6 does not direct States Parties to make unlawful racial discrimination or expression of racial hatred, as these are the respective purposes of Article 2 and Article 4. Given this, and given s 18C does not provide for remedies, s 18C is not reasonably capable of being considered appropriate or adapted to Article 6.

(d) Article 7

Article 7's purpose is to encourage State Parties to take action in the fields of teaching, education, culture and information to combat attitudes that lead to racial prejudice. Article 7 does not direct States Parties to legislate to make unlawful racial discrimination or expressions of racial hatred as, once again, these are the respective purposes of Articles 2 and 4. Given this, s 18C is not reasonably capable of being considered appropriate or adapted to Article 7.

We now consider whether Article 20(2) of the ICCPR could support s 18C under the external affairs power.

G *The International Covenant on Civil and Political Rights*

It appears that s 18C also relies on the ICCPR for its constitutional validity under the external affairs power. The Explanatory Memorandum in support of the RHB noted the following:

> The Commonwealth scheme of human rights administration addresses discrimination in the area of sex, race and disability. Part 3 [which inserted Part IIA into the RDA] will add offensive behaviour because of race, colour and national and ethnic origin as additional grounds for investigation and conciliation under that scheme.[287]

The 'scheme of human rights administration' referred to in the Explanatory Memorandum was, at the time, that created by the *Human Rights and Equal Opportunity Act 1986* (Cth) ('HREOCA'). The HREOCA itself relied on a number of treaties for its constitutional validity under the external affairs power. Among those treaties was the ICCPR.[288] The scheme of human rights administration is now provided under the *Australian Human Rights Commission Act 1986* (Cth) ('AHRC Act'). Like the HREOCA, the AHRC Act relies on a number of treaties for its constitutional validity under the external affairs power, including the ICCPR.[289]

Article 20(2) of the ICCPR[290] appears the most relevant to s 18C. This

---

287 Explanatory Memorandum 8. The Explanatory Memorandum mentions both Article 4 of the Convention and Article 20(2) of the ICCPR to support the criminal provisions proposed in the RHB. However, the Explanatory Memorandum appears to have 'cast a broader net' to support the civil provisions.
288 HREOCA sch 2.
289 AHRC Act sch 2.
290 Once again, please note that in order to distinguish Articles of the ICCPR from Articles of the Convention, the latter are just referred to as "Articles" in our treatise, while those of the ICCPR are termed "[Articles] of the ICCPR".

Article provides that:

> Any advocacy of national, racial or religious hatred that constitutes incitement to discrimination, hostility or violence shall be prohibited by law.[291]

Using the tests noted above for the constitutionally valid enactment of treaties, there is no doubt that Australia entered into the ICCPR in good faith and that the ICCPR directs itself to matters of international concern. Further, Article 20(2) of the ICCPR meets the specificity requirement, as it obliges states to prohibit by law advocacy of national, racial or religious hatred that constitutes incitement to discrimination, hostility or violence.

The key issue here is whether s 18C meets the conformity requirement. That is, is s 18C reasonably capable of being considered appropriate and adapted to the purpose of Article 20(2) of the ICCPR?[292] Our view is that s 18C does not meet the conformity requirement for the following reasons.

1 *The type of speech prohibited by Article 20(2) of the ICCPR*

Like Article 4 of the Convention, Article 20(2) of the ICCPR sets a high "harm threshold". This is demonstrated by the use of terms 'advocacy', 'hatred' and 'incitement' as well as 'hostility' and 'violence'.

The *Macquarie Dictionary* defines 'advocate' (from which 'advocacy' is a noun variant) as follows:

> 1. to plead in favour of; support or urge by argument; recommend publicly... 2. (sometimes fol. by *of*) someone who defends, vindicates, or espouses a cause by argument; an upholder; a defender...[293]

This definition suggests something more than just the expression of opinion or statements made in the course of discussion or argument. Rather, the speaker needs to urge, recommend or espouse the cause of national, racial or religious hatred.

The term 'hatred' suggests something more than the generation of offence, insult or even humiliation as the result of a statement being made. This is so especially in the context of the phrase '*advocacy* of national, racial or religious

---

291 ICCPR Art 20(2).
292 As with the Convention, the test of "reasonable proportionality" may assist in assessing whether s 18C is reasonably capable of being considered appropriate and adapted to Article 20(2) of the ICCPR. See *Industrial Relations Act Case* [1996] HCA 56; (1996) 187 CLR 416, 487 (Brennan CJ, Toohey, Gaudron, McHugh and Gummow JJ).
293 *Macquarie Dictionary* 21.

hatred'.[294] It appears that what is prohibited is the *urging* of intense dislike or detestation of others based on their nationality, race or religion.

However, the advocacy of national, racial or religious hatred *itself* is not enough – it must also amount to *incitement* to discrimination, hostility or violence. As noted above, 'incite' means to 'urge on; stimulate or prompt into action'.[295]

Hence, Article 20(2) of the ICCPR, appears directed to prohibiting speech that urges, recommends or espouses intense dislike or detestation against others on the basis of nationality, race or religion such that it stimulates or prompts others to engage in discrimination, hostility or violence.

Obviously, a wide range of expression concerning matters of nationality, race or religion falls outside the categories prohibited by Article 20(2) of the ICCPR. However, this wide range of expression is exactly what s 18C purports to make unlawful. Section 18C makes unlawful acts reasonably likely to offend, insult or humiliate. Such speech *may* urge or recommend intense dislike or detestation such that it prompts other to engage in discrimination or violence, but in a wide range of cases it simply won't.[296] Hence, the means s 18C uses are not suitable or fitting to the purpose of Article 20(2) of the ICCPR.[297] As with s 18C's approach to implementing Article 4, s 18C is legislative overreach, if not legislative overkill. It therefore fails the conformity requirement for implementing Article 20(2) of the ICCPR.

Section 18D does not remedy the overreach of s 18C. This is because, as with Article 4, acts that offend, insult or humiliate in many cases will not fall into a category that Article 20(2) of the ICCPR prohibits even if those acts are made *unreasonably* and in *bad faith*.

Hence, Article 20(2) of the ICCPR does not support s 18C's constitutional validity under the external affairs power, even when that Article is considered on its own. However, there are other Articles of the ICCPR that make it more difficult to argue that s 18C (and s 18D) are constitutionally valid under the external affairs power.

2   *The effect of other relevant Articles of the ICCPR*

Any analysis concerning whether s 18C conforms to Article 20(2) of the

---

294 ICCPR Art 20(2) (emphasis ours).
295 *Macquarie Dictionary* 750.
296 This analysis is similar to what we conducted for Article 4, see Part IV. E.1.f (page 44).
297 This analysis is strengthened by applying the "reasonable proportionality" principle. The means that s 18C employs are greatly disproportionate to the conduct prohibited by Article 20(2) of the ICCPR.

ICCPR must take into account other relevant Articles of the ICCPR. Indeed, parties to the ICCPR are obliged to ensure the observance of all rights under the ICCPR. Article 2(1) of the ICCPR provides:

> Each State Party to the [ICCPR] undertakes to respect and to ensure to all individuals within its territory and subject to its jurisdiction the rights recognized in the [ICCPR], without distinction of any kind, such as race, colour, sex, language, religion, political or other opinion, national or social origin, property, birth or other status.[298]

Article 3 of the ICCPR provides:

> The States Parties to the [ICCPR] undertake to ensure the equal right of men and women to the enjoyment of all civil and political rights set forth in the [ICCPR].[299]

The Articles that are most relevant to s 18C, along with Article 20(2) of the ICCPR, are Articles 5(1), 19 and 26 of the ICCPR.

Article 5(1) of the ICCPR disallows States Parties from placing limits on rights and freedoms to a greater extent permitted by the ICCPR, providing:

> Nothing in the present Covenant may be interpreted as implying for any State, group or person any right to engage in any activity or perform any act aimed at the destruction of any of the rights and freedoms recognized herein or at their limitation to a greater extent than is provided for in the present Covenant.[300]

Article 26 of the ICCPR concerns equality before the law, providing:

> All persons are equal before the law and are entitled without any discrimination to the equal protection of the law. In this respect, the law shall prohibit any discrimination and guarantee to all persons equal and effective protection against discrimination on any ground such as race, colour, sex, language, religion, political or other opinion, national or social origin, property, birth or other status.

Article 19 of the ICCPR concerns freedom of expression. It provides:

> 1. Everyone shall have the right to hold opinions without interference.
>
> 2. Everyone shall have the right to freedom of expression; this right shall

---

298 ICCPR Art 2(1).
299 ICCPR Art 3.
300 ICCPR Art 5(1).

include freedom to seek, receive and impart information and ideas of all kinds, regardless of frontiers, either orally, in writing or in print, in the form of art, or through any other media of his choice.

3. The exercise of the rights provided for in paragraph 2 of this article carries with it special duties and responsibilities. It may therefore be subject to certain restrictions, but these shall only be such as are provided by law and are necessary:

(a) For respect of the rights or reputations of others;

(b) For the protection of national security or of public order (*ordre public*), or of public health or morals.[301]

The HRC has noted that Article 20(2) of the ICCPR falls within the exceptions in Article 19(3) of the ICCPR.[302] However, the HRC goes on to note:

> It is only with regard to the *specific forms* of expression indicated in article 20 that States parties are obliged to have legal prohibition. In every case in which the State restricts freedom of expression it is necessary to justify the prohibitions and their provisions in strict conformity with article 19.[303]

That is, restrictions on freedom of expression can only be directed at the forms of expression that Article 20(2) of the ICCPR specifically prohibits. As noted in the previous section, these prohibitions only apply to certain, narrow categories of expression.

The HRC noted the following about the conformity requirement under Article 19(3):

> [W]hen a State party imposes restrictions on the exercise of freedom of expression, these may not put in jeopardy the right itself. The [HRC] recalls that the relation between right and restriction and between norm and exception must not be reversed.[304]

It then noted:

> [Article 19(3)] lays down specific conditions and it is only subject to these conditions that restrictions may be imposed: the restrictions must be 'provided by law'; they may only be imposed for one of the grounds set

---

301 ICCPR Art 19.
302 Human Rights Committee, *General Comment 34, Article 19: Freedom of opinion and expression* (12 September 2011) [50].
303 Ibid [52] (emphasis ours).
304 Ibid [21] (citations omitted).

out in [Article 19(3)(a) or (b)]; and they must conform to the strict tests of necessity and proportionality.[305]

Further, The HRC noted that a restriction in Article 19(3) must be:

> [F]ormulated with specific precision to enable an individual to regulate his or her conduct accordingly... A law may not confer unfettered discretion for the restriction of freedom of expression on those charged with its execution. Laws must provide sufficient guidance to those charged with their execution to enable them to ascertain what sorts of expression are properly restricted and what sorts are not.[306]

As to proportionality, the HRC noted:

> Restrictions must not be overbroad. The [HRC] observed in general comment No. 27 that 'restrictive measures must conform to the principle of proportionality; they must be appropriate to achieve their protective function; they must be the least intrusive instrument amongst those which might achieve their protective function; they must be proportionate to the interest protected...'[307]

Given the foregoing, our conclusions concerning whether the ICCPR supports s 18C are similar to those concerning whether the Convention supports it. Section 18C uses legislative overreach, if not legislative overkill, to achieve the purpose of Article 20(2) of the ICCPR. Section 18C substantially intrudes into not only the right to freedom of expression but also (along with s 18D) the right to equality before the law.

We now turn to considering the approach that relevant reports have taken to the Convention and the ICCPR, and the approach taken in *Toben*.

H *The approach of relevant reports*

Prior to the RHB,[308] three influential reports considered whether Australia should enact legislation prohibiting racial hatred pursuant to relevant international treaties. These reports were:

- The Royal Commission into Aboriginal Deaths in Custody in 1991 ('Royal Commission');[309]

---

305 Ibid [22] (citations omitted).
306 Ibid [25] (citations omitted).
307 Ibid [34].
308 The Explanatory Memorandum to the RHD itself refers to the National Inquiry into Racist Violence and the Royal Commission into Aboriginal Deaths in Custody.
309 Commonwealth, Royal Commission into Aboriginal Deaths in Custody, *National Report* (1991).

- The Human Rights and Equal Opportunity Commission's *National Inquiry into Racist Violence* in 1991 ('Inquiry');[310] and
- The Australian Law Reform Commission's ('ALRC's') report, *Multiculturalism and the Law* in 1992 ('ALRC Report').[311]

These reports remain valuable contributions to the issue of race relations in Australia. Each was referred to in Parliamentary debates over the RHB. However, as to each report's analysis concerning legislating to prohibit racial hatred, we note two things. First, each report predates both the full development of the implied freedom of political communication, and the further development of tests for legislating a treaty under the external affairs power.

Each report adopted a "balancing approach" to competing rights. The Royal Commission noted that legislating to make unlawful racial vilification related to the Convention and the ICCPR.[312] It noted that:

> National legislation relating to racial vilification... has to take into account the potential conflict between these two rights in a democratic society: the right to freedom of speech, and the right of the state to limit certain kinds of speech that can lead to overt conflict among its citizens.[313]

It then noted:

> What is at issue in the legislation... is the matter of balancing the individual's rights, in this case to freedom of speech, with the rights of other individuals and groups and the legitimate interests of the state in the promotion of civil order.[314]

The Inquiry stated that '[i]mplementation of Australia's international obligations under [the Convention and the ICCPR]... requires the striking of a balance between potentially conflicting rights and freedoms.'[315] It later stated with regard to legislating against incitement to racist hostility:

> The Inquiry recognises that this is a difficult area which requires the striking of a balance between conflicting rights and values. The right to free speech, for example, needs to be weighed against the value placed on the rights of people from different ethnic backgrounds to enjoy their

---

310 Human Rights and Equal Opportunity Commission, *National Enquiry into Racist Violence* (Australian Government Publishing Service, 1991).
311 Australian Law Reform Commission, *Multiculturalism and the Law*, Report No 57 (1992).
312 Royal Commission [28.3.31].
313 Royal Commission [28.3.33].
314 Royal Commission [28.3.35].
315 Inquiry 295.

lives free of harassment or violence.³¹⁶

The ALRC Report noted that when the Commonwealth legislated to give effect to an international convention that it was sufficient that the legislation gives effect to the principles stated in the convention.³¹⁷ However, it also noted 'There is no requirement of exact equivalence; it is enough that legislation is... "reasonably appropriate"'.³¹⁸ It then noted that, 'It may... be necessary that there is "reasonable proportionality" between the means chosen and the purpose or object of the convention'.³¹⁹ In recommending that incitement to racist hatred and hostility should be unlawful,³²⁰ the ALRC Report commented that freedom of expression must be balanced against other community values:

> In the view of a majority of the Commission, freedom of expression is just one of the values the law protects in a democratic society. In a tolerant society people are entitled to be protected against serious attempts to undermine tolerance by stirring up hatred between groups. Laws prohibiting incitement to racial hatred and hostility protect the inherent dignity of the human person. In a multicultural society, values such as equality of status, tolerance of a wide variety of beliefs, respect for cultural and group identity and equal opportunity for everyone to participate in social processes must be respected and protected by law.³²¹

The "balancing approach" to rights adopted by the Royal Commission, Inquiry and the ALRC Report imposes a lower threshold to meet than the tests we noted above, namely whether a law is reasonably capable of being considered appropriate or adapted to the relevant treaty.³²²

Second, even though each of these reports adopted a lower threshold, *none* of them recommended that speech that offended, insulted or even humiliated be made unlawful. Indeed, the Inquiry noted:

> In recommending the amendment of the Racial Discrimination Act to prohibit the incitement of racial hostility, the Inquiry is not talking about protecting hurt feelings or injured sensibilities. Its concern is with conduct

---

316 Inquiry 299.
317 ALRC Report [7.32].
318 Ibid.
319 Ibid.
320 Ibid [7.45]. Nygh J dissented from this recommendation: see ibid [7.45] fn 88.
321 Ibid [7.44] (citation omitted). It should be noted that Nygh J took the view 'that in a democratic and pluralist society freedom of expression is of special importance which may necessitate tolerance of obnoxious and hateful views which do not incite violence': see ibid [7.44] fn 87.
322 Especially if the test of reasonably proportionality is included in analysis.

with adverse effects on the quality of life and well-being of individuals or groups who have been targeted because of their race.[323]

And later:

> The threshold for prohibited conduct needs to be higher than expressions of mere ill will to prevent the situation in New Zealand, where legislation produced a host of trivial complaints. The Inquiry is of the opinion that the term "incitement to racial hostility" conveys the level and degree of conduct with which the legislation would be concerned.[324]

Thus, s 18C's reach extends far beyond that recommended in any relevant report, even when those reports adopted a lower threshold for balancing rights and freedoms.

I *The approach in* Toben

Toben is the leading decision on the constitutional validity of s 18C. This case held that s 18C is constitutionally valid under the external affairs power. However, the reasoning in *Toben* concerning s 18C's validity under the external affair power contains significant errors. To explore these errors, we will first examine the reasoning of Carr J (with whom Kiefel J agreed) and then examine the reasoning of Allsop J.[325]

1   *The reasoning of Carr J*

The reasoning of Carr J with respect the external affairs power supporting s 18C is the reasoning that carries the most weight. This is because Kiefel J agreed with Carr J's reasoning in this regard.[326] Hence, Carr J's reasoning forms the majority in *Toben*. As to s 18C, Carr J stated, relevantly:

> [I]n my opinion, an assessment of whether Part IIA is within power requires reference not only to Article 4 but also to Articles 2 and 7 of the Convention and to Article 20 paragraph 2 of the [ICCPR] which entered into force for Australia on 13 November 1980. Article 2 of the Convention imposes an obligation on States Parties to take measures to prohibit racial discrimination. The relevant part of Article 4 imposes

---

323 Inquiry 299.
324 Ibid 300.
325 Before going further, and to avoid any doubt, we do not in any way endorse the views or the actions of Frederick Toben.
326 *Toben* [2003] FCAFC 137; (2003) 129 FCR 515, 528-9 [50] (Kiefel J).

an obligation to adopt immediate and positive measures designed to eradicate all incitement to acts of racial hatred and discrimination. Article 7 imposes an obligation to adopt measures with a view to combating prejudices which lead to racial discrimination and to promoting tolerance, particularly in the fields of teaching, education, culture and information. Article 20 paragraph 2 of the ICCPR relevantly requires prohibition by law of any advocacy of racial hatred that constitutes incitement to discrimination, hostility or violence. I accept the Commonwealth's submission that acts done in public which are objectively likely to offend, insult, humiliate or intimidate and which are done because of race, colour or national or ethnic origin are likely to incite other persons to racial hatred or discrimination or to constitute acts of racial hatred or discrimination. In my view, the Convention can be seen to be directed not only at acts of racial discrimination and hatred, but also to deterring public expressions of offensive racial prejudice which might lead to acts of racial hatred and discrimination.

In my opinion it is clearly consistent with the provisions of the Convention and the ICCPR that a State Party should legislate to "nip in the bud" the doing of offensive, insulting, humiliating or intimidating public acts which are done because of race, colour or national or ethnic origin before such acts can grow into incitement or promotion of racial hatred or discrimination. The authorities show that, subject to the requisite connection referred to ... above, it is for the legislature to choose the means by which it carries into or gives effect to a treaty...[327]

We now turn to analysing the errors in Carr J's reasoning. To do this, we will be excerpting relevant parts of the passage quoted above in order to make clear the particular errors in Carr J's reasoning.

(a) Accepting the Commonwealth's submission

Justice Carr accepted the Commonwealth's submission that:

[A]cts done in public which are objectively likely to offend, insult, humiliate or intimidate and which are done because of race, colour or national or ethnic origin are likely to incite other persons to racial hatred or discrimination or to constitute acts of racial hatred or discrimination.[328]

---

327 Ibid 524-5 [19]-[20] (Carr J).
328 Ibid 524 [19] (Carr J).

Carr J does not cite the evidence the Commonwealth presented to support this submission (assuming the Commonwealth presented evidence to support it). This is curious, because the Commonwealth's submission makes an extraordinary claim: that public acts that are objectively likely to offend, insult, humiliate or intimidate and which are done because of race, colour or national or ethnic origin *are likely* to incite other persons to racial hatred or discrimination or to constitute acts of racial hatred or discrimination. Such an extraordinary claim required at least some evidence supporting it. However, the Commonwealth did not provide such evidence or, if it did, Carr J did not cite it.

We submit that, in fact, the Commonwealth's submission is a *non sequitur*. If acts are objectively likely offend, insult or humiliate on the basis of race, colour or national or ethnic origin, it does *not* follow that such acts are likely to incite others to racial hatred or discrimination, or constitute racial hatred or discrimination, *especially as those terms are understood in the Convention and the ICCPR*. As we have demonstrated above, expression that offends, insults or humiliates may be motivated by emotions other than hate. Further, such expression may manifest emotions other than hate, or create emotions in the audience (apart from those offended, insulted or humiliated) far removed from hatred.

Apart from this, the problems with the Commonwealth's submission should have been immediately apparent. As Megan McArdle notes in relation to journalism, falsification is a much more reliable route to the truth than confirmation.[329] The same principle applies to law. To use an example, are offensive, off-colour jokes with a racial connotation *likely* to incite others to racial hatred or discrimination, or constitute racial hatred or discrimination, as those terms are understood in the Convention and the ICCPR? As noted above, 'it is clear enough that one can racially insult or offend another without ever expressing or intending hatred for that person's race or ethnicity'.[330]

As to humiliation, and recalling McArdle, suppose a robust debate involving race (for example, the racial composition of annual immigrant intake) leaves a participant humiliated (owing to poor debating skills or the like). Again, is this humiliation likely to incite others to racial hatred or discrimination, or constitute racial hatred or discrimination, as those terms are understood in the

---

329 Megan McArdle, 'Ex-'60 Minutes' Producer Is No Hollywood Hero', *BloombergView* (on-line), 24 July 2014.
330 Dan Meagher, 'So Far So Good?: A Critical Evaluation of Racial Vilification Laws in Australia' (2004) 32(2) *Federal Law Review* 225, 232. See also our analysis at Part IV.E.1.(f) (page 44).

Convention and the ICCPR? The logical connection between even humiliation and racial discrimination or hatred is, we suggest, tenuous. In any event, such commonplace examples refute the contention that humiliating acts *are likely* to incite others to racial hatred or discrimination, or constitute racial hatred or discrimination.

However, accepting the Commonwealth's submission is not the most significant of Carr J's errors.

(b)   Failing to properly apply principles relevant to interpreting treaties

Carr J concluded:

> In my view, the Convention can be seen to be directed not only at acts of racial discrimination and hatred, but also to deterring public expressions of offensive racial prejudice *which might* lead to acts of racial hatred and discrimination.[331]

The basis for Carr J's conclusion is as follows:

> ...[I]n my opinion, an assessment of whether Part IIA is within power requires reference not only to Article 4 but also to Articles 2 and 7 of the Convention and to Article 20 paragraph 2 of the [ICCPR] which entered into force for Australia on 13 November 1980. Article 2 of the Convention imposes an obligation on States Parties to take measures to prohibit racial discrimination. The relevant part of Article 4 imposes an obligation to adopt immediate and positive measures designed to eradicate all incitement to acts of racial hatred and discrimination. Article 7 imposes an obligation to adopt measures with a view to combating prejudices which lead to racial discrimination and to promoting tolerance, particularly in the fields of teaching, education, culture and information. Article 20 paragraph 2 of the ICCPR relevantly requires prohibition by law of any advocacy of racial hatred that constitutes incitement to discrimination, hostility or violence.[332]

With respect, Carr J's interpretation of Articles 2, 4 and 7 of the Convention, and his application of Article 20(2) of the ICCPR, are in error for the following reasons.

---

331 *Toben* [2003] FCAFC 137; (2003) 129 FCR 515, 524-5 [19] (Carr J) (emphasis ours).
332 Ibid 524 [19] (Carr J).

(i) Failing to account for the text, object and purpose of the Convention

As noted above, it is important to note the text, structure and purpose of a treaty along with the form the treaty takes, the subject to which it relates, its history of negotiations, and the mischief it addresses.[333] In ascertaining these things, extrinsic sources are useful.[334] It appears that Carr J failed to account for the text, structure and purpose of relevant Articles of the Convention along with the mischief each addresses. This may explain his other errors.

(ii) Failing to properly determine the role of Article 4 in the Convention

As also noted above, there was considerable concern when drafting the Convention about the effect racial discrimination legislation would have on freedom of expression. Article 4 was drafted to address this concern. Even then Article 4 was controversial because of its impact on freedom of expression. Ultimately, Article 4's terms included the provision that prohibitions on racial hatred must pay due regard to Article 5, including the guarantee of freedom of expression.

As to freedom of expression, Article 4's terms were directed to prohibiting expression of insults, ridicule or slander of persons or groups or justification of hatred, contempt or discrimination only when it *clearly amounted to incitement* to hatred or discrimination.[335] Article 4 was *not* directed towards (in Carr J's words) 'expressions of offensive racial prejudice *which migh*t lead to acts of racial hatred and discrimination'.[336]

(iii) Failing to properly determine the role of Article 2 in the Convention

Carr J failed to read the text, purpose and history of Article 2 in light of the text, purpose and history of Article 4. As noted above, Article 4 addressed concerns about the effect of racial discrimination legislation on freedom of expression, and Article 2 should not be interpreted to sweep aside Article 4, as it were, by a side-wind.[337]

(iv) Failing to account for the role of Article 5 of the Convention

It should be noted that Carr J overlooked Article 5 in his basis for concluding

---

333 *A v Minister for Immigration and Ethnic Affairs* [1997] HCA 4; (1997) 190 CLR 225, 231 (Brennan J).
334 Ibid.
335 See Part IV.E.1.(e) (page 43).
336 *Toben* [2003] FCAFC 137; (2003) 129 FCR 515, 525 [19] (Carr J).
337 See Part IV.E.3 (page 58).

that the Convention deters public expressions of offensive racial prejudice which might lead to acts of racial hatred and discrimination.[338] This was a critical error.

As we noted above, Article 4 specifically directs State Parties when enacting laws to pay due regard to the guarantee of rights in Article 5, including freedom of expression.[339] As to Article 2, Article 5 itself states that in eliminating racial discrimination in compliance with Article 2, State Parties must also guarantee the right of everyone, amongst other rights, to freedom of expression.[340]

When Article 5 is taken into account in the manner that the Convention requires, it is simply not possible to conclude that the Convention was directed against the type of conduct Carr J suggests. It is not directed against 'public expressions of offensive racial prejudice *which might* lead to acts of racial hatred and discrimination',[341] or which '"nips in the bud" the doing of offensive, insulting, humiliating or intimidating public acts… before such acts can grow into incitement or promotion of racial hatred or discrimination'.[342] The guarantee of freedom of expression provided for in Article 5 sets a much higher threshold for legislative prohibition of expressions of racial hatred.

(v) Failing to properly determine the role of Article 7 in the Convention

In *Toben*, Article 7 was taken to support s 18C. Justice Carr noted:

> Article 7 imposes an *obligation* to adopt measures with a view to combating prejudices which lead to racial discrimination and to promoting tolerance, particularly in the fields of teaching, education, culture and information.[343]

However, as we noted previously, Article 7 is not directed to legislative action making unlawful speech based on racial hatred.[344] Rather, Article 7's purpose was to encourage efforts to combat racism in the fields of teaching, education, culture and information.[345] Article 7's purpose was not to serve as a "catch all" provision. Hence, Article 7 cannot support s 18C.

---

338 *Toben* [2003] FCAFC 137; (2003) 129 FCR 515, 525 [19] (Carr J).
339 Convention Art 4.
340 Convention Art 5.
341 *Toben* [2003] FCAFC 137; (2003) 129 FCR 515, 525 [19] (Carr J) (emphasis ours).
342 Ibid 525 [20] (Carr J).
343 *Toben* [2003] FCAFC 137; (2003) 129 FCR 515, 524 [19] (Carr J) (emphasis ours).
344 See Part IV.D.5 (page 32).
345 Convention Art 7.

(vi) Failing to properly interpret Article 20(2) of the ICCPR

As we noted previously, Article 20(2) of the ICCPR prohibits '[a]ny advocacy of national, racial or religious hatred that constitutes incitement to discrimination, hostility or violence'.[346] The types of expression restricted by Article 20(2) of the ICCPR are strictly limited, especially in light of Articles 2(1), 3, 5(1), 19 and 26 of the ICCPR.[347] Section 18C greatly exceeds the legislative limits that the ICCPR imposes.[348]

(vii) Conclusions concerning Carr J's reasoning

Ultimately, on their proper construction, neither the Convention nor the ICCPR are directed at deterring public expressions of offensive racial prejudice which *might lead* to acts of racial hatred and discrimination. Further, neither the Convention nor the ICCPR support legislation that "nips in the bud" offensive, insulting, humiliating or intimidating public acts before they can grow into incitement or promotion of racial hatred or discrimination. Hence, Carr J was in error on these points.

(c) Failing to properly apply the principles concerning conformity

Justice Carr failed to properly apply the principles concerning conformity when considering whether the Convention supports s 18C. He stated:

> The authorities show that, subject to the requisite connection [being shown], *it is for the legislature to choose the means by which it carries into or gives effect to a treaty*...[349]

Justice Carr correctly identified the test for conformity as the law being reasonably capable of being considered appropriate and adapted to implementing a treaty.[350] However, he then failed to apply it correctly.

Justice Carr's error appears to stem from his incorrect interpretation of the Convention and the ICCPR. It appears that Carr J held that s 18C was reasonably capable of being considered appropriate and adapted to the purpose of the relevant Articles of the Convention and the ICCPR. This is because s 18C makes unlawful 'public expressions of offensive racial prejudice *which might* lead to acts of racial hatred and discrimination',[351] and this "nips in the bud"

---

346 ICCPR Art 20(2).
347 See Part IV.G (page 91).
348 See Part IV.G (page 91).
349 *Toben* [2003] FCAFC 137; (2003) 129 FCR 515, 525 [20] (Carr J) (emphasis ours).
350 Ibid 524 [17] (Carr J).
351 Ibid 525 [19] (Carr J) (emphasis ours).

offensive, insulting, humiliating or intimidating public acts before such acts can grow into incitement or promotion of racial hatred or discrimination.[352] Thus, s 18C is appropriate and adapted to prohibiting offensive racial prejudice that might lead to acts of racial hatred and discrimination.

However, as we demonstrated above, the relevant Articles of the Convention and the ICCPR are *not* directed at offensive racial prejudice which *might* lead to acts of racial hatred and discrimination.[353] Rather, these Articles prohibit conduct that is more immediate and severe. As we also demonstrated above, s 18C is not reasonably capable of being considered appropriate and adapted to the purposes of the relevant Articles.[354] Hence, Carr J is also in error concerning conformity.

2   *The reasoning of Allsop J*

In his judgment, Allsop J provided an overview of the Convention and the origins of Part IIA. That said, Allsop J's overview, and his resulting reasoning, contained errors concerning the approach to be employed when interpreting treaties, as well as errors applying the principles concerning specificity and conformity.

As with our analysis of Carr J's reason's, we will excerpt relevant parts of Allsop J's reasons.

(a)   *Failing to interpret the Convention correctly*

Once again, it is important to note the text, structure and purpose of a treaty along with the form the treaty takes, the subject to which it relates, its history of negotiations, and the mischief it addresses.[355] As with Carr J, Allsop J failed to account for the text, structure and purpose of relevant Articles of the Convention along with the mischief each Article addresses. This led him into error.

(i)   *Interpreting Article 4 narrowly*

In answering a submission that s 18C needed to be confined to instances of racial hatred in light of Article 4 and the heading to s 18C itself, Allsop J stated:

> The first proposition put in support of this submission is that Part IIA is

---

352 Ibid 515, 525 [20] (Carr J).
353 See Part IV.E.1 (page 36), Part IV.E.2 (page 51), Part IV.E.3 (page 58) and Part IV.G (page 91).
354 See Part IV.E.1 (page 36), Part IV.E.2 (page 51), Part IV.E.3 (page 58) and Part IV.G (page 91).
355 *A v Minister for Immigration and Ethnic Affairs* [1997] HCA 4; (1997) 190 CLR 225, 231 (Brennan J).

an intended implementation only of Article 4 of the Convention... It was submitted that the touchstone of the offence contemplated by the Convention is the dissemination of ideas based on racial superiority or hatred.

A number of things can be said in answer to this first proposition. First, the fact that the *offence* contemplated by Article 4 was of the character described in [Article 4(a)] does not, in terms, require *civil provisions* such as ss 18B, 18C and 18D, set in a framework of conciliation in cognate legislation, to be so limited.[356]

Put briefly, Allsop J thought Article 4 provided only for criminal laws against racist speech, not for laws enabling civil claims. However, this narrow view of Article 4 is unsustainable.

As noted above, there was considerable concern about the effect that legislation prohibiting racial discrimination would have on freedom of expression. Article 4 was designed to specifically address these concerns. The solution struck was to allow States Parties flexibility in approaching this issue. A State Party, when considering the rights and freedoms in Article 5 and their own constitutional framework, could elect to do nothing. Alternatively, a State Party could pursue a legislative response *up to and including* criminal prohibition. That is, a State Party in adopting a legislative response could provide for *civil* rather than *criminal* actions.

Of course, civil claims impact freedom of expression, which is an issue we examine in more detail below.[357] Consequently, State Parties must also take into account the rights and freedoms in Article 5 when crafting laws enabling civil claims with respect to racist speech.

This view of Article 4 is supported by the Committee, which noted with specific reference to Article 4:

> The Committee recommends that the criminalization of forms of racist expression should be reserved for serious cases, to be proven beyond reasonable doubt, *while less serious cases should be addressed by means other than criminal law*, taking into account, inter alia, the nature and extent of the impact on targeted persons and groups.[358]

The Committee went on to outline criteria for the type of conduct that may

---

[356] *Toben* [2003] FCAFC 137; (2003) 129 FCR 515, 549 [134]-[135] (Allsop J) (emphasis in original).
[357] See Part V.D.5.(c) (page 175).
[358] Committee on the Elimination of Racial Discrimination, *General recommendation No. 35: Combating racist hate speech* (26 September 2013) [12] (emphasis ours).

attract criminal sanctions.[359]

(ii) Interpreting the elimination of racial discrimination in all its forms too broadly

Justice Allsop stated:

> Secondly, Article 4 is not the only matter in the Convention to which Part IIA can be seen as directed. The context and aim of the Convention were, as I have sought to explain, racial discrimination and its elimination, in *all* its forms. Sections 18B, 18C and 18D can be seen as intended to assist in the endeavour of eliminating racial discrimination in all its forms, including by dealing with racial hatred. Many acts comprehended by ss 18B, 18C and 18D will involve an expression of racial hatred, though other acts may not. The provisions can also be seen as intended to pursue a policy of eliminating racial discrimination and promoting understanding among races (Article 2), prohibiting and bringing to an end by an appropriate means, including legislation, as required by circumstances in Australia, racial discrimination by any person (Article 2 par (d)), eliminating barriers between races and discouraging anything which tends to strengthen racial division (article 2 par (e)), adopting positive measures designed to eradicate all incitement to, or acts of, racial hatred and discrimination in any form (Article 4), assuring everyone in Australia effective protection and remedies through competent tribunals against any acts of racial discrimination which violate human rights and fundamental freedoms contrary to the Convention (Article 6), and adopting an effective measure to combat prejudices which lead to racial discrimination and to promote tolerance and friendship among racial or ethnic groups (Article 7). This is how the Attorney-General and the Explanatory Memorandum explained it. Such explanation was in conformity with the genesis, structure and terms of the Convention.[360]

With respect, Allsop J was in error when interpreting the text, structure and purpose of the Convention.

Citing Schwelb and Lerner, Allsop J provided a general overview concerning the background to the Convention, noting:

> The unexpected recrudescence, in the winter of 1959-60, of some of the most recent and horrific manifestations of racist behaviour enlivened the world community to act swiftly and (with an inevitable degree of variation in political perspective) unanimously, to take steps towards the *elimination* of the perceived evil. The perceived evil was *all* forms of racial

---
359 Ibid [15].
360 *Toben* [2003] FCAFC 137; (2003) 129 FCR 515, 549 [136] (Allsop J) (emphasis in original).

discrimination and racial prejudice, the manifestation of which had been, in recent generations, at times horrifically violent and strident, at times overt, and at times less overt and less brutal, but nevertheless insidiously pervasive. In any form, it was recognised, by all nations in the international community, to strike at the dignity and equality of all human beings.[361]

As a general characterisation of the mischief it addressed, the Convention was indeed directed at the elimination of racial discrimination. However, Allsop J then appeared to suggest that the Convention was directed to the elimination of discrimination such that (in the context of his judgment)[362] it prohibited the making of racially offensive comments:

> Racial hatred was *one* form or manifestation of the perceived evil. Unhappily, it was a form with which the nations in the General Assembly in 1960 to 1965 were all too familiar. It was the form of the perceived evil most likely to lead to brutality and violence, but it was not the only form of the perceived evil antithetical to the dignity and equality inherent in all human beings upon which the Charter of the United Nations was based. It was to *all* such forms and manifestations that the Convention was directed.[363]

In support of this view, Allsop J cited the preamble of the Convention.[364] However, and with respect, Allsop J overlooked that the preamble (amongst other things) also recognised the right of all to fundamental freedoms, including conscience, opinion and expression. He also overlooked that, after the soaring language of the preamble, the Convention descended (as treaties do) to the practicalities of its substantive Articles.

It is true that the preamble assists when interpreting the Convention.[365] However, as both Schwelb and Lerner pointed out, each Article of the Convention was the product of debate and compromise, and each Article served a purpose.

To repeat what we noted above,[366] the structure of the Convention was, relevantly:

- Article 1 provides for definitions;[367]

---

361 *Toben* [2003] FCAFC 137; (2003) 129 FCR 515, 537 [98] (Allsop J) (emphasis in original).
362 Ibid 549 [136].
363 Ibid 538-9 [100] (Allsop J) (emphasis in original).
364 Ibid 537-8 [99] (Allsop J).
365 Natan Lerner, *The UN Convention on the Elimination of all Forms of Racial Discrimination* (Sijthoff & Noordhoff, 2nd ed, 1980) 21.
366 See Part IV.A (page 25).
367 Ibid 25-33.

- Article 2 provides for the obligation of states;[368]
- Article 3 condemns and prohibits apartheid;[369]
- Article 4 provides for measures to prohibit incitement to racial hatred and discrimination and to prohibit racist organisations;[370]
- Article 5 provides for rights specially guaranteed by the Convention;[371]
- Article 6 provides for remedies against racial discrimination;[372] and
- Article 7 provides for steps in the fields of education and information.[373]

We will examine the text and purpose of specific Articles below. However, it is worth noting from the outset that the Allsop J's interpretation – that the Convention was directed at eliminating racial discrimination in *all* its forms – would justify prohibiting *any* robust discussion involving race. This is because, first, such discussion would involve discrimination: that is, distinguishing a person or group based on their race. Second, a robust discussion may make someone listening feel offended or insulted, thereby adversely affecting their dignity. We would like to say that we are making an *argumentum ad absurdum* regarding Allsop J's interpretation. However, given what Allsop J said, we do not think we are. Rather, it appears that Allsop J's interpretation leads easily to such absurd and unworkable results.

Clearly, the Convention was directed to eliminating racial discrimination. However, and equally clearly, it did not lay down an absolute prohibition on making distinctions based on race that may adversely affect one's dignity. Indeed, the Convention allowed such expression to extend to that which may offend, insult or humiliate.

(iii) Failing to consider the limits to Article 1's scope

Justice Allsop stated:

> The definition of 'racial discrimination' in Article 1 of the Convention confirmed the wide aim of the Convention:

---

368 Ibid 33-9.
369 Ibid 40-3.
370 Ibid 43-53.
371 Ibid 54-60.
372 Ibid 60-2.
373 Ibid 63-4.

Article 1
1. In this Convention, the term "racial discrimination" shall mean any distinction, exclusion, restriction or preference based on race, colour, descent, or national or ethnic origin which has the purpose or effect of nullifying or impairing the recognition, enjoyment or exercise, on an equal footing, of human rights and fundamental freedoms in the political, economic, social, cultural or any other field of public life.[374]

It is true that Article 1(1)'s definition of racial discrimination is wide. However it is not unlimited. Schwelb thought that the scope of rights in Article 5 was more comprehensive than those provided in Article 1.[375] However, as noted above, neither the UDHR nor Article 5 provide for an express right not to be offended, insulted or intimidated, and there are significant problems holding that such a right exists within other rights.[376]

(iv) Failing to properly consider Article 5's purpose

Justice Allsop stated the following regarding Article 5:

> The principles embodied in the Universal Declaration of Human Rights and the rights set forth in Article 5 of the Convention... included the rights to freedom of thought, conscience, religion, opinion, expression, assembly and association.[377]

While Allsop J did note that Article 4 referred to Article 5,[378] he did not consider Article 5's purpose, nor how Article 5 worked with Article 4 and Article 2. This was a critical error. As noted above, Article 5 is crucial to calibrating the operation of Article 4 and Article 2.[379]

(b) Failing to hold that relevant Articles of the Convention did not support s 18C

Before examining his errors, it is useful to summarise Allsop J's reasons for finding that Part IIA and s 18C were constitutionally valid.

Justice Allsop cited the following Articles of the Convention as those supporting Part IIA, and in particular s 18C:

---

374 *Toben* [2003] FCAFC 137; (2003) 129 FCR 515, 539 [101] (Allsop J).
375 Egon Schwelb, 'The International Convention on the Elimination of All Forms of Racial Discrimination' (1966) 15 *International and Comparative Law Quarterly* 996, 1004-6.
376 See Part IV.E.3.(a) (page 60).
377 *Toben* [2003] FCAFC 137; (2003) 129 FCR 515, 540 [108] (Allsop J).
378 Ibid 539-40 [107].
379 See Part IV.E.2 (page 51).

- Article 2(1)(d);[380]
- Article 2(1)(e);[381]
- Article 4(a);[382]
- Article 6;[383] and
- Article 7.[384]

Further, Allsop J thought that general statements of principle that commenced Articles 2 and 4 were themselves sufficient to support Part IIA and s 18C,[385] specifically:

- 'States Parties condemn racial discrimination and undertake to pursue by all appropriate means and without delay a policy of eliminating racial discrimination in all its forms and promoting understanding among all races...';[386] and
- 'States Parties condemn all propaganda and all organizations which are based on ideas or theories of superiority of one race or group of persons of one colour or ethnic origin, or which attempt to justify or promote racial hatred and discrimination in any form, and undertake to adopt immediate and positive measures designed to eradicate all incitement to, or acts of, such discrimination...'[387]

Justice Allsop noted the following:

> ...it is plain from the Explanatory Memorandum, the second reading speeches in Parliament and the text of s 18D that careful regard was apparently had to the balancing of what might be seen as conflicting principles in the Universal Declaration of Human Rights and the rights in Article 5.[388]

Justice Allsop concluded with the following statement:

> It is sufficient for me to conclude that there exists the relevant *perceived connection* with the obligations under the Convention and to conclude, as I do, that there is no apparent inconsistency of Part IIA with the Convention.[389]

We now turn to Allsop J's errors.

---

380 Ibid 539 [104], 551 [144] (Allsop J).
381 Ibid.
382 Ibid 539-40 [107], 551 [144] (Allsop J).
383 Ibid 540 [112], 551 [144] (Allsop J)
384 Ibid.
385 Ibid 539 [104], 539-40 [107], 540 [112], 551 [144] (Allsop J).
386 Convention Art 2.
387 Convention Art 7.
388 *Toben* [2003] FCAFC 137; (2003) 129 FCR 515, 551 [143] (Allsop J).
389 Ibid 551 [144] (Allsop J) (emphasis ours).

(i) Failing to apply the relevant principles concerning specificity or conformity

It is useful to reiterate the relevant principles. As to specificity, the principle to be applied is whether the treaty has defined with sufficient specificity the general course to be taken by the signatory states, noting that a broad objective with little precise content and permitting widely divergent policies by parties does not meet the description.[390]

As to conformity, the principle to be applied is whether s 18C is reasonably capable of being considered appropriate and adapted to the relevant Article. This means that s 18C must be a suitable and fitting means of implementing the relevant Article.[391] We note here that while Allsop J did cite the principle, he then stated that the principle requires only a 'relevant perceived connection'.[392] However, the principle requires much more than a 'relevant perceived connection'.[393] Hence, Allsop J is in error on this point.

We will now examine the Articles that Allsop J held supported s 18C.

(ii) The opening sentences of Articles 2 and 4

As we noted above, the opening sentences of Article 2 and Article 4 contain aspirational language.[394] Each also permits a wide range of measures by States Parties to combat racial discrimination. By themselves, they would not be specific enough to justify a legislative response and hence fail the specificity requirement. Hence, Allsop J was in error in holding that these sentences alone may justify s 18C.

However, given that both Article 2 and Article 4 both proceed to outline specific measures, we do not need to spend too much time on this point.

(iii) Article 2(1)(e)

As we also noted above, Article 2(1)(e) of the Convention is broadly and vaguely worded, and appears to exhort States Parties to exert moral influence to combat racial discrimination.[395] There are a number of ways other than

---

390 *Industrial Relations Act Case* [1996] HCA 56; (1996) 187 CLR 416, 486 (Brennan CJ, Toohey, Gaudron, McHugh and Gummow JJ), quoting Leslie Zines, *The High Court and the Constitution* (Butterworths, 3rd ed 1992) 250.
391 Again, we note that the test for reasonably proportionality may also be relevant.
392 *Toben* [2003] FCAFC 137; (2003) 129 FCR 515, 551 [144] (Allsop J).
393 Ibid.
394 See Part IV.D.1 (page 29) and Part IV.D.2 (page 29).
395 See Part IV.D.2 (page 31).

legislation that States Parties may implement Article 2(1)(e). Further, in the context of Article 2, Article 2(1)(d) is directed specifically towards legislation. Given this, Article 2(1)(e) fails in the specificity requirement. Hence, Allsop J was in error holding that Article 2(1)(e) supported s 18C.

(iv) Article 6

Article 6's purpose is to direct States Parties to provide remedies in the event of racial discrimination.[396] It does not specifically provide for prohibitions on racial discrimination, as the relevant prohibitions fall with the scope of Article 2(1)(d) and Article 4. Hence, Article 6 fails the specificity requirement.

Alternatively, given that Article 6 is directed to remedies, and that s 18C (or, indeed, Part IIA) does not provide for remedies, s 18C cannot be reasonably considered to be appropriate and adapted for the purpose of Article 6.

Hence, Allsop J was in error in holding Article 6 supported s 18C.

(v) Article 7

Justice Allsop was in error in holding Article 7 supported s 18C for the same reasons we gave for Carr J being in error in this regard.

(vi) Article 2(1)(d) and Article 4

Justice Allsop was in error in holding the Article 2(1)(d) and Article 4 supported s 18C for the same reasons we gave for Carr J being in error regarding these Articles. Specifically, Allsop J failed to properly interpret Articles 2, Article 4 and Article 5 in light of the history, context and purpose of these Articles. The difference is that, whereas Carr J was in error in holding that Article 2 and Article 4 supported legislation that prohibited conduct that might lead to racial hatred or discrimination, Allsop J was in error in holding that all that was required for these Articles to support s 18C was a relevant perceived connection.

(vii) A final point on Article 5

Justice Allsop stated that Parliament carefully regarded Article 5 in drafting s 18C and s 18D.[397] However, this is not was the conformity principle requires. The conformity principle requires a court to consider whether s 18C was

---

396 See Part IV.D.3 (page 32).
397 *Toben* [2003] FCAFC 137; (2003) 129 FCR 515, 551 [143] (Allsop J).

reasonably capable of being considered appropriate and adapted to (in this case) Article 4. This meant that the relevant test became (in effect) was s 18C reasonably capable of being considered appropriate and adapted to prohibiting instances of racial hatred as prescribed by Article 4, paying due regard to the guarantee of freedom of expression provided in Article 5? Hence Allsop J was in error with respect to Article 5's role in applying the conformity principle.

3   *Conclusions regarding* Toben

Toben is the most authoritative decision concerning s 18C's constitutional validity. It is also a decision that contains significant errors in law. These errors stem principally from a failure to properly apply relevant principles concerning interpreting treaties, and a failure to appreciate the purpose of Article 4 and the concerns that the Convention's drafters intended it to address. We are of the view that *Toben* should be overturned.

J *Section 18C's approach to intimidation*

At first glance, there does not appear to be anything wrong with s 18C making unlawful acts that intimidate. However, there are problems with s 18C's operation and effect regarding intimidation.

Section 18C makes unlawful acts reasonably likely to intimidate on the grounds of race, colour, ethnicity or nationality. As noted above, 'intimidate' means 'to make timid, or inspire with fear, overawe, cow' or 'to force into or deter from some action by inducing fear: *to intimidate a voter*'.[398]

Intimidation differs from offence, insult or humiliation in that intimidation carries with it an element of *threat*. The foregoing definition of intimidation involves an element of inspiring or inducing fear. Such fear results from an express or implied threat being made to force someone to do something that they would rather not.

Unlike offence, insult and humiliation, intimidation is grounded in a right specified under both the UDHR and the Convention, that is, security of person. However, this is where the problems commence.

As noted above, the reasonable representative test requires that the race, colour, ethnicity or nationality of the audience, speaker, or both, be considered. Given this, it is possible that a statement that a reasonable representative from one race or ethnic group would find intimidating may not intimidate a reasonable

---

[398] *Macquarie Dictionary* 777 (emphasis in original).

representative from another race or ethnicity. The race, colour, ethnicity or nationality of the speaker may also be relevant as to whether a statement is intimidating. Once again, someone's legal liability is being made dependent on race, colour, ethnicity or nationality. As with s 18C making unlawful offence, insult or humiliation, making unlawful intimidation does not pay due regard to Article 5's guarantee of equality before the law.

However, as noted above, intimidation involves an element that offence, insult or and humiliation do not: the element of threat. That is, s 18C may *allow* a threat to be made – and thus someone's right to security of person to be jeopardised – on the basis of the race, colour, ethnicity or nationality of the audience, the speaker, or both. Hence, in addition to not paying due regard to equality before the law, s 18C does not appear to be paying due regard to Article 5's guarantee of the right to security of person

Again, s 18D compounds s 18C's problems, as it appears to allow certain classes of people to engage in acts that intimidate others.

Given the foregoing, s 18C making unlawful intimidation does not appear to be reasonably appropriate or adapted to implementing Article 4 while paying due regard to the guarantees of the rights in Article 5.

K *A Summary of s 18C's Constitutional Validity under the External Affairs Power*

In our view, the external affairs power does not provide the necessary constitutional support for s 18C's prohibition of public acts that offend, insult, humiliate or intimidate. This is the case both in relation to the key obligation found under Article 4 of the Convention, but also in relation to the more general obligations outlined in Articles 2, 6 and 7.

However, even if the external affairs power supported s 18C and s 18D in their entirety, these sections nevertheless impermissibly infringe the implied freedom of political communication. It is to this issue that we now turn.

V

THE IMPLIED FREEDOM OF POLITICAL COMMUNICATION

Our analysis concerning whether the external affairs power supported s 18C reconciled rights under the Convention using the test for validly translating treaties into domestic law. However, our analysis concerning the implied freedom of political communication does not depend upon reconciling rights. Rather, the issue is whether s 18C impermissibly infringes a freedom, being the implied freedom of political communication. Answering this requires working through the modified *Lange* test.

A *The modified Lange test*

In *Lange*, a unanimous High Court stated a test[399] that its decisions in *Coleman*,[400] *Unions NSW*[401] and *McCloy*[402] later modified. In *McCloy*, a majority of the High Court stated the modified *Lange* test as follows:

1. Does the law effectively burden the implied freedom of political communication in its terms, operation or effect?
2. If "yes" to question 1, are the purpose of the law and the means adopted to achieve that purpose legitimate, in the sense that they are compatible with the maintenance of the constitutionally prescribed

---
399 *Lange* [1997] HCA 25; (1997) 189 CLR 520, 567-8.
400 *Coleman* [2004] HCA 39; (2004) 220 CLR 1, 50 (McHugh J), 77-78 (Gummow and Hayne JJ), 82 (Kirby J). The *Lange* test modified by *Coleman* was applied in the High Court decisions of *Hogan v Hinch* [2011] HCA 4; (2011) 243 CLR 506 ('*Hogan*'); *Wotton v Queensland* [2012] HCA 2; (2012) 246 CLR 1. ('*Wotton*'); *Monis* [2013] HCA 4; (2013) 249 CLR 92; *Attorney General (SA) v Corporation of the City of Adelaide* [2013] HCA 3; (2013) 249 CLR 1 ('*Adelaide Preacher's Case*').
401 [2013] HCA 58; (2013) 252 CLR 530, 556 [44] (French CJ, Hayne, Crennan, Kiefel and Bell JJ).
402 [2015] HCA 34.

system of representative government?

3. If "yes" to question 2, is the law reasonably appropriate and adapted to advance that legitimate object? If not, then the measure will exceed the implied limitation on legislative power.[403]

In *Wotton*, a majority of the High Court[404] described the constitutionally prescribed system of government with reference to the following quote from *Aid/Watch Incorporated v Federal Commissioner v Taxation*:[405]

> The provisions of the Constitution mandate a system of representative and responsible government with a universal adult franchise, and s 128 establishes a system for amendment of the Constitution in which the proposed law to effect the amendment is to be submitted to the electors. Communication between electors and legislators and the officers of the executive, and between electors themselves, on matters of government and politics is 'an indispensable incident' of that constitutional system.[406]

We will now turn to assessing whether s 18C meets the requirements of each limb of the modified *Lange* test.

B *Does s 18C effectively burden the implied freedom of political communication in its terms, operation or effect?*

All that is required to satisfy this limb of the modified *Lange* test is that the legislation in fact burdens the implied freedom of political communication.[407] The burden need not be substantial to satisfy this limb.[408] However, the extent of the burden may well be relevant to the other limbs of the modified *Lange*

---

403 Ibid [2] (French CJ, Kiefel, Bell and Keane JJ). For High Court decisions using the *Lange* test modified by *Coleman* but prior to *Unions NSW* see *Wotton* [2012] HCA 2; (2012) 246 CLR 1, 13 [20], 15 [25]; *Hogan* [2011] HCA 4; (2011) 243 CLR 506, 542 [47] (French CJ), 555-6 [94]-[97] (Gummow, Hayne, Heydon, Crennan Kiefel and Bell JJ). For High Court decisions using the *Lange* test modified by Coleman and *Unions NSW* but prior to *McCloy* see *Tajjour v New South Wales* [2014] HCA 35 ('*Tajjour*').
404 *Wotton* [2012] HCA 2; (2012) 246 CLR 1, 13 [20] (French CJ, Gummow, Hayne, Crennan and Bell JJ).
405 [2010] HCA 42; (2010) 241 CLR 539 ('*Aid/Watch*').
406 *Aid/Watch* [2010] HCA 42; (2010) 241 CLR 539, 556 [44] (citations omitted).
407 *Unions NSW* [2013] HCA 58; (2013) 252 CLR 530, 555 [40] (French CJ, Hayne, Crennan, Kiefel and Bell JJ); see also *Tajjour* [2014] HCA 35 [33] (French CJ), [61] (Hayne J), [105]-[107] [(Crennan, Kiefel and Bell JJ), [145]-[146] (Gageler J).
408 Ibid.

test.[409]

Section 18C burdens freedom of communication about government and political matters at both the Commonwealth and State[410] level in its terms and effect. As noted above, s 18C makes it unlawful for a person to do an act otherwise than in private that is reasonably likely in all the circumstances to offend, insult, humiliate or intimidate another person or group of people because of the race, colour, or national or ethnic origin of that person or group of people.[411]

It is important to understand the nature of the burden that s 18C imposes on the implied freedom of political communication. Section 18C's burden has three aspects:

1. Its burden on legislative and executive action;
2. Its burden on the political process overall; and
3. Its burden on the popular sovereignty embodied in the *Commonwealth Constitution*.

We will now examine each of these aspects.

1 The burden on legislative and executive action

Many aspects of the Commonwealth government lead to discussions involving race, colour, ethnicity or nationality. For example, Commonwealth legislation with respect to the following heads of power may well involve discussing race, colour, ethnicity or nationality:

- 'the naval and military defence of the Commonwealth and of the several States, and the control of the forces to execute and maintain the laws of the Commonwealth';[412]

---

409 *McCloy* [2015] HCA 34 [81] (French CJ, Kiefel, Bell and Keane JJ), [150], [152] (Gageler J), [255] (Nettle J), [336]-[337] (Gordon J). See also *Unions NSW* [2013] HCA 58; (2013) 252 CLR 530, 555 [40] (French CJ, Hayne, Crennan, Kiefel and Bell JJ); see also *Tajjour* [2014] HCA 35 [33] (French CJ), [105]-[107] [(Crennan, Kiefel and Bell JJ), [148]-[149] (Gageler J).
410 Please note that in this Part, "State" (that is, "State" with an upper-case "S") means "a State of Australia". This is in contrast to the use of "State" and "State Party" in Part III, which meant "nation-state". When we use "state" in this Part (that is, "state" with a lower-case "s"), we mean nation-state.
411 RDA s 18C(1).
412 *Commonwealth Constitution* s 51(vi).

- 'quarantine';[413]
- 'naturalisation and aliens';[414]
- 'the people of any race, ~~other than the aboriginal race in any State,~~ for whom it is necessary to make special laws';[415]
- 'immigration and emigration';[416]
- 'external affairs';[417]
- 'the relations of the Commonwealth with the islands of the Pacific';[418] and
- 'the influx of criminals'.[419]

Other heads of power that may involve discussing race, colour, nationality or ethnicity include:

- 'trade and commerce with other countries, and among the States';[420]
- 'fisheries in Australian waters beyond territorial limits';[421]
- 'census and statistics';[422] and
- 'foreign corporations…'[423]

Legislation made under the heads of power noted above, and especially those noted in the first-mentioned list, often involve issues of great importance and controversy.

For example, the matters of border protection, refugee intake and immigration raise important and controversial issues concerning the level of refugee and immigrant intake, the racial, ethnic or national composition of such intake and the level of integration expected of immigrants. The matter of terrorism raises important and controversial issues concerning the causes of terrorist activity and how such conduct may be prevented. How Australia

---

413 Ibid s 51(ix). This might appear to be an unusual inclusion. However, during the Ebola outbreak in Africa in 2014, commentators noted racial aspects to restricting travel to and from countries in which the Ebola outbreaks were located, and the treatment of those afflicted with Ebola: see, for example, Hannah Kozlowska, 'Has Ebola Exposed a Strain of Racism?', *New York Times* (online), 21 October 2014.
414 Ibid s 51(xix).
415 Ibid s 51(xxvi) (the strike-through appears in official versions of the *Commonwealth Constitution*).
416 Ibid s 51(xxvii).
417 Ibid s 51(xxix).
418 Ibid s 51(xxx).
419 Ibid s 51(xxviii).
420 Ibid s 51(i).
421 Ibid s 51(x).
422 Ibid s 51(xi).
423 Ibid s 51(xx).

conducts its external affairs often involve controversial issues concerning Australia's type and level of engagement with other nations. Even issues like foreign investment in Australia create controversies concerning the desirability of such investment from certain nations.

In addition to Commonwealth legislation, the Commonwealth's executive government is responsible for implementing legislation as well as other executive functions.[424] The manner in which the Commonwealth's executive government does this with respect to matters involving race, colour, ethnicity or nationality also may involve issues of great importance and controversy.

For example, the manner in which Australia's executive government conducts border protection and administers refugee and immigration programs involve controversial issues. To conclude with perhaps the most dramatic (but not uncommon) example, Australia's prosecution of wars involve critical but controversial issues about the nature of the conflict and the enemy.

As to issues at State level, Commonwealth issues often affect the States in terms of the relevant legislation and executive action each State pursues. Further, issues local to the State, such as law and order, health or education, may involve discussion of race, colour, ethnicity or nationality.

At times, discussion amongst electors about relevant Commonwealth or State legislation or executive action will be robust, lively, even heated. In its terms, s 18C burdens the way that Australian electors would discuss issues concerning race, colour, ethnicity or nationality.

2 The burden on the political process overall

Further to the last aspect, legislative and executive action contemplated under the *Commonwealth Constitution* and the State constitutions operates generally. That is, legislation rarely targets specific individuals.[425] Rather, legislation in all but rare cases concerns *groups* of people, ranging from small groups up to the entirety of Australia's population. Executive action may concern individuals directly, but often concern groups.

Hence, when discussing matters that may be subject to government action it is common to make general statements about an issue. It is also common to refer generally to groups of people. Statements concerning groups may

---

424 Ibid s 61.
425 Although a Parliament can enact a law targeting a specific individual: see *Kable v Director of Public Prosecutions (NSW)* [1996] HCA 24; (1996) 189 CLR 51, 64 (Brennan CJ), 73-4 (Dawson J), 109, 121 (McHugh J), 125 (Gummow J).

not apply to individuals in that group. However, that lack of specificity is the inherent price of discussions about proposed or past legislative or executive action.

Section 18C concerns acts that members of a group may find offensive, insulting, humiliating or intimidating based on the group's race, colour, ethnicity or nationality. Hence, s 18C affects political discussions affecting such groups.

3 Popular sovereignty

Under the *Commonwealth Constitution*, sovereignty ultimately resides in the Australian people.[426] It is Australian electors who elect representatives to legislate on their behalf.[427] Representative and responsible government are 'constitutional imperatives intended... to make the legislature and executive branches of the Commonwealth ultimately answerable to the Australian people'.[428]

In addition, plenary powers are vested in Australian Parliaments. This means that Australian Parliaments have very broad powers to make laws. Subject to certain restrictions, State and Territory Parliaments may make laws concerning any matter.[429] The Commonwealth Parliament's powers are confined to those specified in the *Commonwealth Constitution*, but these powers have been interpreted very broadly.[430]

Such sweeping powers can be, and have been, exercised in matters of great controversy. The laws themselves may have terms and effects that members of the public regard as outrageous. Members of the public may also find the executive actions resulting from such laws to be outrageous. Indeed, given that Parliaments must address controversial matters, members of Parliament are shielded from claims by Parliamentary privilege.[431] This is necessary for robust debate on such matters.

---

426 *Unions NSW* [2013] HCA 58; (2013) 252 CLR 530, 548 [17] (French CJ, Hayne, Crennan, Kiefel and Bell JJ). See also *McCloy* [2015] HCA 23, [45] (French CJ, Kiefel, Bell and Keane JJ), [215] (Nettle J), [318] (Gordon J).
427 *Australian Capital Television Pty Ltd v The Commonwealth* [1992] HCA 45; (1992) 177 CLR 106, 137-8 (Mason CJ) ('*ACTV*').
428 *Wills* [1992] HCA 46; (1992) 177 CLR 1, 47 (Brennan J). Brennan J did note that the intention for representative and responsible government was 'imperfectly effected': see ibid.
429 *Union Steamship Company of Australia Pty Ltd v King* [1988] HCA 55; (1988) 166 CLR 1, 10 (Mason CJ, Wilson, Brennan, Deane, Dawson, Toohey and Gaudron JJ).
430 *Amalgamated Society of Engineers v Adelaide Steamship Co Ltd* (1920) 28 CLR 129, 151 (Knox CJ, Isaacs, Rich and Starke JJ).
431 See, for example, *Commonwealth Constitution* s 49; *Parliamentary Privileges Act 1987* (Cth) s 16; *Parliamentary Privileges Act 1891* (WA) s 1.

It follows that, as sovereign, the Australian people must *also* be free to communicate about government and political matters fully and frankly. Such communication is critical to holding the executive and legislature accountable,[432] and to resolving controversial issues democratically at the ballot box. In communicating about government and political matters, the Australian people may be fractious and salty. However, history suggests that such a people make better sovereigns than a people who march in actual or apparent lockstep. Consequently, the extent to which Australian governments may circumscribe the speech of the Australian people as sovereign is strictly limited.

Ultimately, s 18C burdens the implied freedom of political communication. The extent to which it burdens the implied freedom of political communication is further examined below.[433]

C *Does s 18C serve a legitimate purpose?*

Legislation must serve a legitimate purpose in order not to infringe the implied freedom of political communication. To be legitimate, the purpose must be compatible with the system of representative and responsible government prescribed by the *Commonwealth Constitution*. It must also be compatible with the freedom of communication about government and political matters, which is a necessary incident to this system. Determining the purpose of legislation is a matter of statutory construction.

In this section, we find that s 18C does not serve a purpose compatible with the system of representative and responsible government prescribed by the *Commonwealth Constitution*. This is because the purpose that s 18C serves includes making unlawful acts that offend. This is not a purpose compatible with the constitutionally prescribed system of representative and responsible government, or (moreover) the freedom of communication which is its necessary incident. This is so even if s 18C's purpose also involves eliminating racial hatred, promoting racial tolerance, or both. Our argument in this section is presented as follows:

1. Identifying the purpose that s 18C serves.
2. Examining whether prohibiting offence is a legitimate purpose.
3. Examining whether confining offence to that based on race, colour, ethnicity or nationality is a legitimate purpose.

---

432 *Unions NSW* [2013] HCA 58; (2013) 252 CLR 530, 551 [28]-[29] (French CJ, Hayne, Crennan, Kiefel and Bell JJ); *ACTV* [1992] HCA 45; (1992) 177 CLR 106, 138 (Mason CJ).
433 See Part V.D.8 (page 198).

4. Further to the examination of the issues in points 2 and 3, exploring the "body/idea" distinction.

We now examine each of these matters.

1   *The purpose that s 18C serves*

Identifying a provision's purpose is important to resolving the second limb of the modified *Lange* test.[434] The ordinary processes of statutory construction are used to identify the statutory purpose.[435]

Section 18C's interpretation should be in a manner that best promotes the RDA's purpose or object.[436] As noted above,[437] the starting point for interpreting s 18C is the text of the provision itself, and the statutory context in which the provision is found.[438] Regard may be had to extrinsic material[439] but, once again, statements in explanatory memoranda or by Ministers cannot overcome the need to carefully consider the words of the statute itself.[440]

We have already analysed the width of the terms 'offence, insult, humiliate or intimidate' in Part III. However, in order to determine whether s 18C serves an end compatible with the constitutionally prescribed system of representative and responsible government, it is necessary to revisit s 18C's text.

In our view, the end that s 18C serves cannot be separated from its prohibition of offensive, insulting, humiliating or intimidating acts. Starting with the provision itself, s 18C's terms makes unlawful acts that offend, insult, humiliate or intimidate individuals or groups because of their race, colour, or national or ethnic origin.[441] The title of s 18C itself is '[o]ffensive behaviour because of race, colour or national or ethnic origin'. Given that headings form part of the statute,[442] this reinforces the view that s 18C's purpose is to prohibit

---

434 *Unions NSW* [2013] HCA 58; (2013) 252 CLR 530, 557 [50] (French CJ, Hayne, Crennan, Kiefel and Bell JJ).
435 Ibid.
436 Interpretation Act s 15AA ('s 15AA'). The leading decisions interpreting s 18C took place before s 15AA was amended. It may be that these decisions will not need to be reconsidered in light of the amendments. However, we note the amendment to s 15AA and its possible effect on s 18C for the sake of completeness.
437 See Part III.B.2.(a) (page 18).
438 *Project Blue Sky* [1998] HCA 28; (1998) 194 CLR 355, 381 [69] (McHugh, Gummow, Kirby and Hayne JJ).
439 Interpretation Act s 15AB(1).
440 *Saeed* [2010] HCA 23; (2010) 241 CLR 252, 264-5 [31] (French CJ, Gummow, Hayne, Crennan and Kiefel JJ).
441 RDA s 18C.
442 Interpretation Act s 13(1).

offensive conduct.

Section 18C is found in Part IIA. Part IIA is titled '[p]rohibition of offensive behaviour based on racial hatred'. Once again, the purpose of s 18C appears to be to prohibit offensive conduct. It is true that the full text of Part IIA's includes 'based on racial hatred'. However, in our view, the basis of the prohibition (racial hatred) cannot be separated from its purpose (to prohibit offence).[443]

In interpreting a provision, the long title of the act is relevant.[444] The long title of the RDB, which inserted Part IIA into the RDA, read 'An Act to prohibit certain conduct involving the hatred of other people on the ground of race, colour or national or ethnic origin, and for related purposes'. This suggests that the RDA's purpose was to prohibit hatred.[445] However, the long title cannot be interpreted in isolation from the wording of s 18C itself, the title of s 18C and the title of Part IIA. Hence, the purpose of s 18C appears to be to prohibit racial hatred by prohibiting offence based on racial hatred.

As to the mischief against which s 18C is directed, one can and should consider both the Explanatory Memorandum and Second Reading Speech.[446] However, in our view, these extrinsic materials must be treated cautiously. This is because the RHB also included proposed amendments to the *Crimes Act 1914* (Cth).[447] These amendments to the Crimes Act would have made incitement to racial hatred a criminal offence. The Explanatory Memorandum and the Second Reading Speech appears directed more towards the proposed amendments to the Crimes Act than the proposed amendments to the RDA.[448]

That said, there are parts of the Explanatory Memorandum and the Second Reading Speech that concern s 18C's objectives specifically. The Explanatory Memorandum refers to 'the proposed prohibition on offensive behaviour based on racial hatred' being placed in the existing jurisdiction of the Human Rights and Equal Opportunity Commission.[449] It later refers to '[Part IIA adding] offensive behaviour because of race, colour, and national and ethnic origin as additional grounds for investigation and conciliation under [the

---

443 See Part III.B.2.(c) (page 20).
444 Interpretation Act s 13(2)(a).
445 See also Dan Meagher, 'So Far So Good?: A Critical Evaluation of Racial Vilification Laws in Australia' (2004) 32(2) *Federal Law Review* 225, 232.
446 Interpretation Act ss 15AA, 15AB(1), 15(2).
447 Subsequent reference to the *Crimes Act 1914* (Cth) will be to just 'the Crimes Act'.
448 See *Creek* [2001] FCA 1007; (2001) 112 FCR 352, 356 [15] (Kiefel J).
449 Explanatory Memorandum 2.

Commonwealth scheme of human rights administration].'[450] It also states that '[t]he emphasis is therefore to promote racial tolerance by bringing the parties together to discuss the act subject to the complaint and arrive at a conciliated and agreed outcome'.[451] Hence, this extrinsic material supports the view that s 18C was directed against offensive behaviour, but also to promoting racial tolerance.

The objective of promoting racial tolerance finds support in the Second Reading Speech. It was stated that the RHB '…fills a gap in our laws and enhances the social compact which underpins racial harmony in Australia'[452] and '…provides a safety net for racial harmony and sends a clear warning to those who might attack the principle of tolerance'.[453]

However, even if s 18C's aim is to promote racial tolerance, it cannot be separated from prohibition of offence. Put another way, s 18C's aim can, at best, be described as "promoting racial tolerance by prohibiting offence based on racial hatred". This is because the text of s 18C and Part IIA as well as extrinsic material makes clear that prohibiting offence is an aim. A similar rationale applies to any other objective construed to apply to s 18C.

That said, for reasons given above,[454] our analysis assumes that s 18C's aims only involves prohibiting *serious* instances of offence, insult, humiliation or intimidation. We assume that, if s 18C's aims involve less than serious instances of offence, insult or humiliation, then our argument applies with greater force.

2 Is prohibiting offence, insult or humiliation a legitimate end?

Putting aside intimidation for now,[455] s 18C making unlawful serious offence, insult or humiliation is not a legitimate end under the modified *Lange* test. This is so even if such offence, insult or humiliation is based on race, colour, ethnicity or nationality, and even if s 18C's aims also include promoting racial tolerance, prohibiting conduct involving racial hatred, or similar aims.

As noted above, legislative and executive action often involve issues of great importance and controversy. Passions run high. In a representative democracy discussion concerning political matters is often robust, lively and heated. Participants in these discussions may deploy all manner of rhetoric and sophistry.

---

450 Ibid 8; see also ibid 9.
451 Ibid 8; see also ibid 9.
452 Second Reading Speech 3342.
453 Ibid.
454 See Part III.B.2.(c) (page 20).
455 We examine intimidation at Part IV.J (page 115) and Part V.E. (page 211).

In these circumstances, serious offence or insult may be given or taken during the course of discussion even if care is taken to avoid such language. For example, deliberately or inadvertently employing racial stereotypes during discussion of government or political matters may cause serious offence or insult. Similarly, discussions where a person perceives "coded language" or "dog-whistling"[456] may cause serious offence or insult to that person. Ultimately, participants in – and bystanders to – discussions concerning political matters may be offended and insulted, often to a serious extent.

As noted above,[457] people often "stake their pride" to an idea, issue, cause, or position in which they believe. This is especially so in politically controversial matters. Given this, robust, lively and heated exchanges over political matters may not only result in serious offence and insult, but also humiliation.

In *Coleman*, McHugh J noted that insults can be used as weapons of intimidation that may have a chilling effect.[458] However, McHugh J also stated that '[t]he use of insulting words is a common enough technique in political discussion and debates'[459] and '…insults are a legitimate part of the political discussion protected by the Constitution. An unqualified prohibition on their use cannot be justified as compatible with the constitutional freedom.'[460]

In the same case, Gummow and Hayne JJ stated '[i]nsult and invective have been employed in political communication at least since the time of Demosthenes.'[461] Kirby J, disagreeing with Heydon J's views on the level of discourse that should be encouraged in Australians,[462] stated as follows:

---

456 That is, seemingly neutral words or phrases that carry an offensive meaning. The Committee noted that: 'Racist hate speech can take many forms and is not confined to explicitly racial remarks. As is the case with discrimination under article 1, speech attacking particular racial or ethnic groups may employ indirect language in order to disguise its targets and objectives': see Committee on the Elimination of Racial Discrimination, *General recommendation No. 35: Combating racist hate speech* (26 September 2013) [7].
457 See Part III.B.2.(b) (page 20).
458 *Coleman* [2004] HCA 25; (2004) 220 CLR 1, 54 [105] (McHugh J). As noted, we will analyse intimidation further below.
459 Ibid.
460 Ibid. While Part IIA is only a qualified prohibition on offensive speech, s 18C nevertheless impermissibly infringes the implied freedom of communication for reasons stated below.
461 Ibid 78 [197] (Gummow and Hayne JJ).
462 Ibid 121-2 [323]-[324] (Heydon J). Heydon J noted (amongst other things) 'A legislative attempt to increase the standards of civilisation to which citizens must conform in public is legitimate. In promoting civilised standards, s 7(1)(d) not only improves the quality of communication on government and political matters by those who might otherwise descend to insults, but it also increases the chance that those who might otherwise have been insulted, and those who might otherwise have heard the insults, will respond to the communications they have heard in a like manner and thereby enhance the quantity and quality of debate.'

Reading the description of civilised interchange about governmental and political matters in the reasons of Heydon J, I had difficulty in recognising the Australian political system as I know it. His Honour's chronicle appears more like a description of an intellectual salon where civility always (or usually) prevails. It is not, with respect, an accurate description of the Australian governmental and political system in action.

One might wish for more rationality, less superficiality, diminished invective and increased logic and persuasion in political discourse. But those of that view must find another homeland. From its earliest history, Australian politics has regularly included insult and emotion, calumny and invective, in its armoury of persuasion. They are part and parcel of the struggle of ideas. Anyone in doubt should listen for an hour or two to the broadcasts that bring debates of the Federal Parliament to the living rooms of the nation. This is the way present and potential elected representatives have long campaigned in Australia for the votes of constituents and the support of their policies. It is unlikely to change. By protecting from legislative burdens governmental and political communications in Australia, the Constitution addresses the nation's representative government as it is practised. It does not protect only the whispered civilities of intellectual discourse…[463]

In *Monis*,[464] Hayne J stated:

History, not only recent history, teaches that abuse and invective are an inevitable part of political discourse. Abuse and invective are designed to drive a point home by inflicting the pain of humiliation and insult. And the greater the humiliation, the greater the insult, the more effective the attack may be. The giving of really serious offence is neither incidental nor accidental. The communication is designed and intended to cause the greatest possible offence to its target no matter whether that target is a person, a group, a government or an opposition, or a particular political policy or proposal and those who propound it. And any reasonable person would conclude that not only is that the purpose of what was

---

463 Ibid 91 [238]-[239] (Kirby J).
464 *Monis* is a rare case as it was a 3-3 decision in a 6 judge High Court. Three judges (French CJ, Hayne J and Heydon J) held that prohibiting offence was not an end compatible with the constitutionally-prescribed system of representative and responsible government. Three judges (Crennan, Kiefel and Bell JJ) held that it was. The result was governed by the *Judiciary Act 1903* (Cth) s 23(2)(a), which provides that in such cases, the decision of the court appealed from is affirmed. In *Monis*, the Queensland Court of Appeal held that prohibiting offence was a compatible end. Hence, *Monis* has a result but no binding *ratio decidendi*.

said, its purpose has been achieved.

If examples are sought, and recent Australian political history is thought too controversial, consider O'Connell's attack on Disraeli in 1835, with its references to the impenitent thief and what now are rightly seen as racial or religious slurs. Or look to Lloyd George's speech in the House of Commons about Sir John Simon acting 'as if [he] has been a total abstainer all his life and has suddenly taken to drink ... and landed amidst the Tory drunkards'. The examples can be multiplied.[465]

In *Sunol v Collier (No 2)*,[466] Allsop P of the Court of Appeal of New South Wales quoted *Coleman* to re-assert that 'insult, emotion, calumny and invective [we]re part of the "armoury" of political persuasion and the struggle for ideas.'[467] He confirmed the need for the courts to always interpret anti-discrimination laws in light of the important 'Constitutional freedom to discuss matters of wide public interest that may be related to political and governmental matters'.[468]

When asked why one could not just word their criticism of values or ideas politely and respectfully, avoiding scorn, mockery and ridicule, Dworkin replied:

> We can't do that because scorn, mockery and ridicule are specific modes of expression, which present their content in such a way that it cannot be duplicated less offensively without that content being changed...We cannot force some other taste on people, or some different standard as to how they should voice their opinions in the public debate, at the same time as we ask them to accept the decisions of the majority.[469]

Dworkin continued:

> The democratic process is founded on the idea of freedom of speech. In a democracy we discuss things and then vote, and we expect those who lose the discussion and the vote to accept the decision of the majority and uphold the laws it has adopted. That's quite an extraordinary thing to ask of people. My conviction is that the only way we can ask that is if everyone in the democratic process has had the chance to put forward their arguments in exactly the way they wish. If we suppose one group has the special right

---

465 *Monis* [2013] HCA 4; (2013) 249 CLR 92, 136-7 [85]-[86] (Hayne J).
466 [2013] NSWCA 196.
467 *Sunol v Collier (No 2)* [2013] NSWCA 196 [66] (Allsop P).
468 Ibid [64] (Allsop P).
469 Quoted from Flemming Rose, *The Tyranny of Silence: How One Cartoon Ignited a Global Debate on the Future of Free Speech* (Cato Institute, 2014) 117.

not be ridiculed, what that automatically entails is that others are deprived of their right to voice their opinions about that group.[470]

In addition, and as noted above,[471] Australian electors are sovereign. It borders on absurdity to assert that Australian Parliaments may pass outrageous laws, the executive may do outrageous things, and members of Parliament may speak outrageously; but the people in whom sovereignty resides and from whom Parliament, members of Parliament and the executive derive their authority *cannot* speak outrageously. If anything, a sovereign people must be free to speak the unspeakable, especially about government and political matters.

Of course, there are restrictions on an individual's capacity to speak, even as a member of the people in which sovereign power resides. However, three points should be made here. First, many laws restricting freedom of expression have at best a tangential relationship with government and political matters. We explore this in more detail below.[472] Second, the operation of many of these restrictions is often controversial.[473] Third, these restrictions themselves are *heavily restricted*.[474] Yes, rights and freedoms are qualified; but qualification is not *carte blanche*.[475] Far from it. Those purporting to restrict a fundamental freedom must make a clear and compelling (if not overwhelming) case for justifying the restriction.

---

470 Ibid. Judith Lichtenberg notes the following concerning the importance of freedom of expression to democratic participation and dignity: 'Democracy means not only that 'the people' are collectively self-governing, but also that they are equal in an important sense. The democratic equality of persons bears on free speech in two ways. First, democracy functions as it should only when each person's interests are represented in the political forum; freedom of speech and press enhances opportunities for representation. Second, we show the sort of respect for persons associated with democracy both by acknowledging that anyone (regardless of race or class or lack of company) may have a view worth expressing, and by assuming that people can be open-minded or intelligent enough to judge alien views on their merits. Only under these conditions can majority rule become morally respectable and not merely the best of a bad lot of decision procedures.': Judith Lichtenberg, 'Foundations and Limits of Freedom of the Press' (1987) 14(4) *Philosophy and Public Affairs* 329, 337-8.
471 See Part V.B.3 (page 122).
472 See Part V.D.6.(a) (page 184).
473 For example, the chilling effect of defamation law is a perennial topic of controversy in law. The use of copyright law to thwart criticism (for example, by the frivolous use of DMCA takedown notices on YouTube) is an emerging area of concern: see Part IV.E.3.(c).(i) (page 70).
474 For example, one can indeed obtain damages for defamation, as long as an ordinary, fair minded member of the community would think less of the person, and the statement was not (i) true; (ii) fair comment; (iii) privileged; (iv) fair reporting of proceedings of public concern; (v) publishing public documents; (vi) information innocently disseminated; or (vii) trivial.
475 It is disturbing how often the following formulation is heard: "Of course, rights/freedoms are not absolute, so [insert sweeping intrusion into the relevant right/freedom here]".

3   *Is prohibiting offensive, insulting or humiliating acts based on race, colour or ethnic or national origin a legitimate end?*

It might be argued that the scope of offence, insult and humiliation covered in the previous section is too wide. That is, it may be compatible with the constitutionally prescribed system of representative and responsible government to make unlawful a *narrower* range of such language. Hence, making unlawful offence, insult and humiliation based on race, colour, ethnicity or nationality may be compatible with this system.

However, even given this, s 18C still fails this stage of the modified *Lange* test. This is because of the nature of certain concepts mentioned in s 18C, namely race, colour, ethnicity and nationality.

(a)   The idea of race

The Australian Law Reform Commission noted the following about the concept of race:

> One of the most interesting outcomes of the Human Genome Project and other current scientific research is that there is no meaningful genetic or biological basis for the concept of 'race'... any two human beings are 99.9% identical genetically. Within the remaining small band of variation, scientists estimate that there is an average genetic variation of 5% *between* what are called 'racial groups'—which means that 95% of human genetic variation occurs *within* 'racial groups'.
>
> It is now well-accepted among medical scientists, anthropologists and other students of humanity that 'race' and 'ethnicity' are social, cultural and political constructs, rather than matters of scientific 'fact'.[476]

The ALRC's observation is similar to that of Nell Irvin Painter's: 'race is an idea, not a fact, and its questions demand answers from the conceptual rather than the factual realm'.[477]

That said, both State and Commonwealth Parliaments have attempted definitions as to who may be considered to be part of a particular race. In addition, agencies of executive government have also attempted such definitions. For example, the RDA defines 'Aboriginal' as:

> 'a person who is a descendant of an indigenous inhabitant of Australia

---

[476] Australian Law Reform Commission, *The Protection of Human Genetic Information*, Report No 96 (2003) 922 [36.41]-[36.42] (citations omitted).
[477] Nell Irvin Painter, *The History of White People* (W W Norton & Company, 2010) ix.

but does not include a Torres Strait Islander'.[478]

As to agencies of executive government, the ALRC noted:

> In the early 1980s, the Commonwealth Department of Aboriginal Affairs proposed a new three-part definition of an Aboriginal or Torres Strait Islander person.
>
> An Aboriginal or Torres Strait Islander is a person of Aboriginal or Torres Strait Islander descent who identifies as an Aboriginal or Torres Strait Islander and is accepted as such by the community in which he [or she] lives.
>
> Federal government departments adopted the definition as their 'working definition' for determining eligibility to certain services and benefits. The definition continues to be applied administratively in relation to programs such as Abstudy funding for tertiary students.[479]

Whatever the reason that a Parliament or an agency of executive government makes such definitions, the fact that they do is a matter of public concern, and hence, a matter for public discussion.

(b) The definitions employed in s 18C

Somewhat curiously, the RDA does not define race,[480] colour, nationality or ethnicity. As to s 18C, the Explanatory Memorandum stated that Part IIA was intended[481] to employ definitions of 'ethnic origin' found in *King-Ansell v Police*[482] and *Mandla v Dowell Lee*.[483] The Parliamentary Research Service noted the following about this approach:

> If the Parliament 'intends' [to follow the definitions in *King-Ansell* and *Mandla*], it should state it in its legislation, rather than attempting to legislate by an Explanatory Memorandum, which is a government document that is neither passed nor approved by the Parliament. While the courts may take into account the Explanatory Memorandum if there is an ambiguity in the legislation, it is surely the Parliament's role to pass legislation that is not

---

478 RDA s 3(1) (definition of 'Aboriginal').
479 Australian Law Reform Commission, *The Protection of Human Genetic Information*, Report No 96 (2003) 922 [36.14]-[36.15] (citations omitted).
480 As noted above, the RDA does define 'Aboriginal': see RDA s 3(1) (definition of 'Aborigine'). However, there is no general definition of race.
481 Explanatory Memorandum 2.
482 [1979] 2 NZLR 531 (*'King-Ansell'*).
483 [1983] 2 AC 548 (*'Mandla'*).

deliberately ambiguous.[484]

Indeed, it may be arguable that, by leaving it to courts to decide matters of race, colour, ethnicity and nationality, Part IIA breaches the *Commonwealth Constitution's* requirement for separation of powers. This is because, under the *Commonwealth Constitution*, Parliament's role is to legislate and the courts to interpret the law and determine disputes. In *Western Australia v Commonwealth*[485] members of the High Court stated:

> Under the Constitution, the Parliament cannot delegate to the Courts the power to make law involving, as that power does, a discretion or, at least, a choice as to what that law should be.[486]

Resolving ambiguous terms does not create issues concerning separation of powers in all but exceptionally rare instances. However, with s 18C, Parliament is asking courts to do something far beyond resolving an ambiguity in the operation of a law. Rather, Parliament is in effect delegating to courts the task of giving content to a law by providing the definitions of race, colour, ethnicity and nationality. That is, by determining the content of these definitions, courts are deciding the classes of people who have the right to bring an action under s 18C.[487] Making decisions of this nature is the proper role of Parliament.[488]

For example, does s 18C apply to someone who has been subjected to offense or insult because they practice Islam? The text of s 18C itself suggests not, as religion is not expressly covered. This is the position that the AHRC takes when determining disputes.[489] However, the Explanatory Memorandum states that adopting *King-Ansell's* definition of ethnicity 'would provide the

---

484 Parliamentary Research Service (Department of the Parliamentary Library), *Bills Digest: Racial Hatred Bill 1994*, 14 November 1994, 9.
485 [1995] HCA 47; (1995) 183 CLR 373.
486 Ibid 486 (Mason CJ, Brennan, Deane, Toohey, Gaudron and McHugh JJ).
487 Of course, by interpreting ambiguities in the operation of a statutory provision, a court may give that provision content. However, this can be said to be incidental to the normal task of statutory interpretation. Normally, Parliament will have at least attempted to give a provision substantive content. With s 18C, interpreting race, colour, ethnicity or nationality will give content to the law not in an incidental way, but in a substantive way.
488 This is not a case like that considered in *Australian Competition and Consumer Commission v C G Berbatis Holdings Pty Ltd* [2000] FCA 2; (2000) 96 FCR 491. In that case, s 51AA of the *Trade Practices Act 1974* (Cth) gave statutory force to the unwritten law concerning unconscionable conduct as decided by courts from time to time. French J held that Parliament could do this, as the capacity for the court to legislate was very limited given the precedents set by earlier Australian courts: see ibid 509-10 [43] (French J). With s 18C, the capacity for a court to legislate is far greater as its terms have not been determined by previous Australian courts.
489 40th Anniversary Report 43-5.

broadest basis for protection of peoples such as Sikhs, Jews and Muslims'.[490] Australian courts have yet to determine this issue.

One could argue that, under s 15AB of the Interpretation Act, a court may use the Explanatory Memorandum to resolve ambiguities regarding race and ethnicity in s 18C.[491] However, s 15AB of the Interpretation Act confers a discretion on courts to use such material. In other words, a court could ignore the Explanatory Memorandum (which, admittedly, is unlikely), or employ a definition that confers or denies rights to people contrary to Parliament's intentions (which is a real risk).[492] It may be that Parliament expects courts to legislate a certain way (such as by adopting the Explanatory Memorandum's definitions), but the courts are *legislating* nonetheless.

Putting this (potentially very significant issue) to one side, in *Eatock*, Bromberg J approved the definitions given in *King-Ansell* and *Mandla*.[493] It is to an examination of these definitions that we now turn.

In *King-Ansell*, Richardson J stated the following regarding the terms 'race' and 'ethnic origin':

> The real test is whether the individuals or the group regard themselves and are regarded by others in the community as having a particular historical identity in terms of their colour or their racial, national or ethnic origin. That must be based on a belief shared by members of the group...
>
> ...a group is identifiable in terms of its ethnic origins if it is a segment of the population distinguished from others by a sufficient combination of shared customs, beliefs, traditions and characteristics derived from a common or presumed common past, even if not drawn from what in biological terms is a common racial stock. It is that combination which gives them an historically determined social identity in their own eyes and in the eyes of those outside the group. They have a distinct social identity based not simply on group cohesion and solidarity but also on their belief as to their historical antecedents.[494]

In *Mandla*, Lord Fraser of Tullybelton stated the following regarding what

---

490 Explanatory Memorandum 3.
491 Interpretation Act s 15AB(1)(b)(i), s 15AB(2)(e).
492 Courts may draw on other material to interpret an ambiguous provision: s 15AB(2). Of course, courts may also consider definitions used in other jurisdictions.
493 *Eatock* [2011] FCA 1103; (2011) 197 FCR 261, 333-4 [310]-[313] (Bromberg J). See also *Scully* [2002] FCA 1080; (2002) 120 FCR 243, 272 [112]-[113] (Hely J). While Hely J approved the definition of 'race' and 'ethnic origin' stated in the Explanatory Memorandum, this definition was based on the quoted statements from *King-Ansell* and *Mandla*.
494 *King Ansell* [1979] 2 NZLR 531, 542-3 (Richardson J).

constituted an 'ethnic group':

> For a group to constitute an ethnic group… it must, in my opinion, regard itself, and be regarded by others, as a distinct community by virtue of certain characteristics. Some of these characteristics are essential; others are not essential but one or more of them will commonly be found and will help to distinguish the group from the surrounding community. The conditions which appear to me to be essential are these: (1) a long shared history, of which the group is conscious as distinguishing it from other groups, and the memory of which it keeps alive; (2) a cultural tradition of its own, including family and social customs and manners, often but not necessarily associated with religious observance. In addition to those two essential characteristics the following characteristics are, in my opinion, relevant; (3) either a common geographical origin, or descent from a small number of common ancestors; (4) a common language, not necessarily peculiar to the group; (5) a common literature peculiar to the group; (6) a common religion different from that of neighbouring groups or from the general community surrounding it; (7) being a minority or being an oppressed or a dominant group within a larger community, for example a conquered people (say, the inhabitants of England shortly after the Norman conquest) and their conquerors might both be ethnic groups.[495]

These definitions of race and ethnic origin include not only biological but also religious, cultural and historical factors. The issue with incorporating religious, cultural, and historical factors is that each of these factors involves *ideas*. Put broadly, religion involves ideas concerning spirituality; culture involves ideas about how people should conduct themselves individually and socially; the history of a people involves ideas concerning their collective heritage and experiences.

Such ideas are influential in political matters.[496] As the Court noted in *Evans v State of New South Wales*,[497] 'Religious beliefs and doctrines frequently attract public debate and sometimes have political consequences reflected in government laws and policies'.[498] The same reasoning applies not only to culture and history, but also many aspects of ethnicity, nationality and race.

This is an important point, because discussion often stops at the level of religion, culture, ethnicity, nationality or race. In reality, underlying religion,

---

495 *Mandla* [1983] 2 AC 548, 562 (Lord Fraser of Tullybelton).
496 Politics (and political ideology) being ideas concerning government.
497 [2008] FCAFC 130; (2008) 168 FCR 576 (*'Evans'*).
498 *Evans* [2008] FCAFC 130; (2008) 168 FCR 576, 578 [2] (French, Branson and Stone JJ).

culture, ethnicity, nationality[499] and even race[500] are *ideas*, either wholly or in important aspects.[501] All of these ideas may be, and often are, contested. Prohibiting expression that offends, insults or humiliates on grounds of religion, culture, ethnicity, nationality or race puts certain ideas beyond discussion, in effect creating state-enforced taboos. This is fundamentally incompatible with our system of government, in which full and frank discussion of ideas – and especially ideas that influence politics and government – is necessary.

4   The *"body/idea" distinction*

We pause here to note a distinction that may assist with resolving issues concerning the constitutional validity of laws pertaining to race, colour, ethnicity and nationality. The distinction also assists when someone attempts to stop the expression of opinion because of the offence or hurt that the

---

499 Benedict Anderson defined nations as 'imagined political communities', noting: '[the nation] is *imagined* because members of even the smallest nation will never know most of their fellow-members, meet them, or even hear of them, yet in the minds of each lives the image of their communion.': see Benedict Anderson, *Imagined Communities* (Verso, revised ed, 2006) 6 (emphasis in original).
500 We noted above that ALRC's comment that race and ethnicity being social, cultural and political constructs, rather than matters of scientific fact: see Australian Law Reform Commission, *The Protection of Human Genetic Information*, Report No 96 (2003) 922 [36.42] (citations omitted). These "social, cultural and political constructs" are themselves comprised of ideas.
501 Indeed, it is common to reify religion, culture, ethnicity, nationality or race (and social, cultural and political constructs) when, in reality, they are comprised of "clusters" of ideas, with each idea being open to discussion and challenge. We expand on the concept of the "idea cluster" below.

opinion causes.[502] This distinction is the "body/idea" distinction.[503]

As we noted above, Lee and George have argued that what sets human being apart from other animals is the capacity for conceptual thought.[504] It was this capacity that made humans *unique among species*, and each human *unique among humans*. We now want to further explore this latter aspect, how it bears on arguments concerning freedom of expression and, in particular, the manifestation of concepts into *ideas*.

In our view, there is an important distinction between a person's *body* and

---

502 Which, unfortunately, appears to be an increasingly common feature of modern discourse.
503 We note here that the "body/idea" distinction is based on concepts expressed by a variety of authors. First, the work of Lee and George concerning the human capacity for conceptual thought: see Patrick Lee and Robert George 'The Nature and Basis of Human Dignity' (2008) 21(2) *Ratio Juris* 173. Second, John Stuart Mill's 'harm principle': see J S Mill, *On Liberty* (Penguin Classics, first published 1859, 1985 ed) 68. In particular, we wish to explore the level of mental harm required to justify state-imposed restrictions on freedom of expression. This is because, in our view, the harm principle is being twisted to protect against harms that Mill did not intend to be covered by the principle. A good example is the (farcical) concept of "microaggressions". The accusation of "microaggression" purports to recast a benign statement as a threat, and one that may cause mental trauma. Hence, under (this distortion of) the harm principle, the state is justified in restricting speech. Another example is where someone asserts that their mental state is such that speech about certain topics will cause them mental trauma. Hence a speaker needs to take care in broaching the subject. The concept of "trigger warnings" is based on this. This then creates the risk of expression about certain subjects (even expression not intended to cause offence, insult or humiliation) being chilled. (To be clear, we are not denying that post-traumatic stress disorder may be triggered. This phenomenon is well-documented. However, real or perceived psychological triggers should not be used to burden or restrict freedom of expression.) The final example is the notion that offense, insult or humiliation causes psychological harm to such an extent that restrictions on speech are justified. While the exercise of freedom of expression *can* cause psychological harm in certain instances, there must be clarity about where the line is drawn legally. In drawing the line, great weight must be given to the fundamental freedoms of conscience and expression, and in the overwhelming public interest in being able to fully and frankly discuss matters that affect states and societies, even matters that are confronting or distressing. Third, Peter Kreeft's principle: 'be egalitarian regarding persons; be elitist regarding ideas' as cited and employed by Gregory Koukl in Gregory Koukl, 'The Intolerance of Tolerance', *Townhall* (online), 14 December 2006. The work of Kreeft and Koukl is important in refuting cultural relativism, Fourth, Richard Dawkins's concept of "memes" as stated in Richard Dawkins, *The Selfish Gene* (Oxford University Press, 1989) 189-201. Our concept of "ideas" is loosely based on Dawkins's concept of "memes". (Dawkins himself notes that ideas are memes: see ibid 192). In our view, it is critical to distinguish between threats to the physical body on the one hand, and threats to ideas on the other. (One might note the incongruity of drawing on concepts expressed, on the one hand, by a devout Catholic in Kreeft and, on the other, a resolute atheist in Dawkins. However, one can detect an overlap between Dawkins and Kreeft on the subject of the competition between ideas. Isn't it great when believers and skeptics can find common ground?).
504 See Part IV.E.(c).(i) (pages 67-9).

a person's *ideas*.[505] When a person is threatened *bodily*, it is *their own body* that is threatened. Everyone is physically unique. Further, the fact of one's physical uniqueness in time and space is perhaps the one thing an individual can claim against everyone and everything else.[506] This uniqueness is threatened by a physical or mortal danger.

However, *ideas* are a different matter.[507] Individuals can and do hold unique ideas.[508] That said, a great many ideas have an existence beyond one person. Indeed, ideas held in common shape societies and states. As we noted above, religion, culture, ethnicity, nationality and even race are comprised of ideas, either wholly or in important aspects.[509] Indeed, religions, cultures, ethnicities, nationalities and even races may in many instances be usefully thought of as "idea clusters".[510] These clusters grow, diminish and "cross-pollinate" with

---

505 Please note that the "body/idea" distinction we make is not the same as the "mind/body" distinction and "mind/body" arguments encountered in philosophy (for example, the "mind/body" distinction made by René Descartes). Whatever one thinks about the "mind/body" distinction (and we venture no opinion here), it is clear that minds can and do hold more than one idea, and different minds can and do hold the same idea.
506 As noted above, even those who are genetically identical like twins are physically unique, as each has a unique existence and experience in time and space.
507 Ideas being the product of the capacity for conceptual thought.
508 Individuals are free to express (or not express) unique ideas. These ideas may be protected if they pertain to the individual's personal life (for example, laws concerning privacy and breach of confidence). Ideas that have commercial or artistic merit may also be protected (for example, copyright and patent law). However, we hasten to add that even unique ideas are not protected from challenge.
509 We hope the "body/idea" distinction can assist with distinquishing attacks on a person from attacks on what are in fact ideas.
510 Being ideas that are commonly associated with each other, as is the case with the religion, culture, ethnicity or even race. "Idea clusters" are based on the concept of "gene-complexes" and "meme-complexes": see Richard Dawkins, *The Selfish Gene* (Oxford University Press, 1989) 197, 199. That said, ideas within an idea cluster do not necessarily depend on other ideas within the cluster (that is, ideas can be associated with an idea cluster without the need for support from other ideas within the cluster.) These ideas may include beliefs about spirituality, history, identity, or culture. They also include acts and practices associated with a religion, ethnicity or culture. Of course, political ideologies are also "idea clusters". Further, it should be noted that a person may adopt more than one idea cluster. For example, a person may adopt the "Catholic idea cluster" and also adopt the "free market idea cluster". Another person may adopt the "Catholic idea cluster" but adopt the "socialist idea cluster".

other clusters.[511] However, what makes a religion, culture, ethnicity, nationality or even race widespread are ideas (and idea clusters) held in common.

Unique ideas expressed by individuals should be open to challenge. However, ideas held in common – and especially those shaping societies and states – *must* be open to challenge, even if that challenge involves derision or mockery.

Individuals have freedom of conscience. They have a right to hold ideas (both unique and shared) close to them, and to treat them as a fundamental part of their identity. That said, freedom of conscience does *not* mean that these ideas cannot be challenged, even when it results in stress and anxiety to the individual. There is much merit in the claim that a person cannot, save in exceptional circumstances, attack another person physically. However, there is no merit to the claim that feelings can shield an idea from its critic. Put another way, it is fallacious to claim, "you cannot attack this idea because you will hurt my feelings".[512]

We make nine further points about the "body/idea distinction". First, as to bodily threats, there is a material difference between actual or threatened physical violence and hurt feelings. Hurt feelings are a physical response that affects the body. However, the stress and hurt stemming from having one's ideas challenged is different in magnitude and kind to those stemming from physical threats or attacks.[513] An individual can ignore any non-violent challenge to their ideas from the massed ranks of the state and society. The same individual cannot ignore a poke in their eye.

Second, severe mental trauma may equate to a physical threat or attack. However, a distinction must be made between everyday stresses (such as those resulting from having one's ideas challenged) and more severe mental trauma. This distinction has been made in other areas of the law. In negligence cases

---

511 Individuals who adopt an idea cluster may add their own ideas to that cluster. They may also jettison ideas from that cluster. If enough people do this with respect to the same idea cluster, then that idea cluster (say, a religion, culture or nation) may itself change. Of course, a source of ideas for an idea cluster is ideas from other idea clusters. Indeed, as to the last factor, people have been adopting ideas from other idea clusters since time immemorial. Given this, the (asinine) concept of "cultural appropriation" is fundamentally flawed. Humans, as beings capable of conceptual thought, will adopt ideas that they find useful or simply like. That a particular community especially values a particular idea does not change the fact that it is an idea. It may therefore exist in people apart from those who especially value it. To elaborate, once people other than those who especially value the idea are exposed to it, that idea may then exist independently in the people so exposed. These people may then treat the idea how they wish.
512 It is a variant of the old rhetorical fallacy: the *argumentum ad misericordiam*.
513 To take an example, stabbing someone with a knife is worse than threatening to stab someone with a knife. In turn, threatening to stab someone with a knife is worse than talking with someone about people who stab others with knives.

concerning pure mental harm:

> ...[G]rief or sorrow alone, however deeply felt, do not sound in damages. These reactions, anxiety, distress or depression are feelings which most normal people experience when someone they are fond of is injured or killed. The common law does not compensate the victims for this form of emotional distress. The 'very universality of those emotions denies to them the character of compensable loss under the tort of negligence'.[514]

Rather, the negligence must cause a recognised (or recognisable) psychiatric illness to be compensable.[515] If the law does not, as a matter of policy, compensate grief, anxiety, distress or even depression for the losses of loved ones by negligence, then such reasoning applies with greater force to hurt or distress caused by having one's ideas challenged.

Further, in the tort of assault, a person needs to apprehend that they will be subject to physical violence to establish a claim.[516] In the tort of intentional infliction of physical harm, there must be willful act or statement calculated to cause physical harm to a specific person.[517] Even in defamation, which is perhaps the action closest to laws prohibiting racial hatred, mere hurt and distress is not enough. Rather, it is injury to reputation,[518] that is, the way a person has *conducted themself* that enlivens the action.

Third, there will be cases where discussion of certain ideas, issues or topics aggravates an anxiety disorder in a listener and thus meet the criteria of a recognised psychiatric illness compensable in claims of tort. However, and with the deepest of respect to those suffering such disorders, there is an overwhelming public interest in the free and robust exchange of views. Ideas must be challenged, even those ideas held close or sacred to individuals, and even if the challenge involves derision or mockery of those ideas. In a democracy like Australia's, citizenship requires a fair measure[519] of maturity and resilience.

If someone is suffering an anxiety disorder, then the appropriate action is for them to get help. It is not to restrict discussion of ideas, issues or topic that

---

514 See R P Balkin and J L R Davis, *Law of Torts* (LexisNexis Butterworths, 4th ed, 2009) [7.42] (citations omitted).
515 Ibid.
516 Ibid [3.16].
517 Ibid [3.21]-[3.23].
518 Ibid [17.1]. For further comparisons with defamation see Part V.D.6.(c) (page 186).
519 By "fair measure" we mean "fair" in the sense of "not insignificant", but also "not unreasonable".

aggravate the disorder.[520] Restricting discussion on such a basis unacceptably chills discussion. Further, it creates uncertainty: words or phrases that do not aggravate the disorders in some may do so in others. Where is the line drawn?

Finally, these restrictions will not assist in overcoming such disorders. As Greg Lukianoff and Jonathan Haidt argue in relation to campus speech codes, such restrictions actually *create* or *worsen* depression and anxiety.[521] Lukianoff and Haidt's argument in relation to campus speech codes are directly applicable to democratic polities. Restrictions on speech, and the rationale for those restrictions, may in fact feed anxiety.

Fourth, "the body/idea" distinction applies even if members of a group holding the same idea are all hurt emotionally as a result of that idea being challenged. The sum of their feelings does not change the fact that ideas held in common shape societies and states, and hence have a public dimension that must be open to discussion. Indeed, it cannot be overlooked that a group sharing the same ideas has resources that individuals do not. In a society that has freedom of assembly, a group may organise to defend its ideas. Group representatives can speak for weaker members of the group who may not be able to participate in discussion effectively. A group can marshal resources to participate in public discussion and change attitudes. In a society such as Australia's, this dynamic should not be trivialised, as there are many groups representing different cultures, ethnicities and national and religious identities.[522]

Fifth, the "body/idea" distinction should not be taken to preclude feelings from the analysis of ideas. Whether or not an individual or group likes or dislikes an idea, or finds it (amongst other things) satisfying or pleasing – or

---

520 We are not suggesting that mental illness is confined to any particular political philosophy. Indeed, mental illness afflicts people across the political spectrum, and pays no heed to race, colour, sex, sexuality, ethnicity, culture, gender, creed, age, class, or status. In all instances, people should get help.
521 Greg Lukianoff and Jonathan Haidt, 'The Coddling of the American Mind', *The Atlantic* (online), September 2015.
522 To take a contemporary example, a large number of groups participated in AHRC hearings leading up to the publication of the 40th Anniversary Report: see the organisations listed in the 40th Anniversary Report 55-8. It is safe to surmise that this number is a fraction of the total number of groups representing different races, cultures, nationalities and ethnicities in Australia.

offensive or unpleasant – is of course relevant.[523] However, these matters should be confined to the assessing the merits of the idea. They should not be used to forestall or stop an idea being ventured or discussed (or worse, to determine whether or not someone should face legal liability for venturing or discussing it).

Sixth, there is a difference between the intrinsic worth of people on the one hand and ideas on the other. The notion that all *individuals* are equal in inherent worth is salutary. The notion that all *ideas* are equal in inherent worth is untenable. That people are inherently equal, either spiritually, or as members of the human family, or both, is a powerful check on rancid notions of racial superiority. That all ideas are equal in inherent worth is demonstrably false. Ideas stand or fall on their merit.[524]

Further, questions of merit often involve questions of truth. Truth may be difficult to discern or hurtful. However that is no reason to abandon the quest for truth. Further, truth may come under attack by those with an agenda. However, that is not a reason to *ban the attack*. Rather, it is a call to seek and defend truth tirelessly.

Seventh, the fact that many ideas are not unique to an individual, or that an idea does not have a physical existence like an individual, does *not* mean that the state is justified in *banning ideas*.[525] This is because everyone has freedom of conscience. This right is found in both the UDHR and the Convention. As we

---

523 Empathy of course plays a valuable role in making and understanding arguments: on this point, we agree with Soutphommasane: See Tim Soutphommasane, *I'm Not Racist, But… 40 Years of the Racial Discrimination Act* (University of New South Wales Press, 2015) Kindle Ebook Locations 2124-2321. Empathy also plays its role in debates about restrictions on freedom of expression. It is a mistake, however, to present the debate in terms of prioritising an abstract freedom (freedom of expression) over the wounded feelings of those subject to racist abuse. Rather, an empathetic approach demands considering the emotional costs on both sides. Restricting freedom of expression risks creating feelings of alienation and powerlessness in many people who do not speak on certain subjects (even in mild terms) for fear of being labeled racist. Uncertainty in the law risks people being denied due process and hence justice, often at great emotional cost. As we noted above with respect to restrictions to freedom of expression in Communist societies, such emotional costs can be extreme.
524 Kreeft has said, 'Be egalitarian regarding persons. Be elitist regarding ideas.': Peter Kreeft as cited in Gregory Koukl, 'The Intolerance of Tolerance', *Townhall* (online), 14 December 2006. Koukl went on to elaborate Kreeft's principle: "'Treat others as having equal standing in value or worth… When you are elitist regarding ideas, you are acknowledging that some ideas are better than others. And they are. We don't treat all ideas as if they have the same merit, lest we run into contradiction. Some ideas are good, some are bad. Some are true, some are false. Some are brilliant, others are just plain foolish.'": see ibid.
525 The impracticality of banning ideas (a step beyond banning the expression of ideas) has not deterred some: see Devorah Goldman, 'The Closing of the Campus Mind' *The Weekly Standard* (online), 6 April 2015.

have noted above, freedom of conscience is critical to the human capacity for conceptual thought. Freedom of conscience extends to holding an idea even if it is not unique to the individual. Thus, freedom of conscience protects ideas from being *banned*, but it does not prevent them from being *challenged*.

Eighth, as regards restrictions on freedom of expression, there is no difference between ideas *voluntarily* generated or adopted by individuals and ideas *involuntarily* generated or adopted by individuals. What do we mean by this? Ideas that are *voluntarily generated* or *adopted* are those that an individual has consciously created or accepted. These ideas range from the religion individuals profess to the fashions they wear. Here, the idea voluntarily generated or adopted is open to challenge by others. As noted above, each individual has the capacity for conceptual thought, and a unique perspective on concepts. Expressing a concept leads others bring their own perspectives to bear on it.

Ideas that are *involuntarily adopted* are those ideas that an individual has accepted with little or no conscious thought or reflection. A person raised in a certain culture may adopt the ideas of a particular culture (religious beliefs, customs and the like) without ever turning their mind to the merit of the ideas. Given this, it may seem unfair that other people may challenge an idea when it is unconsciously adopted. However, the human capacity for conceptual thought does not stop at concepts consciously created by others. This is because the human capacity for thought extends to *any matter that humans perceive*. Hence, when a person is presented with an idea involuntarily adopted, it is nevertheless an idea to which the person brings a unique perspective as someone capable of conceptual thought. This unique perspective is protected by the fundamental freedoms of conscience and expression.

The same principle extends to ideas *involuntarily generated*. These ideas are those that an individual generates in *other people* without conscious or unconscious effort by that individual. For example, a person's sex or skin colour may generate ideas in others without the conscious effort of that person. Ideas involuntarily generated in others can be particularly problematic. This is because the ideas generated in others may conflict sharply with a person's own conception of themselves. However, once again, the human capacity for conceptual thought extends to *any matter that humans perceive*. One's presence will generate ideas in others as they each exercise their unique capacity for conceptual thought. Again, this unique perspective is protected by the fundamental freedoms of conscience and expression.

In all these cases, the human capacity for conceptual thought is engaged.

In all cases, a person will use their capacity for conceptual thought in a unique way. The person may choose to express their thoughts. If a person chooses to do this then, the right to freedom of expression will protect their choice as, without more, the right extends to all subjects of expression.

Ninth, people can and do form groups on the basis of ideas voluntarily generated or adopted. For example, people organise by religion or political orientation, which are ideas voluntarily generated or adopted. People also form groups based on ideas involuntarily generated or adopted, or attributes that found such ideas. For example, people organise by nationality or culture, which involve ideas that people may have adopted without much conscious thought. They may also organise by race or colour, which are attributes that generate ideas in others despite what members of that group have done.

However, and once again, the fact that these groups have a public dimension – that they may influence attitudes in society as well as government policies and laws – means that their activities *must* be open to public discussion, and robust discussion at that.

To summarise the foregoing, all individuals are physically unique in time and space. The experience of every individual will be like no other before or after them. An individual may use their brief, unique existence in this mortal plane to express ideas that are deeply profound. However, the same individual may also express ideas that are flat-out stupid. Given all this, laws should recognise the fundamental importance of the rights to conscience and expression: individuals are free to adopt, generate and express their ideas; other individuals are free to perceive, consider and challenge the ideas so expressed. The expression of ideas, or the challenge to those ideas, may be confronting and uncomfortable: feelings may be hurt and pride may be wounded. However, as long as their language does not threaten the physical safety of others, individuals should be free to say what they want.

It is for these reasons that freedoms do not end where feelings begin.[526]

---

[526] The origins of this phrase are unclear. An early online iteration of its more familiar formulation 'rights don't end where feelings begin' was in Rachel Marsden, 'Your Rights End Where Mine Begin' *Human Events* (online) 18 September 2011. However, the phrase's antecedents may go much further back, as it is not that far removed from the aphorism 'Your liberty to swing your fist ends just where my nose begins': see Quote Investigator, 'Your Liberty to Swing Your Fist Ends Just Where My Nose Begins', *Quote Investigator* (online), 15 October 2011. It is interesting to note the observation of Arthur Garfield Hays that 'In a society where interests conflict I realize there can be no absolutes. My freedom to swing my arm ends where the other fellow's nose begins. But the other fellow's nose doesn't begin in my brain, or in my soul either, as the religionists would have it.' : see ibid.

More is required to restrict freedom of expression than emotional hurt. As we argue below, the appropriate threshold is incitement to physical harm to persons or their property.

5 Concluding thoughts about this limb of the modified Lange test

The "body/idea" distinction may help resolve the issue as to whether prohibiting offence is a legitimate purpose. In applying the "body/idea" distinction, one should ask: is the offence, insult or humiliation based on an *idea* pertaining to race, colour, ethnicity or nationality? For example, criticism of a particular cultural practice associated with an ethnicity is in fact criticism of an idea.[527] If criticism of the idea causes offence, it is offence being taken on behalf of an idea. In a democracy such as Australia's, governments should not shield ideas from being criticised by threat of legal liability, especially ideas that may influence how people approach politics and government.

Putting aside the "body/idea" distinction, and in any event, prohibiting offence is not a legitimate purpose given the nature of Australia's constitutionally prescribed system of representative and responsible government. As noted above,[528] matters subject to State and Commonwealth legislative and executive action may well involve issues concerning race, colour, ethnicity or nationality. These matters are often controversial. The Australian people as sovereign need to be able to fully, frankly and robustly discuss all aspects of State and Commonwealth legislative and executive action. The giving and taking of offence is an inevitable incident of such discussions.

To be clear, s 18C *could* have been drafted in a way that did not result in the prohibition of offence being one of its purposes, and thus fail this stage of the modified *Lange* test. In our view, prohibiting expressions of racial hatred or promoting racial tolerance are purposes compatible with Australia's constitutionally prescribed system of representative or responsible government. However, legislation pursuing either purpose must be drafted appropriately. Section 18C was not. We propose alternative legislation below.

---

527 We assume that the criticism solely concerns the cultural practice. Of course, there are instances where someone comments about the *inherent worth* of a person based on their race, colour, ethnicity or nationality. That is, because of their race, colour, ethnicity or nationality a person has less (or more) inherent worth as a human. Taken to its extreme, thinking a person has less inherent worth may lead to thinking that they are less than human. In such cases, ideas are not being criticized, rather it is the person (or people) themselves. To cite some depressing examples from history (some of it recent history), likening a people to cockroaches, pigs, apes or monkeys can be considered thinking that a people is less than human.
528 See Part V.B.1 (see page 118).

D *Is s 18C reasonably appropriate and adapted to advance its purpose?*

As noted above, s 18C's purpose appears to be making unlawful offensive acts towards individuals or groups because of their race, colour, or national or ethnic origin. More broadly, s 18C's purpose may be to prohibit racial hatred or promote racial tolerance by making unlawful such acts.

Whatever s 18C's purpose, s 18C is not reasonably appropriate and adapted to advance it. In this section, we explain why this is so. The test used in this limb of the modified *Lange* test sounds similar to that used to determine s 18C's validity under the external affairs power. However, different considerations apply to the modified *Lange* test.

Previous cases considering the modified *Lange* test suggest that there are different approaches to determining whether or not a law is reasonably appropriate and adapted to a legitimate end. At the time of writing, the most recent case is *McCloy*. In this case, as in previous cases, different approaches were employed among members of the High Court.

Given these differences, in this section we propose to consider matters relevant to this limb of the modified *Lange* test, and then return to the approaches in *McCloy*. Hence, we will consider the following matters in turn:

1. The nature of the implied freedom of political communication;
2. The relationship between the common law and the implied freedom of political communication;
3. The tests used in s 18C;
4. The tests used in s 18D;
5. The operation of s 18C and s 18D;
6. How s 18C compares with other protective legislation;
7. The complexity of s 18C and s 18D; and
8. In light of the foregoing matters and considering the approaches in *McCloy*, whether s 18C is reasonably appropriate and adapted to its purpose.

We will now examine each of these matters.

1 *The nature of the implied freedom of political communication*

The implied freedom of political communication is not a personal right; but rather a limitation on the Commonwealth government's ability to legislate. In *Unions NSW*, a High Court majority stated:

> …A legislative prohibition or restriction on the freedom is not to be

understood as affecting a person's right or freedom to engage in political communication, but as affecting communication on those subjects more generally. The freedom is to be understood as addressed to legislative power, not rights, and as effecting a restriction on that power. Thus the question is not whether a person is limited in the way that he or she can express himself or herself, although identification of that limiting effect may be necessary to an understanding of the operation of a statutory provision upon the freedom more generally. The central question is: how does the impugned law affect the freedom?[529]

As to the strength of the implied freedom of political communication, the remarks of Hayne J in *Monis* and McHugh J in *Coleman* are relevant. In *Monis*, Hayne J stated:

> Because freedom of communication on matters of government and politics is an indispensable incident of the constitutionally prescribed system of government, that freedom cannot be curtailed by the exercise of legislative or executive power and the common law cannot be inconsistent with it. But the freedom is not absolute and it follows that the limit on legislative power is also not absolute.
>
> To observe that the freedom is not absolute is not to say that it must yield to accommodate the regulation of conduct which a majority of members of the Australian community may consider to be repugnant. Nor does the observation that the freedom is rooted in implication rather than in the express text of the Constitution make it brittle or otherwise infirm, or make it some lesser or secondary form of principle. Rather, accepting that the freedom is not absolute recognises that it has boundaries. But within those boundaries the freedom limits legislative power.[530]

In *Coleman*, McHugh J stated:

> In determining whether a law is invalid because it is inconsistent with freedom of political communication, it is not a question of giving special weight in particular circumstances to that freedom. Nor is it a question of balancing a legislative or executive end or purpose against that freedom. Freedom of communication always trumps federal, State and Territorial powers when they conflict with the freedom. The question is not one of weight or balance but whether the federal, State or Territorial

---

[529] *Unions NSW* [2013] HCA 58; (2013) 252 CLR 530, 554 [36] (French CJ, Hayne, Crennan, Kiefel and Bell JJ), 571 [109] (Keane J) (citations omitted). See also *McCloy* [2015] HCA 34 [2], [30] (French CJ, Kiefel, Bell and Keane JJ), [119] (Gageler J), [303], [317] (Gordon J).
[530] *Monis* [2013] HCA 4; (2013) 249 CLR 92, 141 [103]-[104] (Hayne J) (citations omitted).

power is so framed that it impairs or tends to impair the effective operation of the constitutional system of representative and responsible government by impermissibly burdening communications on political or governmental matters. In all but exceptional cases, a law will not burden such communications unless, by its operation or practical effect, it directly and not remotely restricts or limits the content of those communications or the time, place, manner or conditions of their occurrence. And a law will not impermissibly burden those communications unless its object and the manner of achieving it is incompatible with the maintenance of the system of representative and responsible government established by the Constitution.[531]

Hence, the freedom of political communication under the Commonwealth Constitution is a "strong freedom". It cannot be conceptualised as a right to balance against other rights. Nor is the freedom something that can be disregarded lightly when determining whether a law can permissibly infringe this freedom.

Rights play an important role in law and in legal theory. However, it is important in a common law legal system not to lose sight of the importance of *freedoms*. As will be shown, common law freedoms have long been regarded as important, and are still regarded as important today at the highest level of the Australian judiciary. The implied freedom of political communication has been regarded, and should be regarded, as a strong freedom.

2 *The relationship between the common law and the implied freedom of political communication*

In our view, it is important to understand the relationship between the common law and the *Commonwealth Constitution* when determining whether a law is reasonably appropriate or adapted to a legitimate end.

(a) A complementary relationship

The common law and the *Commonwealth Constitution* have a complementary relationship. The common law informs the *Commonwealth Constitution* while the *Commonwealth Constitution* informs (and in some areas displaces) the common law. In *Lange*, a unanimous High Court said:

---

[531] *Coleman* [2004] HCA 25; (2004) 220 CLR 1, 49-50 [91] (McHugh J) (citations omitted); see also ibid 77 [195] (Gummow and Hayne JJ).

...The Constitution, the federal, State and territorial laws, and the common law in Australia together constitute the law of this country and form "one system of jurisprudence"... Within that single system of jurisprudence, the basic law of the Constitution provides the authority for the enactment of valid statute law and may have effect on the content of the common law.

Conversely, the Constitution itself is informed by the common law. This was explained extra-judicially by Sir Owen Dixon:

> 'We do not of course treat the common law as a transcendental body of legal doctrine, but we do treat it as antecedent in operation to the constitutional instruments which first divided Australia into separate colonies and then united her in a federal Commonwealth. We therefore regard Australian law as a unit. Its content comprises besides legislation the general common law which it is the duty of the courts to ascertain as best they may. ... The anterior operation of the common law in Australia is not just a dogma of our legal system, an abstraction of our constitutional reasoning. It is a fact of legal history.'

And in *Cheatle v The Queen*, this Court said:

> 'It is well settled that the interpretation of a constitution such as ours is necessarily influenced by the fact that its provisions are framed in the language of the English common law, and are to be read in the light of the common law's history.'[532]

One of the common law principles that the Australian colonies and then the Commonwealth of Australia inherited was what we term "the principle of freedom".

(b) The common law principle of freedom

What do we mean by the principle of freedom? In *Lange*, a unanimous High Court stated the following regarding the common law principle of freedom as it applied to freedom of expression:

> Under a legal system based on the common law, 'everybody is free to do anything, subject only to the provisions of the law', so that one proceeds 'upon an assumption of freedom of speech' and turns to the law 'to

---

[532] *Lange* [1997] HCA 25; (1997) 189 CLR 520, 563-4 (citations omitted).

discover the established exceptions to it'.⁵³³

Hence, the common law principle of freedom is the freedom to do anything, subject only to the provisions of the law.

As regards freedom of expression, the principle of freedom has constitutional importance. In *Minister for Immigration & Citizenship v Haneef*,⁵³⁴ the Full Federal Court stated the following:

> Freedom is not merely what is left over when the law is exhausted. As TRS Allan put it in 1996:
>
>> Liberty is not merely what remains when the meaning of statutes and the scope of executive powers have been settled authoritatively by the courts. The traditional civil and political liberties, like liberty of the person and freedom of speech, have independent and intrinsic weight: their importance justifies an interpretation of both common law and statute which serves to protect them from unwise and ill-considered interference or restriction. The common law, then, has its own set of constitutional rights, even if these are not formally entrenched against legislative repeal.⁵³⁵

In the *Adelaide Preacher's Case*, French CJ stated: 'Freedom of speech is a long-established common law freedom...linked to the proper functioning of representative democracies and on that basis has informed the application of public interest considerations to claimed restraints upon publication of information'.⁵³⁶ As Noel Foster points out with respect to this case:

> the decision...affirms, in very strong terms, the value of freedom of speech as both a common law principle, and also a constitutional constraint on law-making.⁵³⁷

The common law principle of freedom is therefore not to be taken lightly: indeed, it has constitutional importance.

(c)   The origin of the common law principle of freedom

---

533 Ibid 564 (citation omitted).
534 [2007] FCAFC 203; (2007) 243 ALR 606 (*'Haneef'*).
535 [2007] FCAFC 203; (2007) 243 ALR 606, 635 [113] (Black CJ, French and Weinberg JJ). See also *Evans* [2008] FCAFC 130; (2008) 168 FCR 576, 594 [72] (French, Branson and Stone JJ); *Monis* [2013] HCA 4; (2013) 249 CLR 92, 128 [60] (French CJ).
536 *Adelaide Preacher's Case* [2013] HCA 3; (2013) 249 CLR 1, 31 [43] (French CJ).
537 Noel Foster, 'Anti-Vilification Laws and Freedom of Religion in Australia – Is Defamation Enough?' Paper presented at the conference 'Justice, Mercy and Conviction: Perspectives on Law, Religion and Ethics', University of Adelaide School of Law, 7-9 June, 2013, 14.

In addition to the foregoing observations about the significance of the common law principle of freedom, we would add another. The origin of the common law principle of freedom appears to be (quite fittingly, considering that at the time of writing it is in its 800th anniversary year) the *Magna Carta*.[538] In *Ex parte Walsh; In re Yates*,[539] Isaacs J noted the following about its influence:

> It is essential… even at this advanced stage of our political development, and perhaps none the less because of that development, to bear constantly in mind certain fundamental principles which form the base of the social structure of every British community… The principles themselves cannot be found in express terms in any written Constitution of Australia, but they are inscribed in that great confirmatory instrument, seven hundred years old, which is the groundwork of all our Constitutions – *Magna Charta*. Chap. 29 (sometimes cited as Chap. 39) contains them all. Its words, rendered into English, and so far as immediately material here, are: 'No free man shall be taken or imprisoned ... or exiled ... but ... by the law of the land.' The chapter, as a whole, refers to other rights as well, and recognizes three basic principles, namely, (1) primarily every free man has an inherent individual right to his life, liberty, property and citizenship; (2) his individual rights must always yield to the necessities of the general welfare at the will of the State; (3) the law of the land is the only mode by which the State can so declare its will. These principles taken together form one united conception for the necessary adjustment of the individual and social rights and duties of the members of the State.[540]

This statement by Isaacs J lends further support to the constitutional importance of freedom of expression (and common law freedoms generally).

The nature of freedom of expression at common law is not like that of the right to freedom of expression provided under Article 19 of the ICCPR. Article 19(3) of the ICCPR provides that the right to freedom of expression carries with it special responsibilities. However, at common law, an individual

---

538 In June 1215, King John sealed the document that would become known as the *Magna Carta*. Subsequent Kings of England reissued versions the *Magna Carta*. The version most relevant to Australia's legal system is the statute known as 25 Edward I (1297) *Magna Carta* (the '1297 *Magna Carta*'). This version forms part of the received law of Western Australia, South Australia, Tasmania and the Northern Territory. Alternatively, Chapter 29 of the 1297 *Magna Carta* has been re-enacted through Imperial Acts legislation, such as in Victoria, New South Wales, Queensland and the Australian Capital Territory: see David Clark, 'The Icon of Liberty: The Status and Role of Magna Carta in Australian and New Zealand Law' (2000) 24(3) *Melbourne University Law Review* 866, 869-72.
539 (1925) 37 CLR 36.
540 Ibid 79-80 (Isaacs J).

is free to say anything unless restricted by law. Absent restraint by law, it is a complete freedom – and one with constitutional importance.

(d)   The realm of freedom

In light of the foregoing, we also venture another observation: the common law principle of freedom creates what can be conceptualised as a 'realm of freedom':[541] an area of society that the state protects but into which it does not venture. When it does venture there, the realm cedes territory to the state meanly:[542] that is, only when the state expressly and clearly legislates.

As to freedom of expression, the realm of freedom possesses other important qualities: it is *vast* and it is *ever-expanding*. One need only consider the numberless topics that are now or have ever been discussed in documented form to fathom the vastness of the realm of freedom.[543] However, with every scientific discovery, every news item, every tidbit of celebrity gossip and indeed every new act or thing great or small that can be subject of documented discussion, the realm of freedom grows.[544]

It is true that a new act or thing discussed may involve a legal restriction on that particular discussion. That is, the realm of freedom has an area where expression is restricted, and this area grows along with the realm of freedom. However, the pace of growth of this area does not match that of the realm of

---

541 We should note here that the 'realm of freedom' as we use it here is different from Marx's 'realm of freedom'. To Marx, the 'realm of freedom' was what was left when the necessaries of life had been paid for: see Karl Marx, *Capital: A Critique of Political Economy* (Penguin Classics, 1991) vol 3, 958-9. In our view, 'the realm of freedom' is a phrase simply too good to be left to Marxists.
542 We use the term 'meanly' deliberately, recalling what Abraham Lincoln said in an annual message to Congress during the Civil War to 'nobly save or meanly lose the last best hope of earth'. Abraham Lincoln Online, 'Annual Message to Congress – Concluding Remarks, 11 May 2015. We echo the sentiment: all liberty must be meanly lost.
543 And this is putting aside those topics discussed verbally. (We leave for now the "metaphysics" of how the realm of freedom expands and contracts as topics are discussed verbally, then remembered or forgotten. Or how the realm of freedom may expand as topics are discussed verbally and then passed on as some form of oral tradition.)
544 We have used the term "documented form" to mean information that is published or distributed in hard or electronic form and preserved. Of course, such documents can be lost or destroyed. However, it is safe to assume that the number of documents lost each day is dwarfed by the number of documents generated each day. Given the continuing innovation in electronic record generation and record keeping, this dynamic will only strengthen. It would take a cataclysm on the scale of a Carrington event (that is, a solar flare generating an electromagnetic pulse sufficient to short out electrical systems on a global scale) to disrupt this dynamic. (Given that the last Carrington event was in 1859 and shorted telegraphic systems around the world at the time, this cannot be ruled out – the last major event was in 2012: see Phys Org, 'Earth survived near-miss from 2012 solar storm: NASA', *Phys Org* (online) 25 July 2014.) However, once computer systems were restored, the dynamic would resume.

freedom itself. Put another way, in the modern world there will always be far more things that can be discussed than cannot be discussed.

Hence, in *Eatock*, Bromberg J was in was in error when he stated:

> The right of freedom of expression at common law is, by definition, qualified by those exceptions otherwise provided by law. The law of defamation imposes significant limitations on freedom of expression. Other laws imposing limitations include laws dealing with blasphemy, contempt of court and of Parliament, confidential information, the torts of negligent misstatement, deceit and injurious falsehood. Further, a wide range of legislative provisions dealing with obscenity, public order, copyright, censorship and consumer protection place restrictions on the exercise of the right to freedom of expression. These laws recognise that there are legitimate countervailing interests which require the imposition of limitations upon freedom of expression.[545]

With respect, none of the limitations that Bromberg J identifies (let alone defamation) are "significant" limitations on freedom of expression.[546] Rather, they occupy a small area of a vast realm. Further, their boundaries are strictly policed.[547] Hence, one cannot be cavalier about freedom of expression. It is not a right "crowded out" by other equally important rights; it is a fundamental freedom that suffers limited exceptions.

Given the foregoing, when it comes to freedom of expression at common law, two things should be noted. First, it is a freedom that has constitutional importance and to which great weight must be given. Second, it is an error to assume that restrictions of freedom of expression are the rule. They are not. Rather, they are *exceptions*: limited intrusions into a vast realm of free speech – a realm that concedes territory meanly.

(e) The particular relationship between the principle of freedom at common law and the implied freedom of political communication

As to the implied freedom of political communication, the common law principle of freedom must be borne in mind when assessing whether or not s 18C is reasonably considered to be appropriate and adapted to the end it serves. As French CJ noted in the *Adelaide Preacher's Case*:

---

545 *Eatock* [2011] FCA 1103; (2011) 197 FCR 261, 317 [238] (Bromberg J).
546 We examine certain legislative restraints on freedom of speech below.
547 It is an error to assume that, because the realm of freedom is so vast, it can easily afford to lose territory to an intrusive law. Not so. As noted above, in all instances such territory is meanly lost.

The common law freedom of expression does not impose a constraint upon the legislative powers of the Commonwealth or the States or Territories. However, through the principle of legality, and criteria of reasonable proportionality, applied to purposive powers, the freedom can inform the construction and characterisation, for constitutional purposes, of Commonwealth statutes.[548]

We would add that, in common law legal systems, and especially when a common law freedom is at stake, the appropriate state action can be – and often is – *do nothing*. Further, when states do intervene, the intrusion is relatively minimal, and construed to be limited.

However, the state doing nothing does *not* mean that nothing is done. In a common law legal system, action may (and often is) taken by non-state actors in civil society. By "civil society", we adopt Martin Krygier's description of it as:

> ...comprised of multitudes of independent actors, going about their individual or freely chosen cooperative affairs, able to choose to associate and participate (or not) in an independent public realm, with an economy of disbursed actors and markets, undergirded by a socially embedded legal order, which grants and enforces legal rights.[549]

As regards offensive speech, non-state actors may challenge that speech by their own speech. Further, they may organise by free assembly to magnify their voice and to speak out on behalf of those who cannot speak for themselves. That is, in a common law system, those exercising their common law freedoms of speech and association counter others exercising their common law freedom of speech to make offensive remarks. These matters are relevant to whether or not a law is reasonably appropriate or adapted to advance the end it serves.

3 *The tests used in s 18C*

> [W]e have now sunk to a depth at which the restatement of the obvious is the first duty of intelligent men.[550]

Unfortunately, the above quote from George Orwell's review of Bertrand

---

548 *Adelaide Preacher's Case* [2013] HCA 3; (2013) 249 CLR 1, 32 [44] (French CJ).
549 Martin Krygier, 'Virtuous Circles: Antipodean Reflections on Power, Institutions, and Civil Society' (1997) 11(1) *East European Politics and Societies* 36, 75.
550 George Orwell, 'Review of *Power: A New Social Analysis*' *The Adelphi* (January 1939).

Russell's *Power: A New Social Analysis* holds true today.[551] Various commentators have spoken about the "chilling" effect of s 18C. Regrettably, the term "chilling", while useful shorthand, often obscures the damage that s 18C does to freedom of expression. Hence, the purpose of this and the next two sections is to analyse the text and operation of s 18C and s 18D and their effect on freedom of expression.

Section 18C provides that it is unlawful to do an act 'otherwise than in private'[552] that is 'reasonably likely, in all the circumstances, to offend, insult, humiliate or intimidate another person or a group of people'[553] and 'the act is done because of the race, colour or national or ethnic origin of the person or some or all of the people in the group'.[554] Each of these elements will be examined in turn.

(a) 'otherwise than in private'

Section 18C concerns acts directed to the public or done in a public place. For the purposes of 18C 'an act is taken not be done in private if it'[555] 'causes words, sounds, images or writing to be communicated to the public';[556] 'is done in a public place';[557] or 'is done in the sight or hearing of people who are in a public place'.[558]

Section 18C is not directed to private communications. Hence, people are free to talk however they like in private. However, prohibiting public communications is by itself a serious infringement on the implied freedom of political communication. The forum, the town square, the soapbox and now the internet are examples of public spaces that have been or are critical to

---

551 Orwell's quote in context reads: 'If there are certain pages of Mr Bertrand Russell's book, *Power*, which seem rather empty, that is merely to say that we have now sunk to a depth at which the restatement of the obvious is the first duty of intelligent men. It is not merely that at present the rule of naked force obtains almost everywhere. Probably that has always been the case. Where this age differs from those immediately preceding it is that a liberal intelligentsia is lacking. Bully-worship, under various disguises, has become a universal religion, and such truisms as that a machine-gun is still a machine-gun even when a "good" man is squeezing the trigger — and that in effect is what Mr Russell is saying — have turned into heresies which it is actually becoming dangerous to utter.': ibid. In our view, George Orwell's observations about the machine gun apply to laws restricting freedom expression.
552 RDA s 18(1).
553 RDA s 18(1)(a).
554 RDA s 18(1)(b).
555 RDA s 18(2).
556 RDA s 18(2)(a).
557 RDA s 18(2)(b).
558 RDA s 18(2)(c).

the exchange of ideas necessary to a democracy. Further, media organisations are in the business or broadcasting news and opinion, hence s 18C impairs the freedom of political communication as it applies to the press. In addition to media organisations, the internet has resulted in a proliferation of private citizens who proffer news and opinion by publicly accessible websites.

(b) 'reasonably likely, in all the circumstances, to offend, insult, humiliate or intimidate another person or a group of people'

This element raises the following issues:

1. Whether 'reasonably likely' suggests an objective assessment;
2. Whether someone must actually be offended, insulted or humiliated; and
3. How offence, insult, humiliation or intimidation are determined.

(i)   Does 'reasonably likely' suggest an objective assessment?

It is clear that the term 'reasonably likely' suggests an objective assessment of an act that may breach s 18C.

We have noted above the problems with using objective standards.[559] Confining speech to that which is not reasonably likely in the circumstances to offend, insult or humiliate another person or group of people on the grounds of race, colour, ethnicity or nationality substantially fetters the implied freedom of political communication. As noted above, Commonwealth legislative power and Commonwealth executive actions often concern matters involving race, colour, ethnicity and nationality. The principle so stated carries a real risk of deterring someone from speaking about a government or political matter pertaining to race, colour, ethnicity or nationality for fear of being found to have made a comment reasonably likely to offend.

Further, for reasons detailed below,[560] s 18D does not relieve this burden sufficiently, and indeed imposes additional burdens of its own.

(ii) Does someone need to have been actually offended, insulted or humiliated?

This element does not need someone to *actually* be offended, insulted or humiliated. All that is required is that the act be *'reasonably likely*, in all the circumstances' to do this to 'another person or a group of people'.[561] This

---

559 See Part IV.E.1.(b).(ii) (pages 40-2).
560 See Part V.D.4 (page 159).
561 Emphasis ours.

interpretation of s 18C is open on its terms alone. However, case law has confirmed this interpretation.[562]

Given s 18C's terms, there is nothing stopping litigants bringing actions on behalf of potentially aggrieved individuals or groups even though no one is actually offended, insulted or humiliated. The fact that s 18C may subject someone to legal liability when there is no harm to anyone distinguishes it from many criminal and civil actions, where harm to someone must be established.

(iii) How is offence, insult and humiliation to be determined?

There are two aspects here. First, how serious the offence, insult or humiliation must be to breach s 18C. Second, the test used to determine whether the statement actually breached s 18C. Each of these will be examined in turn.

As to how serious offence, insult or humiliation must be to breach s 18C, we have discussed this above.[563] We once again assume that these terms will be given a narrow interpretation, applying only to serious offence, insult or humiliation. However, if the High Court gives them a broad interpretation, then our arguments apply with greater force.

As to the test used to determine a breach, the reasonable representative test is used, which we also have discussed above.[564] The reasonable representative test further burdens the ability to communicate about government or political matters. Determining whether or not s 18C is breached requires considering:

- The race, colour, ethnicity or nationality of the reasonable representative of the group or sub-group; and
- The speaker's own race, colour, ethnicity or nationality.

These considerations will differ from person to person, group to group, or sub-group to sub-group, based on the speaker's, group's or sub-group's respective race, colour, ethnicity or national origin. Thus, Australians face a balkanized landscape where speech may be acceptable to one or some groups or sub-groups but not others. To argue that all other Australians may be similarly burdened is to miss the point. Australians must be able to freely and frankly discuss matters involving race, colour, ethnicity and nationality as Commonwealth and State legislative and executive action often concern these matters.

---

562 *Scully* [2002] FCA 1080; (2002) 120 FCR 243, 269 [99] (Hely J); *Eatock* [2011] FCA 1103; (2011) 197 FCR 261, 318 [241] (Bromberg J).
563 See Part III.B.2.(c) (page 20).
564 See Part IV.E.2 (pages 53-7).

We would also note another outcome of the reasonable representative test that is peculiar but nevertheless open on the terms of s 18C. Members of a particular race, colour, ethnicity or nationality may have views that fall outside the "mainstream" of their particular group or sub-group. Section 18C raises the curious prospect of these individuals being subjected to allegations of "racial hatred" for expressing an opinion about matters relevant to that group with whom the majority of that group disagrees. So much for dissident opinion.

(c) *'the act is done because of the race, colour or national or ethnic origin of the person some or all of the people in the group'*

This element raises the following issues:

1. Causation; and
2. How race, colour, national and ethnic origin are defined.

(i) *'because of' – causation*

As to causation, s 18B of the RDA provides that if an act is done for 2 or more reasons;[565] and one of the reasons is the race, colour or national or ethnic origin of a person (whether or not it is the dominant reason or a substantial reason for doing the act);[566] then, for the purposes of Part IIA, the act is taken to be done because of the person's race, colour or national or ethnic origin.[567] Race, colour or national or ethnic origin need only be a factor in the decision to do the act.[568]

As noted above, s 18C may apply even though no one is actually offended, insulted or humiliated. Hence, someone may have acted for a purpose other than causing offence, insult or humiliation in making a statement involving race, colour, ethnicity or nationality. However they may nevertheless breach s 18C because their act is reasonably likely to offend, insult or humiliate.

(ii) *race, colour, ethnicity or national origin*

As noted in our discussion of whether or not s 18C serves a legitimate purpose, s 18C employs definitions of race, colour, ethnicity and nationality that involve

---

565 RDA s 18B(a).
566 RDA s 18B(b).
567 RDA s 18B.
568 *Creek* [2001] FCA 1007; (2001) 112 FCR 352, 359 [28] (Kiefel J); *Scully* [2002] FCA 1080; (2002) 120 FCR 243, 273 [114], 273-4 [116] (Hely J); *Jones v Toben* [2001] FCA 1150 [98]-[99] (Branson J).

ideas.[569] Challenging such ideas may result in members of the respective race, ethnicity, culture or nationality being offended, insulted or humiliated.

4 The tests used in 18D

ALL ANIMALS ARE EQUAL BUT SOME ANIMALS ARE MORE EQUAL THAN OTHERS.[570]

The tests used in s 18D compound the problems with the tests used in s 18C.

(a) 'reasonably and in good faith'

The RDA does not define what is meant by 'reasonably' and 'in good faith'. However, the meaning of the terms 'reasonably' and 'good faith' appear plain on their face. The *Macquarie Dictionary* defines 'reasonable' as follows:

> 1. endowed with reason. 2. agreeable to reason and sound judgment: *a reasonable choice*. 3. not exceeding the limit prescribed by reason; not excessive: *reasonable terms*. 4. moderate, or moderate or moderate in price: *the coat was reasonable but not cheap*.[571]

The *Macquarie Dictionary* defines 'good faith' as follows:

> '1. honesty of purpose or sincerity of declaration: *to act in good faith*. 2. expectation of such qualities in others: *to take a job in good faith*.'[572]

However, case law suggests that applying these terms in the RDA's context is not straightforward. *Bropho*[573] provides perhaps the most detailed examination of the terms 'reasonably' and 'good faith' as used in the RDA. In *Bropho*, French J stated the following about the term 'reasonably':

> A thing is done 'reasonably' in one of the protected activities in par (a), (b) and (c) of s 18D if it bears a rational relationship to that activity and is not disproportionate to what is necessary to carry it out. It imports an objective judgment. In this context that means a judgment independent of that which the actor thinks is reasonable. It does allow the possibility that there may be more than one way of doing things 'reasonably'. The

---

[569] See Part V.C.3 (pages 135-6) and Part V.C.4 (page 136).
[570] George Orwell, *Animal Farm* (Penguin Group (Australia), first published 1945, 2004 ed) 97 (all capitals are used in the original).
[571] *Macquarie Dictionary* 1224 (emphasis in original).
[572] Ibid 639 (emphasis in original).
[573] *Bropho* [2004] FCAFC 16; (2004) 135 FCR 105.

judgment required in applying the section, is whether the thing done was done 'reasonably' not whether it could have been done more reasonably or in a different way more acceptable to the court. The judgment will necessarily be informed by the normative elements of ss 18C and 18D and a recognition of the two competing values that are protected by those sections.

> An act will be done reasonably in the performance, exhibition or distribution of an artistic work if it is done for the purpose and in a manner calculated to advance the purpose of the artistic expression in question. An act is done reasonably in relation to statements, publications, discussions or debates for genuine academic, artistic or scientific purposes, if it bears a rational relationship to those purposes...[574]

As to 'good faith', French J noted that the term 'good faith' had a variety of constructions according to its particular applications.[575] After considering the history and use of the term,[576] French J stated that applying good faith in the context of the RDA:

> [R]equires a recognition that the law condemns racial vilification of the defined kind but protects freedom of speech and expression in the areas defined in pars (a), (b) and (c) of [s 18D]. The good faith exercise of that freedom will, so far as practicable, seek to be faithful to the norms implicit in its protection and to the negative obligations implied by s 18C. *It will honestly and conscientiously endeavour to have regard to and minimise the harm it will, by definition, inflict.* It will not use those freedoms as a 'cover' to offend, insult, humiliate or intimidate people by reason of their race or colour or ethnic or national origin.[577]

Justice Lee expanded on the notion of harm in determining whether or not the good faith requirement had been met, stating:

> The words 'good faith' as used in s 18D involve more than the absence of bad faith, dishonesty, fraud or malice. Having regard to the context provided by the Act, the requirement to act in good faith *imposes a duty* on a person who does an act because of race, an act reasonably likely to inflict the harm referred to in s 18C, to show that before so acting that person considered the likelihood of the occurrence of that harm and the degree of

---

574 *Bropho* [2004] FCAFC 16; (2004) 135 FCR 105, 128 [79]-[80] (French J).
575 Ibid 129 [84] (French J). In his judgment, French J noted that the term 'good faith' is used in 154 Commonwealth statutes.
576 Ibid 129-31 [83]-[94] (French J).
577 Ibid 131-2 [95] (French J) (emphasis ours).

harm reasonably likely to result. In short the risk of harm from the act of publication must be shown to have been balanced by other considerations. *The words 'in good faith' as used in s 18D import a requirement that the person doing the act exercise prudence, caution and diligence, which, in the context of the Act would mean due care to avoid or minimize consequences identified by s 18C.*[578]

Hence, the majority in *Bropho* held that good faith imported a harm minimisation approach to speech pertaining to race, colour, ethnicity or nationality. The minority was prepared to go further by imposing a duty to avoid or minimise offence, insult or humiliation.

In the first instance decision that ultimately led to the appeal in *Bropho*, Commissioner Innes AM was prepared to allow for relevant history prior to the speech that breached s 18C to be considered in determining whether an exemption under s 18D was established.[579] In *Bropho*, Lee J was not prepared to do so:

> A publisher of a catholic range of opinions could not rely upon past publication of diverse material to show that it acted reasonably and in good faith by publishing, because of race, a work or material that is offensive, insulting, humiliating or intimidating to persons of that race, if it acts without regard to whether the act of publication would cause the harm the Act seeks to prevent, and does not attempt to show how the risk of harm from the otherwise prohibited act, was counterbalanced, or outweighed, by matters showing the act to have been done reasonably and in good faith.[580]

In *Eatock*, Bromberg J applied both French J and Lee J's approaches to harm minimisation.[581]

Hence, in considering whether an exemption under s 18D applies, one must have regard to the following:

1. The degree of harm caused by the speech that would offend, insult, humiliate or intimidate;
2. The steps taken to minimise that harm;
3. Whether the public interest in the speech would counter-balance or outweigh the harm;

There are major problems with confining the exemption to acts that are 'reasonable and good faith'. First, the essence of freedom of expression is that

---

578 Ibid 143 [144] (Lee J) (emphasis ours).
579 *Nyungar Circle of Elders v West Australian Newspapers Ltd* [2001] HREOCA 1 (see in particular the reasoning under heading 8.7.3).
580 Ibid 142 [142] (Lee J).
581 *Eatock* [2011] FCA 1103; (2011) 197 FCR 261, 341 [345]-[347] (Bromberg J).

it extends to acts that are *unreasonable* and made in *bad faith*. As noted above, in democratic polities discussion and debate may involve all manner of rhetoric and sophistry.[582]

Second, there is considerable uncertainty about what good faith and reasonable mean when applied to various circumstances. One person's idea of good faith and reasonableness may vary substantially with another's. Someone may think they are simply presenting their side of the argument, while their opponent thinks they are being disingenuous or tendentious. The considerable uncertainty this creates leads to a real risk of chilling discussion and debate. This problem is not overcome by imposing a 'reasonable person' test or the like. Someone making a heartfelt statement on a controversial matter may think that a reasonable person would agree that the statement was reasonable and in good faith in the circumstances, only to have an AHRC official later disagree and subject them to investigation, or worse, a judge later disagree and subject them to court-ordered remedies.

Third, good faith's requirement for harm to be minimised also creates uncertainty. What steps are required to minimise harm? Once again, a person may believe that they have taken steps to minimise harm only to have an AHRC official or judge later disagree and subject them to the consequences noted above.

(b) 'genuine academic, artistic or scientific purpose or any other genuine purpose in the public interest'

Like 'reasonably' and 'good faith', the RDA does not define 'genuine' or what is an 'academic, artistic or scientific purpose'.

For the purposes of analysing this limb we will examine first what is meant by the word 'genuine'. We will then examine the problems arising from exempting 'academic, artistic or scientific' purposes.

(i) 'genuine'

There does not appear to be any relevant authority considering the meaning of the term 'genuine'. The *Macquarie Dictionary* defines 'genuine' as:

> 1. being truly such; real; authentic: *genuine regret, genuine worth*. 2. properly so called: *genuine leprosy*. 3. sincere; free from pretence or affectation: *a*

---

582 See Part IV.E.1.(f) (pages 50-1).

genuine person.[583]

In the RDA's context, 'genuine' could mean that the person engaging in the academic, artistic or scientific purpose be appropriately credentialed. However, given that people lacking relevant qualifications can nevertheless produce scientific, artistic and academic works, this interpretation is unlikely.

Alternatively, 'genuine' may mean that the academic, artistic, scientific or other purpose not be used as a "sham" to advance otherwise offensive, insulting, humiliating or intimidating conduct. However, we note that this latter interpretation overlaps with French J's interpretation of good faith: that is, that the purpose will not be a "cover" for such conduct.

Hence, it could be argued that works that are not genuine are those considered "fringe" or otherwise falling outside the "mainstream" of scientific, artistic or academic work. If this is the case, then while it is true that many fringe works have no merit, this cannot safely be said for all such works. Even if works have no merit, the critiques of such works often do. Hence, by responding to fringe works, the store of human knowledge and understanding grows.

In any event, in our view it is not for the state to determine the merit of such works when civil society in a representative democracy is far better equipped to do this. Indeed, modern communications make this task far easier than ever before.

(ii)   'academic, artistic or scientific purpose'

Putting aside the issues with the term 'genuine', this limb of s 18D creates a more fundamental problem. That is, s 18D's terms appear to create classes of people (that is, people regularly engaged in work as scientists, artists or academics) whose speech is more likely to be protected than those falling outside these classes.[584]

To analyse the problem with this aspect of s 18D we submit that, in

---

583 *Macquarie Dictionary* 619 (emphasis in original).
584 Dan Meagher quotes Michael Chesterman in noting that the interpretation of the term 'reasonably' in s 18D is concerned with incivility in style and content, and not so much with racist content itself. This leads to 'a two-tier approach: chilling of blue-collar muck and preservation of upper-class mud': Dan Meagher, 'So Far So Good?: A Critical Evaluation of Racial Vilification Laws in Australia' (2004) 32(2) *Federal Law Review* 225, 249 quoting Michael Chesterman, *Freedom of Speech in Australian Law: A Delicate Plant* (Ashgate, 2000) 226. Meagher goes on to note 'In other words, protection is accorded to racist communications so long as it is made articulately, using scholarly language or socially acceptable conventions': see Dan Meagher, 'So Far So Good?: A Critical Evaluation of Racial Vilification Laws in Australia' (2004) 32(2) *Federal Law Review* 225, 249.

addition to the implied freedom of political communication, the *Commonwealth Constitution* implies an *equality* of political communication. That is, Australian electors are equal concerning (i) the *range of issues* they may discuss concerning government and political matters, and (ii) the *range of language* they may employ when discussing these issues. We refer to (i) and (ii) as 'the implied equality of political communication'.

As stated in *Lange*, implications from the *Commonwealth Constitution* must clearly arise from its terms and structure.[585] The implied equality of political communication arises from the same provisions in the *Commonwealth Constitution* giving rise to the implied freedom of political communication.[586] That is:

- Sections 7 and 24, which respectively provide for members of the Senate[587] and the House of Representatives[588] to be chosen directly by the people.
- Section 64, which provides for Commonwealth executive government.[589]
- Section 128, which provides for amendments to the *Commonwealth Constitution*.[590]

These sections imply that Australian electors must be free to discuss matters concerning the election of representatives, the actions of executive government between elections, and potential amendments to the *Commonwealth Constitution*. However, in our view, a further necessary implication arises. That is, in order for Australian electors to chose their representatives and to discuss the actions of Commonwealth executive government, Australian electors must have an equal range of political issues they can discuss and an equal range of language to discuss these issues.

In addition to the provisions of the *Commonwealth Constitution* noted above, we submit that the equality of political communication arises by necessary implication from ss 51 and 52 of the *Commonwealth Constitution*. These sections provide for matters in relation to which the Commonwealth may legislate.[591]

---

585 *Lange* [1997] HCA 25; (1997) 189 CLR 520, 566-7. See also *McGinty* [1996] HCA 48; (1996) 186 CLR 140, 168 (Brennan CJ), 182-3 (Dawson J), 231 (McHugh J), 284-5 (Gummow J) ('*McGinty*').
586 *Lange* [1997] HCA 25; (1997) 189 CLR 520, 567.
587 *Commonwealth Constitution* s 7.
588 Ibid s 24.
589 Ibid s 64.
590 Ibid s 128.
591 Ibid ss 51, 52.

Australian electors must be able to discuss an equivalent range of issues concerning these matters, and be able to employ an equivalent range of language to discuss these issues.

We note that equality of political communication does not encounter the same "structural difficulties" in the *Commonwealth Constitution* that the implied "one-vote one value" argument encountered in *McGinty*. This is for two reasons. First, unlike "one vote one value", there are no provisions in the *Commonwealth Constitution* that provide for "structural inequality" among Australian electors concerning their range of discussion of government and political matters.[592] The only provision that provides for inequality in range of communication is s 49 of the *Commonwealth Constitution*. This section provides for the powers, privileges and immunities of the Senate and House of Representatives.[593] However, we submit that the powers, privileges and immunities that s 49 provides are an exception, being necessary for the Commonwealth Parliament to discharge its legislative functions. These powers, privileges and immunities do not materially affect the range of political communication of Australian electors generally.

Second, the implied equality of political communication does not encounter another difficulty that the 'one vote one value' argument encountered in *McGinty* concerning the qualification of Australian electors at Federation. In *McGinty*, the different qualifications for the franchise among the States at Federation mitigated against a holding that the *Commonwealth Constitution* implied "one vote one value".[594] We submit that the equality of political communication applied at Federation to Australian electors however they were qualified in their respective States. That is, once qualified, each Australian elector had an equal range of issues they could discuss, and an equal range of language they could use to discuss these matters. This equality of political communication continues to apply to Australian electors now that Commonwealth legislation provides for their qualifications.

Further, the implied equality of political communication extends beyond Australian electors to others in the Australian community. This is because political matters not only affect Australian electors but those members of the Australian community who cannot vote, such as children, people disqualified from voting, corporations, unions and other entities. As the High Court stated

---

592 *McGinty* [1996] HCA 48; (1996) 186 CLR 140, 236-8 (McHugh J), 275-8 (Gummow J).
593 *Commonwealth Constitution* s 49.
594 *McGinty* [1996] HCA 48; (1996) 186 CLR 140, 240-5 (McHugh J), 278-4 (Gummow J).

in *Lange* with regards to the implied freedom of political communication:

> [E]ach member of the Australian community has an interest in disseminating and receiving information, opinions and arguments concerning government and political matters that affect the people of Australia. The duty to disseminate such information is simply the correlative of the interest in receiving it. The common convenience and welfare of Australian society are advanced by discussion – the giving and receiving of information – about government and political matters.[595]

In addition, a majority of the High Court stated the following in *Unions NSW*:

> Political communication may be undertaken legitimately to influence others to a political viewpoint. It is not simply a two-way affair between electors and government or candidates. There are many in the community who are not electors but who are governed and are affected by decisions of government. Whilst not suggesting that the freedom of political communication is a personal right or freedom, which it is not, it may be acknowledged that such persons and entities have a legitimate interest in governmental action and the direction of policy. The point to be made is that they, as well as electors, may seek to influence the ultimate choice of the people as to who should govern. They may do so directly or indirectly through the support of a party or a candidate who they consider best represents or expresses their viewpoint. In turn, political parties and candidates may seek to influence such persons or entities because it is understood that they will in turn contribute to the discourse about matters of politics and government.[596]

Please note that the equality that is implied is equality in the range of issues that may be discussed and the range of language used to discuss these issues. The *Commonwealth Constitution* does not imply equality in the *means* by which views may be communicated or the *capacity* to express those views. The means by which Australian electors may broadcast their views, and the capacity to express those views, may differ greatly. However, whatever means adopted or capacity for expression, from the editorial of a broadsheet newspaper to discussion at the pub, the range of issues and range of language that may be employed should be equal.

---

595 *Lange* [1997] HCA 25; (1997) 189 CLR 520, 571.
596 *Unions NSW* [2013] HCA 58; (2013) 252 CLR 530, 551-2 [30] (French CJ, Hayne, Crennan, Kiefel and Bell JJ) (citations omitted). See also 580-1 [145] (Keane J).

We suggest that equality of political communication is perhaps already foreshadowed in defamation law. An example is the qualified privilege derived from the implied freedom of political communication ('*Lange* qualified privilege'). This privilege is available to defendants provided the following criteria are met:

- The defendant's publication was reasonable in all the circumstances. That is, the defendant had reasonable grounds for believing the defamatory imputation was true; took proper steps so far as they were reasonably open to verify the accuracy of the material; and did not believe the imputation untrue; and
- The defendant did not act with ill-will or other improper motive.[597]

Lange qualified privilege does not depend on the occupation of the defendant. All that matters is that the defendant is a natural or legal person who is able to satisfy the criteria.[598]

Further, at common law, the defence of opinion in defamation operates in the same way: it does not matter if the defendant is a sophisticated media organisation or an individual.[599] The defamation statutes in Australia operate in the same way.

We would also note that equality of opportunity to participate in the exercise of political sovereignty is an aspect of the representative democracy guaranteed by the *Commonwealth Constitution*.[600] Implying equality in the range of issues and the range of language supports such equality of opportunity.

With the exception of members of Australian Parliaments,[601] there is no reason to grant greater legal protection to members of certain classes when discussing political matters involving certain topics. An artist is no more

---

597 *Lange* [1997] HCA 25; (1997) 189 CLR 520, 574.
598 As a matter of practicality, it is only a natural or legal person who would be subject to an action for defamation.
599 *Langlands v Leng* [1916] SC (HL) 102, 110 (Lord Shaw).
600 *McCloy* [2015] HCA 34, [45] (French CJ, Kiefel, Bell and Keane JJ). In *McCloy*, Gageler J endorsed Harrison Moore's observation that the 'great underlying principle' of the *Commonwealth Constitution* was 'that the rights of individuals are sufficiently secured by ensuring, as far as possible, to each a share, and an equal share, in political power': Harrison Moore, *The Constitution of the Commonwealth of Australia* (John Murray, 1902) 329 cited in *McCloy* [2015] HCA 34, [110] (Gageler J). See also *McCloy* [2015] HCA 34, [27] (French CJ, Kiefel, Bell and Keane JJ), [219] (Nettle J), [318] (Gordon J).
601 Members of Australian Parliaments should, as law-makers and the people's representatives, be free to robustly discuss proposed laws.

qualified than plumbers, hairdressers, engineers or medical professionals (to name but a few examples) to discuss political matters involving race, colour, ethnicity or national origin. Each person will have their own perspective on political matters. Each person should be equal regarding the range of issues they may discuss, and the language they may use to discuss these issues.

We would make three further observations concerning the implied equality of political communication. First, the test for the implied equality of political communication would not, except with the necessary changes, be different from the implied freedom of political communication. That is:

1. Does the law effectively burden the implied equality of political communication in its terms, operation or effect?
2. If "yes" to question 1, are the purpose of the law and the means adopted to achieve that purpose legitimate, in the sense that they are compatible with the maintenance of the constitutionally prescribed system of representative government?
3. If "yes" to question 2, is the law reasonably appropriate and adapted to advance that legitimate object?

For example, laws restricting the communication of secrets important to the defence or security of Australia would pass the test. These laws would burden the equality of political communication by restricting the communication of secrets to certain persons. However, these would be for a legitimate end: the defence or security of Australia, which is a critical function of the Commonwealth government. Further, given the necessity of restricting such information, these laws would be reasonably appropriate and adapted to that end.

Second, the implied equality of political communication can exist either separately from the implied freedom of political communication, or as an aspect of the implied freedom of political communication. In our view, the implied equality of political communication should be treated separately from the implied freedom of political communication. While freedom and equality are not necessarily antithetical concepts,[602] there is much to be said for conceptually distinct tests of constitutional validity. That said, implied equality could be an aspect of the existing test for freedom of political communication, as freedom of association is held to be.[603] However, for the reasons we have

---

602 Something which we have argued elsewhere in this work. See Part IV.E.3.(c).(ii) (pages 73-5).
603 See *Wainohu v New South Wales* [2011] HCA 24; (2011) 243 CLR 181, 230 [112] (Gummow, Hayne, Crennan and Bell JJ), 220 [72] (French CJ, Kiefel J), 251 [186] (Heydon J).

stated, there is more constitutional basis for implying equality of political communication than implying freedom of association.

Third, if it is ultimately held that equality of political communication cannot be implied from the *Commonwealth Constitution*, then this does not mean that s 18C is constitutionally valid. As we have argued elsewhere in this work, s 18C impermissibly infringes the implied freedom of political communication for reasons apart from s 18D's exemption for academic, artistic or scientific works.

(iii) 'A fair and accurate report of any matter in the public interest'

Like 'reasonably', 'good faith' and 'genuine', the RDA does not define 'fair', 'accurate' or 'public interest'.

The *Macquarie Dictionary* defines 'fair', relevantly, as follows:

> 1. free from bias, dishonesty, or injustice: *a fair decision; a fair judge*. 2. that is legitimately sought, pursued, done, given etc.; proper under the rules: *a fair game; a fair stroke; a fair fight*...13. courteous; civil: *fair words*.[604]

In case law, the meaning of 'fair' is the same as in defamation law, that is, it needs to be based on facts.[605]

Further, there is also the requirement for accuracy.[606] The *Macquarie Dictionary* defines 'accuracy', relevantly, as follows:

> In exact conformity to the truth, to a standard or rule, or to a model; free from error or defect...[607]

Finally, there is also the requirement for 'public interest'. The *Macquarie Dictionary* defines 'public interest' as:

> ...the benefit or advantage to a whole community, as opposed to the individual.[608]

Given that the words 'reasonably' and 'good faith' appear in s 18D and qualify s 18D(c)(i), we further suggest that the requirement of fairness and accuracy in this context requires balance, measured use of words, or both. Doing so would be consistent with the 'harm minimisation' approach that French J and Lee J took in *Bropho*.

However, freedom of expression necessarily entails the freedom to present

---

604 *Macquarie Dictionary* 527 (emphasis in original).
605 *Creek* [2001] FCA 1007; (2001) 112 FCR 352, 360 [32] (Kiefel J).
606 Ibid.
607 *Macquarie Dictionary* 10.
608 Ibid 1185.

facts tendentiously. Indeed, speech concerning political matters is often partisan. Certain facts are stated but others omitted in order to cast the opposition in a bad light. Historically, if such an approach is employed, then the proper response is to reply with facts mitigating or refuting those presented earlier. The response has not been for the state to intervene to ensure fairness.

Further, in some cases measured language is plainly unsuitable to stating facts establishing the truth. Sometimes facts are not just inconvenient but grave, horrific, or both. If these facts concern people or their practices, speaking them will cause great offence or insult. However, these facts should be spoken.

(iv) *'a fair comment on any event or matter of public interest if the comment is an expression of a genuine belief held by the person making the comment'*

Like 'reasonably', 'good faith', 'genuine', 'fair', 'accurate' and 'public interest', the RDA does not define 'fair comment'.

In considering this particular exemption, case law appears to have adopted legal principles relevant to the defence of fair comment in defamation. The *Macquarie Dictionary* defines 'fair comment' as:

> [A] defence to an action for defamation; the defendant must show that the statement, if not published maliciously, was fair comment on a matter of public interest and substantially true.[609]

In *Eatock*, Bromberg J stated:

> ...The fair comment defence only applies to a comment as distinct from a statement of fact... The comment must be recognisable as comment and the facts upon which the comment is based must be expressly stated, referred to or notorious. The facts upon which the comment is based must be, at least in general terms, explicitly or implicitly stated. The purpose of that requirement is so that the reader or hearer is put in a position to judge for him or herself whether the comment is well founded...
>
> Honesty requires that the maker of the comment genuinely believe the comment made. If the maker knew the comment was untrue, or was recklessly indifferent to the truth or falsity of the comment, the maker would be acting dishonestly... Section 18D(c)(ii) deals with that aspect expressly by requiring that the comment be "an expression of a genuine belief held" by the maker of the comment.[610]

---

609 *Macquarie Dictionary* 527.
610 *Eatock* [2011] FCA 1103; (2011) 197 FCR 261, 343 [355]-[357] (Bromberg J) (citations omitted).

Given that the words 'reasonably' and 'good faith' appear in s 18D and qualifies s 18D(c)(ii), we further suggest that the requirement of fair comment in this context requires the 'harm minimisation' approach that French J and Carr J outlined in *Bropho*.

A difficulty with the defence of opinion in defamation law is distinguishing between opinion and assertions of fact. Statements intended to be opinion may be held to be assertions of fact.

In defamation law, if a statement could be construed either as an opinion or an assertion of fact then a defendant can "cover their bases" by pleading opinion or truth as alternatives. However, this option is not available to defendants to s 18C claims. That is, if a statement is construed to be asserting fact, then the defendant has no exemption under s 18D *even though their statement is true*. The closest that the defendant can plead is that their statement was a fair and accurate report of an event or matter of public interest[611] (with the limitations of this exemption as noted above).

Hence, statements asserting fact, and statements intended to be opinion but construed to assert fact, are not exempt from s 18C. This is a major burden on the implied freedom of political communication.

This brings us to our next point.

(v) Truth is not an exemption to s 18C

Truth is a defence to defamation. However, truth is not an exemption to s 18C. The absence of this exemption to s 18C is a critical defect in the law. The ALRC noted the following with respect to the defence of truth in defamation:

> Widespread literacy and universal suffrage in 20th century Australia have given all citizens the opportunity to interest themselves in community and political affairs. Steadily rising educational standards enable them to do so effectively. Individuals tend to be more actively involved in the political process than formerly. They are more likely to need and demand correct information... American judges have long appreciated the importance of free speech to democracy.
>
> "When ideas compete in the market for acceptance, full and free discussion exposes the false and they gain few adherents. Full and free discussion, even of ideas we hate, encourages the testing of our own prejudices and preconceptions. Full and free discussion keeps a society from becoming stagnant and unprepared for the stresses and

---

611 RDA s 18D(c)(i).

strains that work to tear all civilizations apart... self-governance in this country perseveres because of our profound national commitment to the principle of debate on public issues should be uninhibited, robust and wide open."

The very fact of self government, of individual responsibility for community affairs, imposes a greater need for freedom of speech. But there is no value in falsehood; intelligent participation in civic affairs depends upon correct information.[612]

The ALRC's comments are also relevant to s 18C. Basing decisions on truth, or the closest one can get to truth, clearly has merit.

However, s 18C allows for a curious result, namely the perpetuation of "flattering falsehoods" at the expense of truth. We will illustrate what we mean with an example. Suppose an Australian website forum is run by and for Cuban expatriates sympathetic to Cuba's communist regime.[613] In the course of thread praising Che Guevara as a hero of the communist revolution in Cuba, a "habitual troll"[614] posts the following:

Che Guevara once said 'the black is indolent and a dreamer; spending his meager wage on frivolity or drink; the European has a tradition of work and saving, which has pursued him as far as this corner of America and drives him to advance himself, even independently of his own individual aspirations'.[615]

Suppose also that a Cuban expatriate reading the post is offended as, in their view, Guevara is a hero of the Cuban people. Further, that the professional

---

612 Australian Law Reform Commission, *Unfair Publication: Defamation and privacy*, Report No 11 (1979) 19 [33] (citations omitted).
613 We are aware of (i) the fact that many Cuban expatriates are anti-communist and are against the communist regime in Cuba; and (ii) the irony of people sympathetic to communism using the internet. We ask the reader to stipulate these things for the sake of argument.
614 Trolling is the internet phenomenon of people posting comments on websites with the intent of provoking a reaction from others. Exchanges with the troll often descend into "flame wars".
615 Lest anyone think we are taking Guevara out of context, his full quote reads: 'The blacks, those magnificent examples of the African race who have maintained their racial purity thanks to their lack of an affinity with bathing, have seen their territory invaded by a new kind of slave: the Portuguese. And the two ancient races have now begun a hard life together, fraught with bickering and squabbles. Discrimination and poverty unite them in the daily fight for survival but their different ways of approaching life separate them completely: the black is indolent and a dreamer; spending his meager wage on frivolity or drink; the European has a tradition of work and saving, which has pursued him as far as this corner of America and drives him to advance himself, even independently of his own individual aspirations.': see Ernesto Che Guevara, *The Motorcycle Diaries: Notes on a Latin American Journey* (Ocean Press, 2003) 161. Guevara's point appeared to be that while the Portuguese were trying to lift themselves out of their circumstances through hard work and saving, the Africans were not disposed to even try.

troll is unrepentant as they *wanted* to provoke outrage among Cuban communist sympathisers who profess to be concerned about anti-racism.

Under s 18C, the relevant sub-group are Cubans sympathetic to the communist regime in Cuba. A "reasonable representative" of this group would be reasonably likely to be offended, as a revered figure to this group is being impugned.[616] The other exemptions under Section 18D do not apply because (i) the person posting has a reputation as a "habitual troll"; (ii) the person wanted to provoke outrage (as opposed to adopting a "harm minimisation" approach in their post), thereby not meeting the requirement for the post to be in good faith;[617] (iii) the "trolling" may also have been unreasonable, given that it is a gratuitous intrusion on a website run by and for Cuban expatriates sympathetic to Cuba's communist regime; and (iv) the post cannot be construed as an opinion but as a bare statement of fact, hence making fair comment unavailable.[618]

However, *Guevara actually said this*.[619] It is a historical fact. Further, it is a fact that Guevara's admirers should know about him, even if it is pointed out by a smartarse. However, truth is not available as a defence under s 18C.

The perpetuation of "flattering falsehoods" by, in effect, penalising truth is not compatible with the maintenance of the constitutionally prescribed system of representative and responsible government. In such a system, truth should be defence to any cause of action that directly affects the implied freedom of political communication.

5   *The operation of s 18C and s 18D*

Sections 18C and s 18D not only burden the freedom of political communication implied from the *Commonwealth Constitution* by their terms. Their operation also burdens this freedom. Hence, it is necessary to review the conciliation process

---

616 Ethnic or national identity may involve valuing or even revering historical events, historical figures, or both.
617 An interesting point regarding the 'harm minimisation' approach in this scenario is this: would the person posting the quoted comment be obliged to include evidence that Guevara may have recanted these views? If someone is so obliged, and case law concerning harm minimisation suggests that they might be (see above at Part V.D.4.(a) (pages 160-1)), then this illustrates the burden that s 18C and s 18D places on the implied freedom of political communication. (For evidence that Guevara may have recanted his views see: Amy Sherman, 'Did Che Guevara write "extensively" about the superiority of white Europeans? Rubio says yes', *Poltifact* (online), 17 April 2013.)
618 Aside from fair comment being unavailable, the lack of good faith and reasonableness would make every other defence in s 18D unavailable.
619 Ernesto Che Guevara, *The Motorcycle Diaries: Notes on a Latin American Journey* (Ocean Press, 2003) 161.

as well as the powers of the AHRC, the Federal Court and the Federal Circuit Court.

Before going further, we should emphasise that our critique of AHRC processes concerning s 18C does not mean we think the AHRC is unnecessary. On the contrary, we think the AHRC does important work in redressing harassment and discrimination in employment, education and accessing accommodation, goods and services. What the AHRC should not be involved with, however, is investigating expression outside these areas, and especially expression about government and political matters.

(a)   A brief overview of the complaint process

The AHRC Act provides the procedure for handling breaches of the RDA. This process is as follows:

- A complaint is lodged with the AHRC.[620]
- The complaint is referred to the AHRC President.[621]
- The AHRC President inquires into the complaint.[622]
- If the matter is not terminated,[623] the AHRC conducts a conference[624] with the aim of conciliating the complaint.
- If the matter is not conciliated at the conference or at some later point, the AHRC President may terminate the complaint.[625]
- If the matter is terminated for any reason then the person complaining may apply to the Federal Court or Federal Circuit Court alleging unlawful discrimination.[626]

(b)   The powers of the AHRC

The AHRC through the AHRC President has the following powers when handling a complaint:

- Require a person to provide relevant information[627] or produce

---

[620] AHRC Act s 46P.
[621] AHRC Act s 46PD.
[622] AHRC Act s 46PF.
[623] The matter may be terminated prior to conciliation for reasons stated in AHRC Act s 46PH(1)(a)-(i).
[624] AHRC Act s 46PJ.
[625] AHRC Act s 46PH(i).
[626] AHRC Act s 46PO(1).
[627] AHRC Act s 46PI(2)(a).

relevant documents.[628]
- Direct the complainant(s) and the respondent(s) to attend a compulsory conference.[629]
- Direct any person able to provide relevant information,[630] or conducive to settling the matter,[631] to attend a compulsory conference.

If a person fails to attend to attend a compulsory conference as directed,[632] then they are subject to an offence of strict liability,[633] carrying a penalty of 10 penalty units.[634]

If a person refuses or fails to give information[635] or produce a document[636] then they are liable to a penalty of 10 penalty units.[637]

A person who knowingly gives false or misleading information to the AHRC, the AHRC President or any other person exercising powers or performing functions under the AHRC Act is liable for imprisonment for 6 months.[638]

(c) The powers of the Federal Court and the Federal Circuit Court

As noted above, if the AHRC President terminates a complaint then the person complaining may apply to the Federal Court or the Federal Circuit Court. The proceedings in these courts are civil (as opposed to criminal) proceedings and the civil standard of proof applies.

Ultimately, these courts have the power to order the following remedies:

- Grant an interim injunction to maintain the status quo[639] or the rights of a complainant, respondent or an affected person.[640]
- Declare that a respondent committed unlawful discrimination;[641]
- Direct a respondent not to repeat or continue such unlawful

---

628 AHRC Act s 46PI(2)(b).
629 AHRC Act s 46PJ(3).
630 AHRC Act s 46PJ(4)(a).
631 AHRC Act s 46PJ(4)(b).
632 AHRC Act s 46PJ(1)(a).
633 AHRC Act s 46PL(3).
634 AHRC Act s 46PL(1). A single penalty unit equals $170: Crimes Act s 4AA(1).
635 AHRC Act s 46PM(1)(a).
636 AHRC Act s 46PM(1)(b).
637 AHRC Act s 46PM(1).
638 AHRC Act s 46PN.
639 AHRC Act s 46PP(1)(a).
640 AHRC Act s 46PP(1)(b).
641 AHRC Act s 46PO(4)(a).

discrimination;[642]
- Direct the respondent perform any reasonable action to redress any loss or damage the applicant suffered;[643]
- Order the respondent employ or re-employ the applicant;[644]
- Order the respondent pay damages for any loss or damage the applicant suffered;[645]
- Order a respondent to vary the termination of a contract or agreement to address the applicant's loss or damage;[646] and/or
- Declare that it would be inappropriate for any further action to be taken in the matter.[647]

The Federal Court and the Federal Circuit Court are not bound by technicalities or legal forms.[648] This measure no doubt facilitates the swifter resolution of proceedings. That said, it is likely that proceedings for breaching the RDA require the following:

- Each party state their case in sufficient detail.
- Each party produce documentary evidence and witness statements; and
- Each party examine and cross-examine witnesses at a hearing.

It has been said that civil proceedings are less serious than criminal proceedings, thereby imposing less of a burden on free speech. However, civil proceedings under the RDA impose burdens on free speech that, while different from the criminal process, are nevertheless serious. Unlike criminal proceedings, a lower standard of proof is required. There is no prosecutorial discretion on the part of the government to drop a case. Rather, it is up to those complaining to decide to bring proceedings. The respondent incurs costs in time, money and stress in meeting cases. Ultimately, if a remedy is awarded, it is enforceable by the government.

In *Theophanous v Herald & Weekly Times Ltd*,[649] Mason CJ, Toohey and Gaudron JJ noted that civil proceedings for defamation could chill discussions even more effectively than criminal proceedings. They cited with approval the

---
642 Ibid.
643 AHRC Act s 46PO(4)(b).
644 AHRC Act s 46PO(4)(c).
645 AHRC Act s 46PO(4)(d).
646 AHRC Act s 46PO(4)(e).
647 AHRC Act s 46PO(4)(f).
648 AHRC Act s 46PR.
649 [1994] HCA 46; (1994) 182 CLR 104 (*'Theophanous'*).

following statement in *City of Chicago v Tribune Co*:[650]

> While in the early history of the struggle for freedom of speech the restrictions were enforced by criminal prosecutions, it is clear that a civil action is as great, if not a greater, restriction than a criminal prosecution. If the right to criticize the government is a privilege which ... cannot be restricted, then all civil as well as criminal actions are forbidden. A despotic or corrupt government can more easily stifle opposition by a series of civil actions than by criminal prosecutions.[651]

They also cited with approval the following statement from *Derbyshire C.C. v Times Newspapers*:[652]

> While these decisions [in *Tribune Co* and *New York Times Co. v Sullivan*[653]] were related most directly to the provisions of the American Constitution concerned with securing freedom of speech, the public interest considerations which underlaid them are no less valid in [England]. What has been described as 'the chilling effect' induced by the threat of civil actions for libel is very important. Quite often the facts which would justify a defamatory publication are known to be true, but admissible evidence capable of proving those facts is not available.[654]

They commented:

> The statements quoted above, as well as the decision in *Sullivan*, speak eloquently of the tendency of the law of defamation to inhibit the exercise of the freedom of communication – 'the chilling effect' - in the United States and the United Kingdom. In Australia also the existence of that tendency has been noted.[655]

Chief Justice Mason, Toohey and Gaudron JJ noted that the defences of truth, privilege and fair comment had been developed to balance the public interest in freedom of speech and the public interest in protecting individual reputation.[656] However, they also noted that these defences had not been developed in view of the implied freedom of political communication, and

---

650 (1923) 139 NE 86 (*'Tribune Co'*).
651 *Tribune Co* (1923) 139 NE 86, 90 (Thompson CJ); *Theophanous* [1994] HCA 46; (1994) 182 CLR 104, 130-1 (Mason CJ, Toohey and Gaudron JJ).
652 [1993] AC 534 (*'Derbyshire'*).
653 (1964) 376 US 254.
654 *Derbyshire* [1993] AC 534, 548 (Lord Keith); *Theophanous* [1994] HCA 46; (1994) 182 CLR 104, 131 (Mason CJ, Toohey and Gaudron JJ).
655 *Theophanous* [1994] HCA 46; (1994) 182 CLR 104, 131 (Mason CJ, Toohey and Gaudron JJ) (citations omitted).
656 Ibid 131-2.

that these defences may be inconsistent with this freedom.⁶⁵⁷ They observed:

> The common law defences of fair comment and qualified privilege are not always available. Fair comment is available only for the expression of opinion and, then, only if the comment is based on facts which are notorious or truly stated. Qualified privilege depends on the absence of malice and on the person who makes the communication having an interest or duty in its making and on the recipient having a corresponding interest or duty in receiving it. The requirement for reciprocity of interest has the effect that common law qualified privilege is usually not available where the information has been disseminated to the public generally… Thus the need to prove truth can often arise in practice.⁶⁵⁸

However, they also observed with regard to the defence of truth:

> It is often difficult to prove the truth of the alleged libel in all its particulars. And the necessity of proving truth as a defence may well deter a critic from voicing criticism, even if it be true, because of doubt whether it can be proved or fear of the expense of having to do so.⁶⁵⁹

Of course, truth is not an exemption provided in s 18D. The absence of this exemption is a critical defect to the operation of s 18C. As Mason CJ, Toohey and Gaudron JJ noted, the defence of truth is necessary given the difficulties with fair comment – considerations that apply equally to the exemption for fair comment provided in s 18D. That said, even if truth was available in s 18D, the doubts about proving truth, the fear of incurring expense to prove truth, or both, also apply to this exemption. Thus, these doubts and fears would create a chilling effect. Further, in our view, the chilling effect of such doubts and fears apply to other defences to defamation and, by analogy, to the other exemptions in s 18D.

Hence, it is not only the terms of s 18C and s 18D that impose burdens on the implied freedom of political communication. Putting aside any remedies ultimately awarded, the operation of these sections also imposes substantial burdens in time, money and stress. As columnist Mark Steyn has noted concerning such cases 'the process is the punishment'.⁶⁶⁰

We now illustrate the foregoing with several examples.

(i)   Eatock

---

657 Ibid 132.
658 Ibid 133.
659 Ibid 132.
660 Mark Steyn, 'Lars Hedegaard, Defender of Freedom', *SteynOnline* (online), 16 December 2014.

Eatock is perhaps the most high-profile s 18C case. In this case, the Federal Court found that Andrew Bolt had breached s 18C when the *Herald Sun* (the paper for which he wrote) published two articles in which he was critical of certain people with Aboriginal heritage claiming employment or assistance meant for people of Aboriginal heritage.

The Federal Court did not award damages. However, among the other things the Federal Court ordered were the following:

1. That a corrective notice be printed adjacent to the two articles;
2. Andrew Bolt and the Herald and Weekly Times Pty Ltd (the publishers of the *Herald Sun*) pay the bulk of the applicant Pat Eatock's legal costs of the proceedings.[661]

Adrienne Stone has commented that the remedy provided in *Eatock* was expressive rather than coercive. That is, instead of awarding damages, 'the state signal[ed] its disapproval of the message conveyed'.[662] Stone goes on to note that 'in his response to the decision, Bolt wrote "Silencing Me Impedes Unity", a commentary in which he argues that his ideas have been "banned" and yet goes on to repeat, at quite some length, his argument that Aboriginal people of mixed heritage should not claim Aboriginal identity.'[663]

We have two points in response. First, that damages were not awarded does *not* mean no costs were incurred. *Eatock* was a Federal Court trial which lasted seven days and at which Queens Counsel represented each side.[664] We can safely surmise that The Herald and Weekly Times Pty Ltd spent a low six-figure sum in legal fees to defend the action (and we are being somewhat optimistic with this estimate). Further, given the Federal Court is a "loser pays" jurisdiction, Andrew Bolt and The Herald and Weekly Times Pty Ltd were liable to pay Ms Eatock's legal costs. Ms Eatock's legal costs would also be a low six-figure sum. Most people simply cannot afford to defend such an action in court. Even well-funded companies and individuals would prefer to spend their money elsewhere. The prospect of incurring legal costs alone creates a chilling effect.

Second, while Bolt did comment on the decision in *Eatock*, there appear to be occasions subsequent to the decision where he was deterred from

---

661 *Eatock v Bolt (No 2)* [2011] FCA 1180.
662 Adrienne Stone, 'The Ironic Aftermath of *Eatock v Bolt*' (2015) 38 *Melbourne University Law Review* 926, 939.
663 Ibid 938-9.
664 See the headnote of *Eatock v Bolt* [2011] FCA 1103; (2011) 197 FCR 261.

commenting on a matter involving race.[665] With respect, the evidence suggests that the decision had a chilling effect.[666]

(ii)   Prior v Queensland University of Technology

At the time of writing, this case is before the Federal Circuit Court.[667] According to reports and documents filed in the Federal Circuit Court,[668] three students entered a computer laboratory at the Queensland University of Technology ('QUT'). Cynthia Prior, a QUT employee, asked the students whether they were indigenous. The students said they weren't. Prior then asked the students to leave the computer laboratory because it was for indigenous students, and there were other places on the QUT campus that the students could use. The students left.

Later, comments appeared regarding the incident on "QUT Stalkerspace", a Facebook webpage. The comments included the following:

- A QUT student commented 'Just got kicked out of the unsigned Indigenous computer room. QUT stopping segregation with segregation'.[669]
- Another QUT student commented 'I wonder where the white supremacist computer lab is'. And later, in response to other posts, 'It's white supremacist, get it right. We don't like to be affiliated with those hill-billies', and '… today's your lucky day, join the white

---

665 See, for example, Andrew Bolt, 'I wish I could say more, but this is dangerous', *Herald Sun* (online), 4 April 2012, Andrew Bolt, 'No comments', *Herald Sun* (online), 8 April 2012; Andrew Bolt, 'No comment', *Herald Sun* (online), 13 October 2012; Andrew Bolt, 'My own words can be quoted, but not by me', *Herald Sun* (online), 25 February 2013 ; and Andrew Bolt, 'No comment from me, but pray Dallas may discuss' *Herald Sun* (online), 26 March 2013.
666 In case anyone is wondering: no, we are not Bolt boosters. The Bolt articles we have cited are relevant to s 18C's effect, and were easily located on the *Herald Sun* website. Stone also notes that the campaign against s 18C was selective: s 18C was criticised, but not laws with equal or greater impact, such as defamation: Adrienne Stone, 'The Ironic Aftermath of *Eatock v Bolt*' (2015) 38 *Melbourne University Law Review* 926, 941. As we have noted elsewhere in this treatise, the chilling effect of defamation law has long been of concern in law. For the record, we are concerned about any law that chills freedom of expression. Given our argument that the implied freedom of political communication is a strong freedom, defamation law as well as other laws directly affecting this freedom may well need to be reconsidered.
667 *Prior v Queensland University of Technology & Ors*, Federal Circuit Court of Australia Case no. BRG990/2015.
668 See below.
669 Hedley Thomas, 'QUT Oodgeroo Unit race row: staffer "aggressive, unpleasant"', *The Australian* (online), 23 February 2016.

supremacist group and we'll take care of your every need.'⁶⁷⁰
- Another QUT student commented 'ITT niggers'.⁶⁷¹
- A QUT lecturer commented that it 'seems a bit silly to kick someone out of an indigenous computer lab for not being indigenous when there are computers not being used.' The QUT lecturer further noted that Prior may be in breach of QUT policy by asking the students whether they were indigenous.⁶⁷²
- Another QUT student commented to the effect that a computer lab for indigenous students encouraged division and was 'more retarded than a women's collective'.⁶⁷³
- Another QUT student commented 'Whatever, im pierce (sic), I've got so much casual racism I need to let it out of my system'.⁶⁷⁴
- Another QUT student commented:

> My Student and Amenity Fees are going to furbish rooms in the university where inequality reigns supreme? I believe if we have to pay to support these sorts of places, there should be at least be more created for general purpose use, but again, how does these sorts of facilities support interaction and community within QUT? All this does is encourage separation and inequality.⁶⁷⁵

The student continued:

> The psychology of living in the past is dangerous, and these 'disadvantaged' people will only stay in their given 'seat' in society if that situation is reinforced.⁶⁷⁶

After comments with similar tone and content to their comments

---

670 The student alleged to have made these comments has denied that anyone reading them in context would find them offensive, insulting, humiliating or intimidating: see Hedley Thomas, 'Racial stoush erupts over QUT computer lab', *The Australian* (online), 4 February 2016. The student has said that he was making these comments ironically: Hedley Thomas, 'Watchdog kept 18C respondent in dark about QUT complaint', *The Australian* (online), 8 February 2016.
671 This is the most incendiary comment. However, the student alleged to have made this comment strongly denies having made it: see Hedley Thomas, 'Offer to drop QUT race "slur" case for $5,000', *The Australian* (online), 5 February 2016.
672 Hedley Thomas, 'Racial stoush erupts over QUT computer lab', *The Australian* (online), 4 February 2016.
673 Hedley Thomas, 'Offer to drop QUT race "slur" case for $5,000', *The Australian* (online), 5 February 2016.
674 *Prior v Queensland University of Technology & Ors*, Federal Circuit Court of Australia Case no. BRG990/2015.
675 Ibid.
676 Ibid.

quoted above, the student concluded:

> [T]here is a hypocrisy and bureaucratic taint in all attempts at making 'special' things for people who are 'deemed unequal' in order 'to help make them equal'. If you deem them unequal, well those poor bastards have no hope now. You've tainted them. I think the worst thing to do to a human is to tell them they are unequal. They will forever doubt their integrity and ability…[677]

Some of the comments were mild; some weren't.[678] However, all concerned a matter of public concern: whether publicly-funded universities should set aside facilities for the use of particular racial groups.

However, staff and students are now subject to a claim for $247,570.52 for, amongst other things, breaching s 18C.[679] It should be noted that in this case some students have settled – even though s 18D's exemptions appear to apply to them – because they cannot afford to defend themselves in court.[680] At least one student appears to have had to represent themselves because they cannot afford legal representation.[681]

(iii) Islamic Council of Victoria v Catch the Fire Ministries, Inc

This is an example from related legislation.[682] Paul Sheehan reported:

> The Equal Opportunity Commission [of Victoria] hired May Helou, of the Islamic Council of Victoria, to begin a large program advising

---

677 Ibid.
678 The 'ITT' comment is the most controversial. The n-word is a vile racial epithet (and we will refrain from expressly stating it from now on, as we do not like using the term). But what does 'ITT' mean? The abbreviation appears to be slang, and according to the *Urban Dictionary* has a number of meanings including, perhaps most relevantly 'in this thread' see *Urban Dictionary* (online), 2 May 2003. If this is the case, then the comment is indeed incredibly abusive albeit apparently directed at others on the thread. (We add that the fact that a comment was directed at another person does not stop someone bringing an claim under s 18C.) There are also a number of other definitions of 'ITT' ranging from 'intense testicular tension' to 'I'd tap that': see ibid. If one of these other meanings was intended, then at the very least the comment remains incredibly crude. However, with respect to all these variations in meaning, would it make a difference to the commenter's legal liability under s 18C if the commenter was black? Some black people use the n-word as slang. This recalls the concerns we raised in Part IV.E.2 (pages 53-6). That there is no straightforward answer to this question is a major problem with s 18C.
679 Hedley Thomas, 'Racial stoush erupts over QUT computer lab', *The Australian* (online), 4 February 2016. Two QUT staff members, along with QUT itself, are facing claims under other provisions of the RDA.
680 Hedley Thomas, 'Offer to drop QUT race "slur" case for $5,000', *The Australian* (online), 5 February 2016 .
681 Ibid.
682 *Racial and Religious Tolerance Act 2001* (Vic).

Muslims of their rights under the new anti-vilification law. It was Helou who recruited three Muslims to attend a seminar, "The Nature Of Islam", organised by Catch The Fire Ministries, a national, non-denominational evangelical group.

After attending the seminar, the three observers prepared a 52-count complaint for the Islamic Council of Victoria. The council then lodged the complaint with the Equal Opportunity Commission against the ministry and two of its pastors, thus completing the ideological circle between bureaucratic agitation and litigation.

A mediation session was arranged. It lasted seven hours and 40 minutes. It produced an ideological impasse. The Islamic Council commenced legal proceedings. Hearings began in the Victorian Civil and Administrative Tribunal in October last year. The hearings went for 40 days, spread over nine months. Final submissions were made in June. The maximum penalties under the act are a $30,000 fine and six months' jail. However, the prospect of jailing people for their religious beliefs has proved so divisive that Judge Michael Higgins felt obliged to announce he saw no grounds to jail anyone.[683]

Here, the parties ultimately settled. However, before this, the matter went to a hearing,[684] and then to an appeal.[685] Sheehan noted the costs:

> The price for [Catch the Fire's] views, so far, has been $300,000 in legal costs. The ministries' solicitors, acting *pro bono*, assess their costs at $400,000. With the costs of the complainant, plus the publicly funded cost of the hearings, total legal costs exceed $1 million.[686]

If these cases are victories for laws promoting tolerance, then they are victories that make Pyrrhus look good.[687]

(iv) Overview

The excessive cost of litigation can easily result in the denial of justice. Since it may lie far beyond the financial capacity of most individuals and small

---

683 Paul Sheehan, 'Spreading the Word of Intolerance', *Sydney Morning Herald* (online), 4 October 2004.
684 [2004] VCAT 2510.
685 *Catch the Fire Ministries, Inc v Islamic Council of Victoria* [2006] VSCA 284.
686 Paul Sheehan, 'Spreading the Word of Intolerance', *Sydney Morning Herald* (online), 4 October 2004.
687 For a full analysis of this case, see: Augusto Zimmermann, 'The Constitutionality of Religious Vilification Laws in Australia: Why Religious Vilification Laws are Contrary to the Implied Freedom of Political Communication Affirmed in the Australian Constitution' (2013) *Brigham Young University Law Review* 457, 461-8.

organisations, defendants accused of discrimination may be compelled to settle cases with unfair concessions in the hope of avoiding costly litigation. This is in itself a form of punishment and a further denial of freedom of expression, meaning that the most vulnerable in this battleground are those who lack the resources and organisational clout to fund litigation.

6 *How does s 18C's effect on discussion of political matters compare with other protective legislation?*

At this point, it is useful to compare s 18C with other protective laws. The most obvious comparison is to other anti-discrimination laws and defamation laws.[688] We will also consider other legislation, specifically child pornography and consumer protection legislation, as comparisons were made to these laws in debates concerning the RHB.[689]

---

688 Soutphommasane has pointed out other examples where speech is restricted. Noting that Australian Parliaments all have standing orders addressed to the use of offensive words or language, he asks 'Why is it acceptable for parliamentarians to object to merely offensive language, but not for others to object to speech that offends, insults, humiliates or intimidates because of race?': Tim Soutphommasane, *I'm Not Racist, But... 40 Years of the Racial Discrimination Act* (University of New South Wales Press, 2015) Kindle Ebook Location 1588. With respect, Parliamentary standing orders are far narrower in application than s 18C. Only a limited number of people are affected, that is, the members of the respective Australian Parliament. By contrast, s 18C affects everyone in Australia. Further, there is some justification for order to be kept in Parliaments so they can deal with many items of often contentious business in the limited time they have at each sitting. (Although, echoing Kirby J's observation in *Coleman*, Parliamentary decorum is often honoured more in the breach than in the observance: *Coleman* [2004] HCA 25; (2004) 220 CLR 1, 91 [238]-[239] (Kirby J).) The Australian people as sovereign are not so limited in their discussions of government or political matters. Soutphommasane then asks: 'Where is the public outrage about all the offensive language provisions in the various criminal summary offences legislation that exist in New South Wales, Queensland, Victoria, South Australia, Tasmania and the Northern Territory. If there is to be such zealous interest in freedom of expression in Australia, surely attention would be properly devoted to summary offence laws that impose fines and possible sentences of community work or imprisonment on the use of merely offensive language': see Tim Soutphommasane, *I'm Not Racist, But... 40 Years of the Racial Discrimination Act* (University of New South Wales Press, 2015) Kindle Ebook Location 1589. There are several points in answer. First, these statutes are laws of equal application. They do not purport to make distinctions based on race, colour, ethnicity and nationality. They may, therefore, be more palatable to a society that values, amongst other things, equality before the law. Second, these laws apply to all manner of abusive speech, not just racist speech. Third, these laws *are* being reviewed because of their potential effect on communication about government and political matters. For example, in *Coleman*, a majority of the High Court overturned a conviction under the *Vagrants, Gaming and Other Offences Act 1931* (Qld) regarding the use of insulting words. In overturning the conviction, the majority held that the relevant provisions concerning insulting words should be interpreted narrowly: see *Coleman* [2004] HCA 25; (2004) 220 CLR 1. Also, in *Monis*, the High Court was split concerning whether the *Criminal Code 1995* (Cth) s 471.12, which prohibited sending offensive material through the post, was constitutional: see *Monis* [2013] HCA 4; (2013) 249 CLR 92.

689 See, for example, Commonwealth of Australia, *Parliamentary Debates*, House of Representatives, 15 November 1994, 3337 (Michael Lavarch), 3348 (Garrie Gibson), 3355 (Lindsay Tanner).

(a) Sexual harassment

Sexual harassment under the *Sex Discrimination Act 1984* (Cth) ('SDA') is confined to conduct directed towards an individual.[690] This conduct involves unwelcome sexual advances,[691] unwelcome requests for sexual favours,[692] or other conduct of a sexual nature.[693] This conduct must be such that a reasonable person in all the circumstances would anticipate the possibility of the person subjected to it being offended, humiliated or intimidated.[694]

Further, the SDA applies to specific situations. The SDA prohibits sexual harassment in employment situations,[695] accreditation bodies,[696] organisations registered under the *Fair Work (Registered Organisations) Act 2009* (Cth),[697] employment agencies,[698] educational institutions,[699] providing or seeking goods, services or facilities,[700] providing accommodation,[701] disposing or acquiring land,[702] clubs,[703] or performing any power under or administering a Commonwealth law or program.[704]

Given its terms, it is difficult to see how prohibiting sexual harassment burdens the implied freedom of political communication. Discussing government or political matters in ways relevant to this freedom would not involve making unwanted sexual advances to someone, requesting sexual favours from someone or engaging in conduct of a sexual nature towards someone.[705] By contrast, discussing government or political matters concerning

---

690 SDA s 28A(1).
691 SDA s 28A(1)(a).
692 Ibid.
693 SDA s 28(1)(b).
694 SDA s 28(1).
695 SDA s 28B.
696 SDA s 28C.
697 SDA s 28D.
698 SDA s 28E.
699 SDA s 28F.
700 SDA s 28G.
701 SDA s 28H.
702 SDA s 28J.
703 SDA s 28K.
704 SDA s 28L.
705 This is not to rule out situations where sex and politics may mix. We will not speculate about how such situations may arise, except to say that if sexual harassment prohibited under the SDA arose in a political context (however conceived), it is almost certain that, because of its personal and limited effect, SDA s 28A(1) would be held to serve a legitimate end, and be reasonably appropriate and adapted to a legitimate end in a manner compatible with the implied freedom of political communication.

race, colour, or national or ethnic origin may quite easily result in someone feeling offended, insulted or humiliated.

(b)   Harassment on grounds of disability

Similarly, the DDA is confined in its operation. The DDA prohibits harassment of a person in relation to that person's disability in employment situations,[706] education,[707] or providing goods, services or facilities.[708] Like the SDA, discussing government or political matters in ways relevant to the implied freedom of political communication would not entail discussing a person's disability.[709]

(c)   Defamation

There are two aspects of the action for defamation[710] that are relevant here. One is defamation of individuals. There other is so-called "group defamation" or "group libel".

(i)   The individual action

In Australia, defamation can be a civil claim or a criminal charge. However, both the civil claim and the criminal charge are concerned with protecting an

---

706 DDA s 35.
707 DDA s 37.
708 DDA s 39.
709 There may be situations that involve commenting about someone's disability when discussing politics. For example, suppose in a workplace an employee knew that a fellow employee suffered a mental illness and commented "no wonder you're crazy, you vote [Greens/Labor/Liberal]" and a complaint under the DDA was lodged. In this and similar situations the DDA may burden the implied freedom of political communication. However, it is certain that the DDA would be held to serve a legitimate end, and was reasonably appropriate and adapted to a legitimate end in a manner compatible with the implied freedom of political communication. The DDA's burden on the implied freedom is at best incidental.
710 As to defamation, and further to the questions that we quoted above concerning parliamentary and criminal prohibitions on offensive language, Soutphommasane asks 'And, if we were to identify areas of the law that may seriously impinge on freedom of speech, why do champions of absolutist free speech not appear to be troubled by the impact of the law of defamation?': see Tim Soutphommasane, *I'm Not Racist, But… 40 Years of the Racial Discrimination Act* (University of New South Wales Press, 2015) Kindle Ebook Location 1599. With respect, the effect of defamation law on freedom of expression has long been the subject of considerable concern in law: see, for example, Australian Law Reform Commission, *Unfair Publication: Defamation and privacy*, Report No 11 (1979) 17-8 [30]-[31]; Western Australian Law Reform Commission, *Defamation*, Project No 8 – Part II (1979) 15-17 [2.1]-[2.7]. Further, Soutphommasane's phrase 'absolutist free speech' appears to conflate free speech with its historical antagonist, absolutism. Historically, proponents of free speech have set their face against absolutism, be it religious, moral or political absolutism. Here's a tip: in any debate, the more a position relies upon telling someone to be quiet, the more absolutist it is.

individual's reputation.

It is important to keep in mind the personal nature of the defamation action: it is the *individual's* reputation that is damaged; it is *their* standing in the community that is lowered; it is *they* who are being exposed to ridicule or contempt; and it is *their* capacity to earn income that is threatened.[711] Even then, a person must suffer damage to their reputation without remedy if a statement about them is true, fair comment or is otherwise privileged.[712]

As to criminal defamation, the ALRC noted the following about the rationale for its retention:

> There is force in the argument of those advocating total abolition of criminal libel. The use of the criminal law to punish the expression of opinion was one of the less attractive features of the English common law. Criminal libel was, in earlier days, repressively used to inhibit free speech and, particularly, attacks on government. Nonetheless a majority of the Commission favours the retention in a restricted form of some criminal sanction... [T]he majority feels that the publication of a libel may cause serious harm to *an individual*... [C]ases may be imagined in which no civil remedy is adequate. They will include cases where the publisher in bankrupt or has no means at all to meet a verdict. A criminal sanction to deter such cases is justified.[713]

(ii) The group action

In Australia, an allegation against a group is not actionable in defamation unless this allegation is referable to an individual within that group.[714] The common law has not allowed civil sanctions for vilifying classes of people 'distinguishable by race, colour, creed or calling... in part for fear of unduly

---

711 Members of the High Court cited with approval the following passage from Spencer Bower concerning the breadth of an individual's reputation: "'[T]he esteem in which he is held, or the goodwill entertained towards him, or the confidence reposed in him by other persons, whether in respect of his personal character, his private or domestic life, his public, social, professional, or business qualifications, qualities, competence, dealings, conduct, or status, or his financial credit ...'": Spencer Bower, *A Code of the Law for Actionable Defamation* (Butterworth, 2nd ed, 1923) 3 cited in *Radio 2UE Sydney Pty Ltd v Chesterton* [2009] HCA 16; (2009) 238 CLR 460, 466 [2] (French CJ, Gummow, Kiefel and Bell JJ) ('*Radio 2UE*').
712 See for example, the defences in the *Defamation Act 2005* (WA) pt 4 div 2; see also the *Criminal Code 1913* (WA) s 345(3). Australia now has uniform defamation laws, so the legislation in WA is emblematic of legislation elsewhere in Australia.
713 Australian Law Reform Commission, *Unfair Publication: Defamation and privacy*, Report No 11 (1979) 105 [203] (emphasis ours).
714 *David Syme & Co v Canavan* [1918] HCA 50; (1918) 25 CLR 234, 238.

inhibiting political discussion and criticism'.⁷¹⁵

In addition, we noted above that one aspect of Australia's system of representative and responsible government was that legislative and executive action was primarily directed towards *groups* of people.⁷¹⁶ The implied freedom of political communication would therefore extend to protecting discussions about groups who are or may be subject to legislative or executive action.⁷¹⁷

That said, Jeremy Waldron has argued for laws prohibiting racial hatred on the basis of group libel. The basis of legislation would not be protection of individual reputation but upholding and vindicating the legal and social status of citizens as a matter of public order. These laws:

> ...are set up to vindicate public order , not just by pre-empting violence, but by upholding against attack a shared public sense of the basic elements of each person's status, dignity and reputation as a citizen or member of society in good standing – particularly against the characteristic of some particular social group.⁷¹⁸

With respect, Waldron's proposal suffers from a number of fundamental problems. First, despite Waldron's call for 'well drafted' hate speech laws,⁷¹⁹ such laws pose considerable drafting difficulties of the kind we noted above.⁷²⁰

Second, Waldron's justification for group libel rests on a public order basis. That is, the concern is not so much protecting individual reputation but public order. However, this basis for defamation is now regarded as anachronistic. Criminal defamation was used to preserve public order.⁷²¹ However, as noted above, criminal defamation had a sorry history of being used to repress free speech.⁷²² As to using criminal libel to maintain public order, the New Zealand

---

715 Australian Law Reform Commission, *Unfair Publication: Defamation and privacy*, Report No 11 (1979) 52-3 [95] quoting John G Fleming, *The Law of Torts* (Law Book Company, 5ᵗʰ ed, 1977) 536.
716 See Part V.B.2 (page 121).
717 Ultimately, in a democracy, individuals must be able to say that a group is wrong. Hence, laws restricting an individual's capacity to do so may be restricted under the implied freedom of political communication.
718 Jeremy Waldron 'Dignity and Defamation: The Visibility of Hate' (2010) 123 *Harvard Law Review* 1596, 1605. See also Jeremy Waldron, *The Harm in Hate Speech* (Harvard University Press, 2012) 47.
719 It is worth reiterating that Waldron rejects using offence in hate speech laws: see ibid 1613; see also Jeremy Waldron, *The Harm in Hate Speech* (Harvard University Press, 2012) 105-8. Somewhat curiously, in 'Dignity and Defamation' Waldron later praises s 18C despite it making unlawful acts that offend based on race, colour, ethnicity and nationality: see Jeremy Waldron 'Dignity and Defamation: The Visibility of Hate' (2010) 123 *Harvard Law Review* 1596, 1645-6.
720 See Part IV.E.1.(b).(ii) (pages 40-2).
721 Australian Law Reform Commission, *Unfair Publication: Defamation and privacy*, Report No 11 (1979) 105 [203].
722 Ibid 102 [194].

Committee on Defamation concluded that other statutory provisions better dealt with breaches of the peace.[723] Other law reform bodies have recommended the retention of criminal libel only on the basis that it protects *individual reputation* in situations where the civil action for defamation may not.[724]

Further, maintaining public order is not a sufficient reason to restrict freedom of expression, even if it protects 'each person's status, dignity and reputation as a citizen or member of society in good standing'.[725] As we noted above, there must be a clear and compelling (if not overwhelming) case to restrict freedom of expression.[726] This is met when allegations have been made against a specific individual such that it would cause ordinary, reasonable, fair-minded people to lower their estimation of that individual.[727] An individual's right to protect their reputation justifies the restriction of freedom of expression (though, to reiterate, even here the individual has no recourse if the allegations are true, fair comment or otherwise privileged).

Unlike individuals, groups are not capable of possessing a reputation. The best that can be is that a group is comprised of individuals who *are* capable of possessing a reputation. However, the attack on an individual's reputation as part of a group is different in kind and degree than a direct attack on an individual's reputation. The individual is not being singled out. The individual may not in fact have the qualities being attributed to the group. Further, the fact that freedom of expression is being restricted for the sake of a group cannot be ignored. Once again, there is a risk of unduly inhibiting political discussion and criticism, and Australia's system of representative and responsible government requires discussion of groups that have been or may be the subject of legislative or executive action.

---

723 The Committee on Defamation (New Zealand) noted: '[Criminal defamation's] functions in the criminal law are now catered for by other statutory provisions or are outside the scope of other criminal offences and it is a harsh provision from the point of view of the defendant. The most compelling reason for its abolition, in our view, is that the civil action for defamation is provides adequate protection for defamatory statements and renders criminal action superfluous.' Committee on Defamation, Recommendations on the Law of Defamation (1977) [447]-[448] cited in Australian Law Reform Commission, *Unfair Publication: Defamation and privacy*, Report No 11 (1979) 105 [202].
724 See Australian Law Reform Commission, *Unfair Publication: Defamation and privacy*, Report No 11 (1979) 105 [203]; see also Western Australian Law Reform Commission, *Defamation*, Project No 8 – Part II (1979) 107 [22.5].
725 Jeremy Waldron 'Dignity and Defamation: The Visibility of Hate' (2010) 123 *Harvard Law Review* 1596, 1605.
726 See Part V.C.2 (page 126).
727 *Radio 2UE* [2009] HCA 16; (2009) 238 CLR 460, 467 [6] (French CJ, Gummow, Kiefel and Bell JJ) (citations omitted).

(d) Child pornography

Laws against the production and distribution of child pornography are narrowly confined.[728] These laws protect children, who cannot consent to the exploitation to which they are subjected. Further, prohibiting the production and distribution of child pornography does not affect discussion about government or political matters.

(e) Consumer protection

Consumer protection laws also have narrow application. For example, laws prohibiting misleading or deceptive conduct or unconscionable conduct are confined to the provision of goods or services.[729] Further, prohibiting these activities does not affect discussion about government or political matters.

(f) An overview

Most of the protective laws examined above have only an incidental impact (if any) on the implied freedom of political communication. They also have a far narrower scope than s 18C. Unlike s 18C, conduct prohibited by these laws is directed a person affected by that conduct, not a group. Sexual harassment is directed at a person; harassment on the ground of disability is directed at a person; defamatory allegations concern a person; children are harmed in the production and distribution of child pornography; a person is harmed by being sold a defective good or service. In addition, unlike the legislation noted in this section, someone may breach s 18C even though no one is actually offended, insulted, humiliated or intimidated.

7 *The complexity of s 18C and s 18D*

(a) *An overview of the mechanism under s 18C*

The ALRC noted the following with regards to the complexity of defamation law and the need for simplicity:

> If defamation defies simplicity it nonetheless demands it. Defamation is an inhibition of an important freedom, freedom of speech. Accepting that publication which affects reputation should be subject to legal sanction it is desirable that the limits of the restriction should be clearly stated. If people are unable to understand and apply the laws themselves

---

728 *Criminal Code 1995* (Cth), div 273, ss 471.16, 471.17, 471.22, 474.19, 474.20, 474.24A.
729 *Competition and Consumer Act 2010* (Cth), sch 2, ss 18, 21.

one of two consequences may follow. Either they will publish the material without legal justification, effecting private damage, or else, in fear and uncertainty, they will restrain themselves from publication of material which might properly have been published and which the public is entitled to have...[730]

Given that s 18C concerns matters more general than individual reputation, we submit that the ALRC's comments apply with greater force to s 18C's complexity. When speaking publicly about an issue concerning race, colour, ethnicity or nationality, under s 18C and s 18D a person will need to undertake the following Rube Goldberg-like[731] exercise:

- Consider whether their act is public or private.
- Consider the circumstances in which they are acting, including their own race, colour, ethnicity or nationality.
- Consider whether their act is reasonably likely to offend, insult, humiliate or intimidate a person, group or sub-group of people. As to these groups or sub-groups, they must consider whether a reasonable representative of that group would be reasonably likely to be offended, insulted, humiliated or intimidated.
- Consider whether their act falls within an exception. Hence:
  o For an act done for a scientific, artistic or scientific purpose or other purpose in the public interest:
    - Consider whether the act is reasonable;
    - Consider whether the act is in good faith (and remember to take a harm minimisation approach);
    - Consider whether the act was in the course of any statement, publication, discussion or debate;
    - Consider whether the act was genuine;
    - For an act done for an other purpose in the public interest, consider whether the act is in fact in the public interest
  o For report of an event or matter of public interest:

---

[730] Australian Law Reform Commission, *Unfair Publication: Defamation and privacy*, Report No 11 (1979) 28 [49].
[731] Rube Goldberg devices (named after cartoonist and author Rube Goldberg) are complex mechanisms that perform simple tasks: Rube Goldberg, *Rube Goldberg Biography* (20 December 2014) Rube Goldberg: Home of the Official Rube Goldberg Machine Contests. To use such complexity to perform simple tasks is charming; to use it to regulate a fundamental freedom is perverse.

- Consider whether the report is reasonable;
- Consider whether the report is in good faith (and remember to take a harm minimisation approach);
- Consider whether the report is fair;
- Consider whether the report is accurate;
- Consider whether the report concerns an event or matter that is in fact in the public interest;
- Note that truth is not an exemption;
  - For a fair comment on an event or matter of public interest:
    - Consider whether the comment is reasonable;
    - Consider whether the comment is in good faith (and remember to take a harm minimisation approach);
    - Consider whether the comment is fair;
    - Consider whether the comment is in fact comment;
    - Consider the possibility that, if the comment is construed as a statement, then truth is not an exemption;
    - Consider whether the event or matter is in fact in the public interest;
    - Consider whether their comment is an expression of their genuine belief;
- Consider that, despite taking care to avoid offence, they may nevertheless be subject to state power for making a statement *that may not actually offend anyone.*[732]

If any or all of the foregoing exercise strikes one as odd, disturbing or even stupid then it should. This Kafkaesque farce is antithetical to any democracy worth the name, especially one with a common law legal tradition.

To be clear, we are not saying that the law cannot be complex where warranted. The point is: it is not warranted here. Sections 18C and 18D impose restrictions far more onerous than those imposed by other protective legislation.

(b) *Are s 18C and s 18D too vague?*

The analysis above raises another issue relevant to the constitutional validity of s 18C and s 18D: whether they are too vague to be constitutional.

---

[732] Further, if someone spontaneously acts without such prior consideration, then they will need to go through the preceding steps of the exercise if they are concerned about their actions after the event.

In *Keegstra*, McLachlin J in dissent noted the concept of vagueness as developed in United States constitutional law. Citing the works of Laurence Tribe, her Honour stated the following regarding vagueness:

> As a matter of due process, a law is void on its face if it is so vague that persons 'of common intelligence must necessarily guess at its meaning and differ as to its application'. Such vagueness occurs when a legislature states its proscriptions in terms so indefinite that the line between innocent and condemned conduct becomes a matter of guesswork.[733]

Her Honour noted:

> The rationale for invalidating statutes that are... vague is that they have a chilling effect on legitimate speech. Protection of free speech is regarded as such a strong value that legislation aimed at legitimate ends may be struck down, if also tends to inhibit protected speech.[734]

Dworkin noted the following regarding vague laws:

> Conviction under a vague criminal law offends the moral and political ideals of due process in two ways. First, it places a citizen in an unfair position of either acting at his peril or accepting a more stringent restriction on his life than the legislature may have authorized... it is not acceptable, as a model of social behavior, that in such cases he ought to assume the worst. Second, it gives power to the prosecutor and the courts to make criminal law, by opting for one or the other possible interpretations after the event. This is a delegation of authority that is inconsistent with our scheme of separation of powers.[735]

Lon Fuller, in arguing that vagueness is one of the eight ways for a law to fail,[736] stated:

> The desideratum of clarity represents one of the most essential ingredients of legality. Though this proposition is scarcely subject to challenge, I am not certain it is always understood what responsibilities are involved in meeting this demand.[737]

Fuller noted that legislation could impose standards like "good faith" and "due

---

733 *Keegstra* [1990] 3 SCR 697, 819 quoting Laurence Tribe, *American Constitutional Law* (Foundation Press, 2nd ed, 1988) 1033-4.
734 *Keegstra* [1990] 3 SCR 697, 819.
735 Ronald Dworkin, *Taking Rights Seriously* (Duckworth, 1977) 221-2.
736 Lon Fuller, *The Morality of Law* (Yale University Press, 1964).
737 Ibid 63 (citations omitted).

care" in appropriate circumstances.[738] However, he went on to note:

> [I]t is a serious mistake – and a mistake made constantly – to assume that, though the busy legislative draftsman can find no way of converting his objective into clearly stated rules, he can always safely delegate this this task to the courts or to special administrative tribunals. In fact, however, this depends on the nature of the problem with which the delegation is concerned. In commercial law, for example, requirements of 'fairness' can take on a definiteness of meaning from a body of commercial practice and from principles of conduct shared by a community of economic traders. But it would be a mistake to conclude from this that all human conflicts can be neatly contained by rules derived, case by case, from the standard of fairness.[739]

Further to Fuller's comments, we note that the range and complexity of matters subject to political discussion far exceed that encompassed by commercial law.

Of course, great care must be exercised in applying concepts relevant to US or Canadian constitutions to an Australian context. Indeed, we have criticised Bromberg J for not paying due regard to the differences between Canadian and Australian law. That said, we suggest vagueness is a concept useful to determining whether a law impermissibly infringes the implied freedom of political communication. This is because, first, these concepts are readily applicable to an analysis under the modified *Lange* test. The implied freedom of political communication is a restriction on lawmaking. It follows that laws that are too vague should be restricted.

On this point, we further note that the void for vagueness doctrine has been used in the United States to create 'an insulating buffer zone of added protection at the peripheries of several of the Bill of Rights freedoms', including freedom of speech.[740] The implied freedom of political communication does not protect freedom of expression as expansively as the First Amendment of the US Constitution. However, and as noted above, the implied freedom of political communication is a strong freedom. There is much to be said for erecting a 'buffer zone' around the implied freedom of political communication. Doing so encourages legislators to avoid enacting vague or overbroad legislation, and

---

738 Ibid 64.
739 Ibid.
740 Note, 'The Void for Vagueness Doctrine in the Supreme Court' (1960) *University of Pennsylvania Law Review* 67, 75.

to enact legislation that clearly prescribes prohibited conduct.[741]

Second, vagueness involves a principle stemming not just from US and Canadian constitutions but common law. This common law principle is due process.[742] In addition to procedural fairness (which arguably is common law due process' principal manifestation), due process involves certainty as to the law. That is, an individual must be certain what the law is in order to avoid unlawful conduct. As noted above, the common law shapes and is shaped by the *Commonwealth Constitution*. Hence, common law due process should inform whether a law impermissibly infringes the implied freedom of political communication.[743]

Third, while vagueness has been employed primarily against criminal laws, it has been used when analysing provisions that make certain activities unlawful.[744] Of particular relevance is McLachlin J's dissent in *Taylor v Canadian Human Rights Commission*.[745] *Taylor* concerned a civil provision: s 13(1) of the *Canadian Human Rights Act*. This section made unlawful discriminatory telephonic communication likely to expose any person to hatred or contempt on the basis of (amongst other things) race, national or ethnic origin. Relating her reasons back to *Keegstra*, McLachlin J noted:

> [Hatred and contempt] are vague and subjective, capable of extension should the interpreter be so inclined. Where does dislike leave off and hatred or contempt begin? The use of these words in s 13(1) opens the door to investigations and inquiries for matters which have more to do

---

741 We would prefer not to put this in another, more blunt way. However, we feel that the approach of some people who craft and interpret the law warrant it. The mark of a well-drafted law is not how clever it makes the drafter feel in drafting it, or the interpreter feel in interpreting it, but whether the layperson can readily understand it. The law is not made by lawyers, for lawyers; but by lawyers, for laypeople.

742 Following the approach of Isaacs J noted above, due process is one of the fundamental principles Australia has inherited. Its sources are not only 25 Edward I (1297) *Magna Carta* ch 29, but also 28 Edward III (1354) and 3 Charles I (1627) *Petition of Right*. As with the Magna Carta, the latter statutes are either received law in certain States, or applied by Imperial Acts legislation in other States.

743 This appears to be a situation that Brennan J described in *Re Bolton; Ex Parte Beane*: 'Many of our fundamental freedoms are guaranteed by ancient principles of the common law or by ancient statutes which are so much part of the accepted constitutional framework that their terms, if not their very existence, may be overlooked until a case arises which evokes their contemporary and undiminished force.': see *Re Bolton; Ex parte Beane* [1987] HCA 12; (1987) 162 CLR 514, 520-1 (Brennan J).

744 Note, 'The Void for Vagueness Doctrine in the Supreme Court' (1960) *University of Pennsylvania Law Review* 67, 77, 81-5.

745 [1990] 3 SCR 892 ('*Taylor*'). *Taylor* was decided along with *Keegstra*. Like *Keegstra*, the Canadian Supreme Court split 4:3, this time holding that s 13 of the *Canadian Human Rights Act* did not violate the Charter.

with dislike than discrimination. The phrase does not assist in sending a clear and precise indication to members of society as to what the limits of impugned speech are. In short, by using such vague, emotive terms without definition, the state necessarily incurs the risk of catching, within the ambit of the regulated area expression falling short of hatred.[746]

We suggest that her Honour's comments apply to s 18C's use of 'offend', 'insult' and 'humiliate'. McLachlin J continued:

> The breadth of the section is further widened by the absence of any requirement of intent or foreseeability of the actual promotion of hatred or contempt. While this is consistent with the remedial as opposed to the punitive focus of human rights legislation, it has the effect of extending the section's application. Any expression 'likely to expose' persons to hatred or contempt... regardless of whether the expression was intended or could be foreseen to have this effect.[747]

We further suggest that her Honour's remarks apply to s 18C's use of 'reasonably likely in the circumstances'. Her Honour said by way of conclusion on this point:

> [T]he chilling effect of leaving overbroad provisions "on the books" cannot be ignored. While the chilling effect of human rights legislation is likely to be less significant than that of criminal prohibition, the vagueness of the law means that it may well deter more conduct than can legitimately targeted, given its objectives.[748]

Section 18C is not a criminal provision. That said, s 18C makes unlawful an act, subjecting those breaching it to remedial action. Further, given the social opprobrium attached to racism, a court finding that someone has breached s 18C carries with it a significant stigma. In these circumstances, it is important that s 18C be clear so that people can avoid acting in a way that breaches it.

As we noted above, the law can be complex where warranted. However, s 18C is not directed to the merger of public companies. Rather, an individual may breach s 18C by the *mere act of speaking in public*. This is an area of the law that demands certainty and simplicity.

To be clear, we are not suggesting that US or Canadian principles concerning vagueness must be imported into the modified *Lange* test for s 18C and s 18D to be held unconstitutional. Our view is that, quite apart from any principle of vagueness derived wholly or partly from US or Canadian constitutional law,

---

746 *Taylor* [1990] SCR 892, 961-2.
747 Ibid 962.
748 Ibid.

s 18C and s 18D are too complex to be reasonably appropriate and adapted to the end they serve. However, we note that vagueness is a concept that has been considered in other common law jurisdictions and which may assist with resolving issues concerning s 18C, s 18D, or similar legislation.

(c)   A sample of words that may infringe s 18C

In order to illustrate the uncertainties involved in the operation of s 18C, we note here two words that may infringe it. These words are "civilisation" and "civilised". We have chosen these words because, first, they are words that are commonly employed in discourse. Second, the Convention itself uses 'civilization'.[749] However, they are words that, when employed may well cause offence, insult or even humiliation.

The *Macquarie Dictionary* defines 'civilisation' as, amongst other things:

> 1. an advanced state of human society, in which a high level of art, science, religion, and government has been reached.[750]

The *Macquarie Dictionary* also defines 'civilised' as:

> '1. having an advanced culture, society,   etc 2. Polite, well-bred, refined'.[751]

When these terms (and in particular 'civilised') are employed, they invite a comparison of one group with another.

For example, suppose someone said in public, with reference to certain conduct by members of a particular ethnic group: "their behaviour is not civilised". This implicitly suggests that people in the group were not meeting a civilised standard. This may result in members of that group being offended or insulted, and breach s 18C. It would then be a matter whether one of the exemptions in s 18D applied.

The problems only multiply if commonly used terms related to "civilisation" and "civilised" are used, like "uncivilised", "barbaric" or "savage".

Unfortunately, our example is not an exaggeration. Allison Pearson has

---

749 Convention, Article 8(1): 'There shall be established a Committee on the Elimination of Racial Discrimination (hereinafter referred to as the Committee) consisting of eighteen experts of high moral standing and acknowledged impartiality elected by States Parties from amongst their nationals who shall serve in their personal capacity, consideration being given to equitable geographical distribution and to the representation of the different forms of *civilization* as well as of the principal legal systems' (emphasis ours).
750 *Macquarie Dictionary* 278.
751 Ibid.

written about another word the use of which may cause problems for our progressive friends:

> 'At least that's progress,' I said to Adam [who lectures in African history] about one notably dysfunctional African country. 'Getting more girls into school is progress, isn't it?'
> 'I'm not allowed to use the word "progress",' he said. 'I'd be sacked if I called it "progress".'
> 'Why?'
> 'Because it would imply that the culture that was there already needed improvement.'
> 'But it *does*. If you keep a girl in education, she won't be married off at 12, which means her chances of getting Aids and dying young are reduced. Her country will become more civilised once it has more educated women. That's what I call progress.'
> 'Obviously, that's true', winced the professor, 'it's just not OK to say so.'[752]

So much for progress. We suggest that a civilisation that can no longer use the word "civilised" without the risk of creating legal issues needs to review its laws.

8   *Ultimately, is s 18C reasonably appropriate and adapted to its purpose?*

We will now weave the threads of the foregoing analysis. To do this, we will consider the approaches in *McCloy*. We will then apply them to the matters we noted above.

(a)   *The approaches in McCloy*

McCloy contains the judgment of the majority (French CJ, Kiefel, Bell and Keane JJ), and three other judgments (each from Gageler J, Nettle J and Gordon J). We will consider each of these judgments.

(i)   *The majority*

In *McCloy*, the majority of the High Court remarked that this limb of the modified *Lange* test required 'proportionality testing'. They stated the following about this requirement:

---

[752] Allison Pearson, 'We must listen to Trevor Phillips and his inconvenient truths about race' *The Telegraph* (online), 19 March 2015.

The proportionality test involves consideration of the extent of the burden effected by the impugned provision on the freedom. There are three stages to the test – these are the enquiries as to whether the law is justified as suitable, necessary and adequate in its balance in the following senses:

> *suitable* – as having a rational connection to the purpose of the provision;
>
> *necessary* – in the sense that there is no obvious and compelling alternative, reasonably practicable means of achieving the same purpose which has a less restrictive effect on the freedom;
>
> *adequate in its balance* – a criterion requiring a value judgment, consistently with the limits of the judicial function, describing the balance between the importance of the purpose served by the restrictive measure and the extent of the restriction it imposes on the freedom.[753]

As to suitability, the majority stated:

> Suitability is also referred to as "appropriateness" or "fit". Despite this language, it does not involve a value judgment about whether the legislature could have approached the matter in a different way. If the measure cannot contribute to the realisation of the statute's legitimate purpose, its use cannot be said to be reasonable. This stage of the test requires that there be a rational connection between the provision in question and the statute's legitimate purpose, such that the statute's purpose can be furthered… It is an enquiry which logic requires.[754]

As to necessity, they stated:

> The second stage of the test – necessity – generally accords with the enquiry… as to the availability of other, equally effective, means of achieving the legislative object which have a less restrictive effect on the freedom and which are obvious and compelling. If such measures are available, the use of more restrictive measures is not reasonable and cannot be justified.[755]

As to the law being adequate in its balance, the majority stated that this stage:

---

753 *McCloy* [2015] HCA 34 [2] (French CJ, Kiefel, Bell and Keane JJ) (citations omitted).
754 Ibid [80] (French CJ, Kiefel, Bell and Keane JJ) (citations omitted).
755 Ibid [81] (French CJ, Kiefel, Bell and Keane JJ) (citations omitted).

> [C]ompares the positive effect of realising the law's proper purpose with the negative effect of the limits on constitutional rights or freedoms. It requires an 'adequate congruence between the benefits gained by the law's policy and the harm it may cause', which is to say, a balance. Balancing is required because it is rare that the exercise of a right or freedom will be prohibited altogether. Only aspects of it will be restricted, so what is needed, to determine whether the extent of this restriction is reasonable, is a consideration of the importance of the purpose and the benefit sought to be achieved. Logically, the greater the restriction on the freedom, the more important the public interest purpose of the legislation must be for the law to be proportionate…
>
> …the methodology to be applied in this aspect of proportionality does not assume particular significance. Fundamentally, however, it must proceed upon an acceptance of the importance of the freedom and the reason for its existence. This stands in contrast to the basic rule of balancing as applied to human rights, which has been subject to criticism for failing to explain the reasons underlying the creation of the right in order to put the reasons for its protection, or which justify its limitation, in perspective.[756]

In summary, the importance of the statute's purpose needs to be considered against its restriction on the implied freedom of political communication, noting the latter's importance and reason for existence.

Given that the majority endorsed this approach, we will employ it in this section. However, it is important to also note the approaches of the three other judges in *McCloy*.

(ii) The three single judgments

Gageler J agreed that with the majority that the existence of less restrictive alternatives was important, noting:

> The existence of other means of achieving the objectives of the law that are less restrictive of political communication will always be relevant to the inquiry, and will sometimes be decisive.[757]

However, Gageler J expressed reservations about the majority's approach to the balancing exercise between the purpose of a law and its restriction on

---

756 Ibid [87]-[88] (French CJ, Kiefel, Bell and Keane JJ) (citations omitted).
757 Ibid [135] (Gageler J).

the implied freedom of political communication. He was concerned especially about leaving this exercise to the very end of the analysis,[758] stating:

> In my view, it is imperative that the entirety of the *Lange* analysis is undertaken in a manner which cleaves to the reasons for the implication of the constitutional freedom which it is the sole function of the *Lange* analysis to protect. Whatever other analytical tools might usefully be employed, fidelity to the reasons for the implication is in my view best achieved by ensuring that the standard of justification, and the concomitant level or intensity of judicial scrutiny, not only is articulated at the outset but is calibrated to the degree of risk to the system of representative and responsible government established by the Constitution that arises from the nature and extent of the restriction on political communication that is identified at the first step in the analysis.[759]

Gageler J noted:

> No unitary standard of justification can or should be applied across all categories of cases. To date that has repeatedly been recognised when it has been accepted that a law which operates to impose a content-based restriction will demand closer scrutiny than a restriction based on the form or manner of communication, just as when it has been recognised that a law which operates to prohibit or regulate communications which are inherently political will demand closer scrutiny than a law which operates incidentally to restrict political communication. Those distinctions are not complete dichotomies, and each distinction may or may not have analytical utility in a particular case. Other considerations which bear on the degree of risk which a particular legislative or executive restriction on political communication poses to the making of an informed electoral choice will also bear on the standard of justification applicable to that restriction.[760]

Nettle J noted the differences in approaches to the proportionality test in recent cases. However, he went on to note:

> For present purposes, it is unnecessary to attempt to resolve such differences. It is enough to observe that each approach involves questions of judgment. Each implies that a direct or severe burden on the implied freedom requires a strong justification in order to satisfy the second limb

---

758 Ibid [145]-[149] (Gageler J).
759 Ibid [150] (Gageler J).
760 Ibid [152] (Gageler J) (citations omitted).

of the *Lange* test. And each is consistent with the view that a burden which discriminates between segments of the electorate, political parties, candidates or political viewpoints requires no less as strong a justification to satisfy the [modified *Lange* test].[761]

Hence, for Nettle J, direct or severe burdens on the implied freedom of political communication require strong justification.[762] However, in apparent contrast to the majority and Gageler J regarding the necessity of less restrictive alternatives to achieve the law's purpose, Nettle J noted that 'the availability of alternative means is a relevant but not determinative consideration'.[763]

Gordon J thought that the existence of less restrictive alternatives to achieve the law's purpose may be relevant:

> The answer to [whether a law is reasonably appropriate and adapted to serve a legitimate end] *may* involve and be assisted by a consideration of whether there are alternative, reasonably practicable and less restrictive means of achieving the same end which are obvious and compelling. To qualify as a true alternative for this purpose, a hypothetical law must be as effective as the impugned law in achieving the identified objects and ends. The requirement that the alternative means be 'obvious and compelling' ensures that consideration of the alternatives remains a tool of analysis in applying the required criterion and that the courts do 'not exceed their constitutional competence by substituting their own legislative judgments for those of parliaments'. If no other hypothetical legislative measure that would be as effective can be identified it may be concluded that the impugned law goes no further than is reasonably necessary in achieving its object or end.[764]

However, while Gordon J thought the nature and extent of the effect of the law on the implied freedom of political communication was relevant, she was reluctant to engage in balancing exercises:

> Because there are no criteria or rules by which a "balance" can be struck between means and ends, the question is not one of balance or *value* judgment but rather whether the impugned law *impermissibly* impairs or tends to impair the maintenance of the constitutionally prescribed system

---

761 Ibid [255] (Nettle J).
762 Nettle J noted that 'authority establishes that burdens which discriminate between, or have an unequal effect upon, segments of the community, political parties and candidates or certain political viewpoints require strong justification': ibid [251] (Nettle J).
763 Ibid [222] (Nettle J). See also ibid [262] (Nettle J).
764 Ibid [328] (Gordon J) (emphasis in original, citations omitted).

of representative and responsible government having regard not only to the *end* but also to the *means* adopted in achieving that *end*. That, of course, is a question of judgment. It is a question of judgment about the nature and extent of the effect of the impugned law on the maintenance of the constitutionally prescribed system of representative and responsible government.

The extent and nature of the burden on the implied freedom of political communication imposed by the means adopted to achieve an identified end will be case specific and, therefore, any analysis must be case specific. This common law approach has at least two distinct advantages. It recognises that we are dealing not with protected individual rights but with negative restrictions on legislative powers and, secondly, it permits the development of different criteria for different constitutional contexts.[765]

Hence, there were differences between the three judgments concerning whether a less restrictive alternative was available and the requirement for balancing. However, every judgment appeared to hold that the nature and extent of the effect of the law on the implied freedom of political communication was relevant when assessing whether it was reasonably appropriate and adapted to its purpose.

We will now examine the stages set out by the majority in *McCloy*.

(b) Suitability

As the majority in *McCloy* stated, a rational connection between the provision in question and the statute's legitimate purpose is required.[766] While stretched, there is nevertheless a rational relationship between s 18C making unlawful offence, insult and humiliation and its purpose of prohibiting racial hatred. A rational relationship can also be said to exist between making unlawful offence, insult and humiliation and promoting racial harmony.

(c) Necessity

Before applying the test, we have two preliminary comments to make about the necessity requirement

First, the necessity requirement is arguably inconsistent with previous

---

765 Ibid [336]-[337] (Gordon J) (emphasis in original, citations omitted).
766 Ibid [80] (French CJ, Kiefel, Bell and Keane JJ).

approaches to "proportionality testing".[767] In *Davis v Commonwealth*,[768] the majority's approach to the validity of the impugned legislation did not depend on there being alternative legislation. Rather, they held the relevant legislation invalid owing to its gross disproportion to the purpose it served.[769] There was no consideration of whether less restrictive legislation could achieve the same end.

Second, analysis under this approach appears to depend on the existence of alternative legislation. This is an odd approach where freedoms, such as the implied freedom of political communication is concerned.[770] Where an express or implied freedom restricts legislative intervention, the best alternative may well be *less or even no legislation*.

This approach is in line the common law principle of freedom noted above. That is, in a common law legal system, the state's best approach to a problem may be to do nothing. However, as also noted above, just because the state does nothing does *not* mean nothing is done. Rather, the work is left to civil society. In the case of freedom of expression, we suggest any application of the proportionality test must consider whether less or even no legislation is an appropriate response.

In light of this, we suggest that there is merit in Nettle J's observation that the availability of alternative means to fulfill the law's purpose is a relevant but not determinative consideration.[771]

That said, and assuming that proportionality testing requires the existence of alternative legislation, we suggest that s 18C (and s 18D, which provides exemptions to the unlawful conduct s 18C describes) could be better drafted in the following ways:

---

767 As the majority has called this stage of the modified *Lange* test: ibid [2] (French CJ, Kiefel, Bell and Keane JJ).
768 *Davis v Commonwealth* [1988] HCA 63; (1988) 166 CLR 79 ('*Davis*'). The impugned legislation in *Davis* was enacted pursuant to an incidental power. However, in our view, the approach to proportionality taken in *Davis* does not materially differ from a proportionality analysis with respect to infringing the implied freedom of political communication. Indeed, given the impugned legislation in *Davis* concerned infringing common law freedom of speech, there are obvious parallels to any proportionality analysis concerning infringing the implied freedom of political communication.
769 *Davis* [1988] HCA 63; (1988) 166 CLR 79, 99-100 (Mason CJ, Deane and Gaudron JJ).
770 We would also note that it is an odd approach to assessing the proportionality of laws with respect to the freedom of interstate trade provided in s 92 of the *Commonwealth Constitution*. The proportionality test for the implied freedom of political communication was modeled on that for laws infringing s 92: see *Monis* [2013] HCA 4; (2013) 249 CLR 92, 190 [268], 194 [282], 213 [344] (Crennan, Kiefel and Bell JJ). Where freedom of interstate trade is concerned, the best approach may be less restrictive laws or no laws at all.
771 *McCloy* [2015] HCA 34 [222] (Nettle J). See also ibid [262] (Nettle J).

In s 18C(1)(a):
1. The law should specifically target racial hatred. That is, if Parliament wants a law targeting racial hatred, *it should make a law targeting racial hatred*. It should not make a law targeting emotions that, in many cases, have little if anything to do with racial hatred.
2. The phrase 'reasonably likely, in all the circumstances…' should be removed. As noted above, s 18C's terms impose liability even though no one may actually be offended, insulted or humiliated.
3. The terms 'offend', 'insult' and 'humiliate' should be removed. This is because even if these terms were expressly qualified by terms like 'serious', 'severe' or 'extreme' they would remain too vague. As demonstrated above, case law has differed over the scope of the term 'offence' in particular. Section 18C thereby creates confusion where clarity is required.
4. An objective test based on a reasonable member of the general community should be used to determine breaches of 18C. Using such a standard avoids the problems that the 'reasonable representative' test creates, as noted above.[772]
5. In s 18C(1)(b), the terms 'race' and 'ethnic' need statutory definitions in order to better guide courts as to who falls into these definitions and who does not.

In s 18D:
1. The terms 'reasonably' and 'good faith' should be removed from s 18D(1). Not only is the ambit of these terms uncertain, they also appear to impose a 'harm minimisation' approach to offensive speech[773] that is incompatible with the implied freedom of political communication. As noted above, the implied freedom of political communication applies even to expression made *unreasonably* and in *bad faith*.[774] Further, we note that in defamation, the defence of fair comment does not require that it be reasonable or in good faith.[775]
2. The word 'genuine' should be removed from s 18D(b). This is because of the uncertainty generated by what is meant by

---
772 See Part IV.E.2 (pages 53-6).
773 Part V.D.4.(a) (pages 160-1).
774 Part V.D.4.(a) (pages 161-2).
775 See, for example, the *Defamation Act 2005* (WA) s 31.

'genuine'.
3. Truth should be an exemption. As noted above, s 18C affects discussion about Commonwealth and State legislative and executive action such that it imposes a heavy burden on the implied freedom of political communication. Truth, or the closest one can get to truth, is crucial to such discussions. Section 18C cannot impose such a heavy burden on the implied freedom of political communication and not have truth as an exemption.

(d) Adequacy in its balance

This stage requires balancing the positive effect of realising the law's proper purpose with the negative effect of the limits on constitutional rights or freedoms.

(i) The purpose of s 18C

Section 18C's purpose is laudable. It is either to prohibit expressions of racial hatred, or to promote racial harmony. From our analysis above, it appears that s 18C's purpose also includes prohibiting offence, which is problematic. However, for the purpose of our analysis in this section, we put s 18C's case "at its highest and best", and proceed on the assumption that its purpose is either to prohibit expressions of racial hatred or promote racial harmony.

Prohibiting expressions of racial hatred and promoting racial harmony are very important goals, especially considering that Australia is a multicultural society. It is important that hatred based on race, colour, ethnicity or nationality be curbed so as to minimise the risk of conflict between groups. Laws that enable civil claims against those who promote racial hatred have a role to play in curbing expressions of racial hatred, and provide a method of redress for the considerable harm that racist speech may cause. Such laws also have symbolic value: signaling to Australians by means of law that expressions of racial hatred will not be tolerated.

(ii) The effect of s 18C on the implied freedom of political communication

Section 18C cannot be considered a law that has only an indirect or incidental effect on communication about government and political matters. Section 18C's burden on the implied freedom of political communication is direct, sweeping, and heavy. Section 18C affects the Australian people's communications about matters that are the subject of Commonwealth and State legislative and executive action. Further, as s 18C protects groups, it affects discussion about government and political matters to a far greater extent than other protective laws. While racist speech may cause harm, experience elsewhere suggests that abridging freedom of expression may also inflict harm by chilling expression about matters of public importance. The risk of such harm increases when laws abridging freedom of expression are too broad and too vague, as s 18C appears to be.

It is true that Australian governments have pursued policies promoting multiculturalism for a considerable period of time. However, to contend that laws impinging the implied freedom of political communication are justified because multiculturalism is government policy, or that Australian society is multicultural, is to put the cart before the horse. The freedom of political communication extends to *all* matters that may be subject to government policy and action. This includes multiculturalism. Hence, the freedom of political communication extends to all aspects of multiculturalism, including (but not limited to) the following, all of which are contentious and prone to heated debate:

- The number of immigrants accepted, and from where immigrants will be accepted.
- The level of integration expected of immigrants.
- The level of integration expected of existing ethnic populations.
- The provision of welfare and other government support to immigrants.
- Whether or not someone's race, colour or ethnicity entitles them to particular government benefits or support.
- Issues facing first and subsequent generations of immigrants.
- Whether multiculturalism should continue as a policy.

As to s 18C's symbolic value, and echoing Warren Sandmann, it is hardly a supportable proposition to restrict a constitutionally important freedom like freedom of expression on the grounds of symbolism.[776]

Regardless of whether s 18C's purpose is to prohibit racial hatred, to promote racial harmony, or both, it is not reasonably appropriate and adapted

---

[776] Warren Sandmann, 'Three Ifs and a Maybe: Mari Matsuda's Approach to Restricting Hate Speech Laws' (1994) 45 (3-4) *Communication Studies* 241, 251. Sandmann's comment was in regard to restricting the First Amendment of the United States Constitution. However, for the reasons noted above, freedom of expression in Australia has similar constitutional significance.

to achieve these ends. Section 18C is not valid for the following reasons:

1. As we noted in Part IV, for a law purporting to combat racial hatred, s 18C targets the wrong feelings in the wrong people.[777] As we demonstrated in Part IV, acts that offend, insult or humiliate may be motivated by or manifest emotions substantially different from hate. Further, such acts may create emotions in the audience (apart from those offended, insulted or humiliated) that are far removed from hatred, and would not lead to hatred.[778]

2. *How race and ethnicity is defined*: Section 18C encounters problems with how it defines the terms 'race' and 'ethnicity'.[779] As demonstrated above,[780] s 18C's prohibition of offensive, insulting or humiliating acts extends to *ideas* about spirituality, culture and history. To extend the prohibition from factors that one cannot control (one's genetic antecedents and expression of genetic structure) to those that one can (one's ideas) is not appropriate in a representative democracy, even if the aim is to eliminate hatred or promote tolerance. This is especially so when those ideas influence opinions and action on government and political matters.

3. *Uncertainty over s 18C's and s 18D's terms that affect free speech*: The operation of the law in this area demands certainty so that people know when they 'cross a line' and consequently be subject to legal action. This is especially so given the ease with which this line is crossed – all a person has to do is speak in public.

There are many terms employed in s 18C that are not defined in the legislation itself, and whose scope remains uncertain despite being judicially considered. Hence, there is considerable uncertainty concerning what may be offensive, insulting or humiliating to groups or sub-groups. There is also uncertainty as to how certain groups or sub-groups would react to certain speakers in certain circumstances. Added to this is the uncertainty over terms in s 18D like 'reasonable', 'good faith', 'genuine' and 'fair'. If these terms cause (as they have) uncertainty among the Australian judiciary, then it is likely that laypeople will also be uncertain. This creates

---

[777] See Part IV.E.1.(f) (page 49)
[778] See Part IV.E.1.(f) (pages 44-50).
[779] RDA s 18C(1)(b).
[780] See Part V.C.3 (page 131), Part V.C.4 (page 136) and Part V.C.5 (page 145).

a chilling effect in areas that are the proper subject of public debate.

4. *No actual harm need be suffered:* No one needs to actually offended, insulted, humiliated to breach s 18C. All that is required is an act be reasonably likely to offend, insult or humiliate or intimidate someone because of their race, colour or national or ethnic origin. For the reasons stated above,[781] s 18C is a sweeping intrusion into the freedom of political communication. Even if the aim is to prohibit hatred or promote racial harmony, such an intrusion cannot be considered reasonably appropriate or adapted when the prohibited speech does not in fact adversely affect anyone.

5. *Truth is not an exemption:* Truth is not an exemption to s 18C. The freedom of political communication is regarded as an indispensible incident to Australia's constitutional system. This is because such freedom promotes accountability and the full consideration of actual or proposed policies and laws. Truth, and debate by which truth is best discerned, is critical to both accountability and full consideration of actual or proposed policies and laws.

Ultimately, any law creating a civil action affecting communication about government and political matters that does not have truth as an exemption to otherwise unlawful conduct is fundamentally flawed.[782] Hence, s 18C simply cannot be considered to be reasonably appropriate and adapted to any kind of end, even that of prohibiting racial hatred or promoting racial harmony.

6. *A comparison with defamation law:* In *Lange*, a unanimous High Court held that the *Defamation Act 1974* (NSW) ('the NSW Defamation Act') was consistent with the implied freedom of political communication:

> In New South Wales, the principal defences to the publication of defamatory matter concerning government and political matters are truth in respect of a matter that is related to a matter of public interest or an occasion of qualified privilege, fair comment on a matter relating to the public interest, fair report of parliamentary and similar proceedings, common law qualified privilege and the

---

781 Please see part V.B (page 118).
782 Truth is a defence to defamation, which is perhaps s 18C's closest analogue (although narrower in application than s 18C).

statutory defence of qualified privilege contained in s 22 of the [NSW Defamation Act).

Without the statutory defence of qualified privilege, it is clear enough that the law of defamation, as it has traditionally been understood in New South Wales, would impose an undue burden on the required freedom of communication under the Constitution.[783]

After developing a form of qualified privilege implied from the *Commonwealth Constitution*,[784] the High Court stated:

> Once the common law is developed in this manner, the New South Wales law of defamation cannot be said to place an undue burden on those communications that are necessary to give effect to the choice in federal elections given by ss 7 and 24 and the freedom of communication implied by those sections and ss 64 and 128 of the Constitution. It is true that the law of defamation in that State effectively places a burden on those communications although it does not prohibit them. Nevertheless, having regard to the necessity to protect reputation, the law of New South Wales goes no further than is reasonably appropriate and adapted to achieve the protection of reputation once it provides for the extended application of the law of qualified privilege.[785]

As noted above, s 18C is far more sweeping in scope than defamation law. Further s 18C, unlike the NSW Defamation Act[786] examined in *Lange*, does not have truth, statutory or common law qualified privilege or *Lange* qualified privilege as defences. If anything, the range of exemptions in s 18D are more limited in scope when compared to the defamation defences examined in *Lange*.

For example, s 22 of the NSW Defamation Act provided a defence of qualified privilege if (amongst other things) the publisher's conduct was reasonable in the circumstances. In s 18D, the requirement is that (amongst other things) the publisher's[787] act be reasonable *and* in good faith.[788] Further, s 22 of the NSW Defamation Act did not stipulate that the information needs

---

783 *Lange* [1997] HCA 25; (1997) 189 CLR 520, 569 (emphasis ours).
784 Ibid 571-4.
785 Ibid 575. The High Court went on to note that, even if *Lange* qualified privilege did not apply, the operation of s 22 of the *Defamation Act 1974* (NSW) would mean that NSW's defamation law was constitutional.
786 The NSW defamation law has now been repealed.
787 We use 'publisher' here for the sake of comparison with the NSW defamation law examined in *Lange*.
788 Please see our discussion at Part V.D.4.(a) (pages 159-62).

to be in the public interest. All that was required in that the recipient have an interest in receiving the information.[789] However, in s 18D the exemption only applies if the act is in the public interest *and* an expression of genuine belief.

Given the High Court's comments that the NSW Defamation Act would have been constitutionally invalid were it not for the range of defences available, there is some precedent for suggesting that s 18C is constitutionally invalid.

Ultimately, and put simply, s 18C's scope is too broad and too vague to be constitutional.

E *Intimidation and the implied freedom of political communication*

In our view, s 18C's prohibition impermissibly infringes the implied freedom of political communication. Applying the modified *Lange* test, s 18C makes unlawful intimidation. Intimidation need not be physical – it can involve other forms of expression that creates fear or apprehension in those subject to the intimidation.[790] Such expression may occur in discussing government or political matters. Section 18C thereby burdens the implied freedom of political communication.

Further, s 18C's prohibition of intimidation is a purpose compatible with the constitutionally prescribed system of representative and responsible government. This is because ensuring that people are not subject to physical threats is a legitimate purpose of government.

However, 18C's prohibition of intimidation is not reasonably appropriate or adapted to achieve its purpose when s 18D is considered. Section 18D's exemptions give rise to manifest absurdities when applied to s 18C's prohibition of intimidation. Intimidation may involve physical or verbal threats being made to individuals or groups. On s 18D's terms, such conduct may be lawful if, among other things, they are made in the context of academic, scientific or artistic work. It is likely that competently executed works would meet the tests

---

789 Under the NSW Defamation Act s 22(2A), the court could take into account whether the information was a matter of public concern. However, it was not obliged to. Further, public concern was a number of discretionary factors the court could consider.

790 For example, in *Bropho*, French J noted that the performance, exhibition or distribution of artistic works 'may offend or insult or even humiliate and intimidate some. And such acts may have that effect in relation to people of a particular race, colour or national or ethnic origin.': see: *Bropho v Human Rights and Equal Opportunity Commission* [2004] FCAFC 16; (2004) 135 FCR 105, 134 [106] (French J).

of being in good faith, reasonable and genuine.[791]

As a matter of policy, the law sets its face against threats. There are laws in all jurisdictions prohibiting threatening behaviour.[792] Further, there are torts providing remedies for threatening behaviour, such as assault and intentional infliction of physical harm. Reiterating our arguments concerning the implied equality of political communication,[793] it is remarkable – and indeed patently unreasonable from a constitutional standpoint – to allow certain classes a wider range of language to express themselves *up to and including intimidating minorities*.

To be clear, we are not saying that all Australians should be free to intimidate. Rather, we are saying that Australians should be (as they are now save for s 18C and s 18D) equally bound by laws prohibiting threatening behaviour.

---

[791] For example, the films *Birth of a Nation* and *Triumph of the Will* have been noted for their artistic merit despite their vile messages. Given this, it is not hard to conceive of artistic works whose content intimidates outright.
[792] See, for example, the *Criminal Code 1913* (WA) chs XXXI, XXXIIIA and XXXIIIB.
[793] Please see Part V.D.4.(b).(ii) (pages 163-9).

VI

A PROPOSAL FOR LEGISLATIVE REFORM

This Part outlines a proposal for legislative reform in light of the limitations imposed by the Convention and the implied freedom of political communication. We will first outline our proposal for legislative reform. We will then explore other means by which racism can be combatted, including enforcing existing laws, more specific targeting legislative and executive solutions, and the "intersectional" approach.

A *A proposal for legislation prohibiting racial hatred*

Our analysis suggests that any law prohibiting speech promoting racial hatred must be narrowly focused. A broad prohibition is unlikely to satisfy the external affairs power's conformity requirement for implementing the Convention, and would impermissibly infringe the implied freedom of political communication.

A law prohibiting racial hatred could be more narrowly focused in the following ways. First, like protections under the DDA and SDA, the law could be confined to particular contexts like employment, education or providing accommodation, goods or services. Second, the law could be confined to expression manifesting or creating hate. Third, the processes employed in enforcing the law could be confined, such as making the law a criminal offence provable beyond reasonable doubt with actions brought by the state alone.

Fortunately, a good template already exists for a narrowly focused law prohibiting racial hatred. In 1974, when the Whitlam Labor government introduced the RDB, it proposed clause 28. The Commonwealth Parliament enacted much of the RDB as the RDA. However, the Commonwealth

Parliament did not enact cl 28. Clause 28 was intended to enact Australia's obligations under Article 4 of the Convention, and provided as follows:

> A person shall not, with intent to promote hostility or ill-will against, or to bring into contempt or ridicule, persons included in a group of persons in Australia by reason of the race, colour or national or ethnic origin of the persons included in the group –
>
> (a) publish or distribute written matters;
>
> (b) broadcast words by means of radio or television; or
>
> (c) utter words in any public place, or within the hearing of persons in any public place, or at any meeting to which the public are invited or have access,
>
> being written matter that promotes, or words that promote, ideas based on -
>
> (d) the alleged superiority of persons of a particular race, colour or national or ethnic origin over persons of a different race, colour or national or ethnic origin; or
>
> (e) hatred of persons of a particular race, colour or national or ethnic origin.
>
> Penalty: $5,000

We note that cl 28 embodies the terms of Article 4 of the Convention better than s 18C. This should not be surprising given that cl 28 was drafted not long after Australia signed the Convention. The text and purpose of the Convention was no doubt fresh in the minds of the RDB's drafters.

The Commonwealth Parliament did not enact cl 28, owing to concerns about its impact on freedom of speech. However, we submit that if the Commonwealth Parliament enacted a modified version of cl 28, it would likely be constitutionally valid. Our proposed modified provision is as follows:

> (1) It is an offence for a person, with intent to incite enmity or violence against a person or persons included in a group of people by reason of their racial identity, colour, ethnicity or nationality, to –
>
> (a) publish or distribute written matters;
>
> (b) broadcast words by means of radio or television; or
>
> (c) utter words in any public place, or within the hearing of persons in any public place, or at any meeting to which the public are invited or have access,

that advocates -

(d) that persons of a particular racial identity, colour, ethnicity or nationality have more inherent worth than other humans;

(e) that persons of a particular racial identity, colour, ethnicity or nationality have less inherent worth than other humans; or

(f) enmity towards persons of a particular racial identity, colour, ethnicity or nationality.

Penalty: $20,000 or six months imprisonment

(2) In subsection (1):

enmity means either:

(a) Hatred creating an imminent danger of violence; or

(b) Contempt creating an imminent danger of violence.

ethnicity means the definitions of ethnicity given in *Mandla v Dowell Lee* [1983] 2 AC 548 and *King-Ansell v Police*[1979] 2 NZLR 531.

intent means either:

(a) The person's purpose or desire is to incite enmity or violence; or

(b) The person knows or foresees that it is virtually certain that doing an act described in subsection (1)(a), (1)(b) or (1)(c) will incite enmity or violence.

racial identity means a person of a particular racial descent who identifies as that race and is accepted as such by the community with whom he or she associates who identifies by that race..

violence and **violent**:

(a) includes actual or threatened unlawful damage to property;

(b) excludes acts not involving:

(i) actual or threatened unlawful physical violence against a person or persons; or

(ii) actual or threatened unlawful damage to property.

We have the following comments about this proposed law:

First, to avoid doubt concerning whether Article 4 supports the proposed provision, the operative word is not "hate" but a term beyond hate: "enmity". Further, we have defined enmity with reference to an imminent danger.

Second, to avoid the constitutional issues noted above regarding not defining race or ethnicity,[794] these terms have been defined within the proposed legislation itself.[795]

---

794 See Part V.C.3.(b) (pages 132-4).
795 We have defined "racial identity" in place of "race".

Third, there is no defence to this provision. However, the offence itself is narrowly confined. This is because it is a criminal offence. The state will need to prosecute the offence and prove each element beyond a reasonable doubt. Further, and critically, the state would need to prove beyond reasonable doubt the element of intent to incite enmity or violence.[796] This is a substantial change from cl 28's element of 'intent to promote hostility or ill-will against, or to bring into contempt or ridicule'. However, in light of our analysis in Parts IV and V, cl 28's scope for intent is too broad. As noted above, discussions concerning government and political matters are often heated. Such discussion may involve value judgments about particular races, cultures, ethnicities and nationalities that are apt to generate ill-will or ridicule. It is an often regrettable – but inherent – incident of such debate in a democracy where ideas clash.[797]

If cl 28 were enacted unamended, it would impermissibly infringe the implied freedom of political communication because it would expose to criminal prosecution heated or robust debate about government and political matters, or expressions of opinion about controversial issues. It would also not pay due regard to the guarantee of freedom of opinion and expression under Article 5 of the Convention for the same reason.

The risk we have outlined is not fanciful. The experience of other countries demonstrates it. For example:

- Harry Taylor: Self-described 'militant atheist'. In 2010, Taylor was convicted in Britain for religiously aggravated intentional harassment, alarm or distress.[798] Taylor had left provocative cartoons concerning Christianity and Islam at a multi-faith prayer room at Liverpool's John Lennon Airport in 2008.[799] These cartoons depicted 'a smiling Christ on the cross next to an advert for a brand of "no nails" glue. In another, the Pope is shown wearing a condom on his finger. Others featured Islamic suicide bombers at the gates of paradise who are told "Stop, stop, we've run out of virgins."'[800]

---

796 The test for intent is based on that in *R v Woollin* [1999] 1 AC 82.
797 Our proposed reforms will still, in effect, protect ideas. However, this will happen in a far narrower range of cases.
798 While the relevant criminal provision did not concern race, we note that religious belief may be an aspect of ethnicity under s 18C. Please see our discussion in Part V.C.3.(b) (pages 132-6).
799 William Crawley, '"Militant Atheist" found guilty of religious harassment', on William Crawley, *BBC Will & Testament: William Crawley's Blog*, (online) 4 March 2010.
800 Ibid.

- Brigitte Bardot: Animal rights activist, actress and model. In 2008, Bardot was convicted a fifth time in France for inciting racial hatred. Her fifth conviction concerned comments about the slaughter of animals for Eid al-Adha, a Muslim festival.[801] Demanding that the animals be stunned before slaughter, Bardot said 'she was "tired of being led by the nose by this population that is destroying us, destroying our country by imposing its acts"'.[802]
- Bob Dylan: Singer and counterculture icon. In 2013, Dylan was subject to a hate speech investigation in France for comments he made about Croats in *Rolling Stone* magazine in 2012.[803] Dylan was quoted as saying, 'If you got a slave master or Klan in your blood, blacks can sense that. That stuff lingers to this day. Just like Jews can sense Nazi blood and the Serbs can sense Croatian blood'.[804] In 2014, the court dropped the case against Dylan. However, the judge in the case ordered that the editor of *Rolling Stone* stand trial for the article.[805]
- Lars Hedegaard: Marxist, historian and author. In 2009, Hedegaard was charged under Danish hate speech laws for commenting during an interview that 'girls in Muslim families are raped by their uncles, their cousins or their dad'. While originally acquitted in January 2011, the prosecutor appealed and Hedegaard was convicted on appeal later in 2011.[806] In 2012, the Danish Supreme Court acquitted him on appeal.[807]
- Oriana Fallaci: Feminist, author and journalist. In 2002, Fallaci was subject to a Swiss arrest warrant for her comments concerning

---

801 'Bardot fined over racial hatred', BBC News, 3 June 2008.
802 Ibid.
803 'Croats in France insist in a court case with Bob Dylan', Croatian Times, 25 November 2013. On an ironic note, Christopher McCrudden's excellent article on human dignity opens with lyrics from Bob Dylan: 'So many roads, so much at stake/So many dead ends, I'm at the edge of the lake/Sometimes I wonder what it's gonna take/To find dignity': Bob Dylan, *Dignity* (1963) quoted in Christopher McCrudden, 'Human Dignity and Judicial Interpretation of Human Rights' (2008) 19(4) *European Journal of International Law* 655, 656. It appears the Revolution continues to eat its own (the times they are a changin' indeed…).
804 'French court drops 'hate speech' case against Bob Dylan', *France24* (online), 15 April 2014.
805 Ibid.
806 'President of Danish Free Press Society convicted for "Racism"', *EuropeNews* (online), 3 May 2011.
807 Ann Snyder, 'Danish Supreme Court Acquits Hedegaard', *The Legal Project* (online), 21 April 2012.

Islam. In her book, *The Rage and the Pride*, Fallaci claimed there was 'an unbridgeable gap between Christian and Muslim worlds',[808] warning of 'a Pearl Harbor against the West'[809] and accusing Europe of being 'blind to the problems of Islamic immigration'.[810] The Italian Justice Ministry refused to prosecute or extradite her.[811] However, in 2005, an Italian judge ordered that she stand trial for defaming Islam. Fallaci died before her trial was concluded.[812]

- Aides Haute-Garonne: An organisation in France aimed at AIDS prevention. In 2005, Aides Haute-Garonne was convicted of using an image offensive to Catholics. The organisation issued a prospectus that 'contained an image of the bosom of a religious woman wearing heavy pink make-up who – apart from a headscarf and a necklace with a cross – was naked. On her right there are two pink condoms.'[813] The text that accompanied the image read 'St Capote Protect Us'.[814] This conviction was upheld on appeal, but was later overturned on a subsequent appeal to the Supreme Court.
- *Charlie Hebdo*: French satirical magazine. In 2005, an issue of *Charlie Hebdo* showed cartoons depicting Mohammed published in the Danish newspaper *Jyllands-Posten*. In the same issue, *Charlie Hebdo* showed its own cartoons about Islam. In 2006, Phillipe Val, *Charlie Hebdo's* editor, was subject to criminal prosecution in France for several of these cartoons. He was not convicted at first instance or on appeal.[815]

These are only some examples of such prosecutions.[816]

We have some further comments concerning these examples. First, we ask the reader: do these examples constitute racial hatred worth prosecuting? Some readers may say all of them do. Others may say none of them do. Some readers

---
808 'Swiss Muslims File Suit Over "Racist" Fallaci Book', *The Milli Gazette* (online) 1 July 2002
809 Ibid.
810 Ibid.
811 Soeren Kern, 'Free Speech on Trial in Europe', *Gatestone Institute* (online) 27 January 2011.
812 Ibid.
813 Esther Janssen, 'Limits to expression of religion in France' (2009) 5(1) *Agama & Religiusitas di Europa, Journal of European Studies* 22.
814 Ibid.
815 Ibid 39.
816 For an overview of hate speech laws, and prosecutions under these laws, see 'European Hate Speech Laws', *The Legal Project* (online); see also Soeren Kern, 'Free Speech on Trial in Europe', *Gatestone Institute* (online), 27 January 2011.

may say certain examples do but other examples don't. Different readers will reach different conclusions. However, this illustrates the problem: there is no certainty in the application of the law if the law is broad or vague. If the state is to hurl its power at an individual, subject that individual to the costs of an investigation or trial, and potentially deprive that citizen of property or liberty, then there must be certainty concerning where the line is drawn so an individual can avoid crossing that line.

However, hate speech laws are prone to arbitrary application – dependent too much on the particular views of prosecutors. The risk of arbitrary application increases where loose definitions of hatred are used in the relevant laws. This is an unacceptable risk in circumstances where someone may breach the law by the mere act of speaking in public. In such an environment an individual may make a statement believing on reasonable grounds that it does not cross a line, only to have a prosecutor disagree and prosecute. Such arbitrariness must be avoided in any nation that values the rule of law.

Second, in some of the examples cited above there was either no conviction, or the conviction was ultimately overturned. However, the fact that people were subject to criminal prosecution in the first place is a cause for grave concern. This is because people subject to such prosecutions incur costs in time, money and stress in defending these charges. In short, having the state "feeling your collar" has a chilling effect.

Third, supporters of hate speech laws often cite examples like women receiving abuse on the street because they are wearing a hijab or vile racial epithets being called out to passers-by. However, and with respect, such examples demonstrate the truth of the legal aphorism that "hard cases make bad law". The law risks being "bad" practically and legally.

Practically, hate speech laws are applied to situations beyond street encounters to those like the examples listed above. This creates a serious chilling effect on free speech. Indeed, hate speech laws are more likely to target written news and opinion given that written evidence makes proving breaches of the law much easier. Legally, the problem is that while such laws may start by intending to only prohibit instances of extreme race hate, they never end there. As the examples listed above suggest, such laws have been extended to a wide range of comments.

Our proposed amendment recognises that during the course of discussions about government and political matters there are people who, inadvertently or deliberately, express extreme or distasteful views, but who would never advocate or condone enmity or violence against anyone. The state should leave these people be.[817] However, where circumstances demonstrate that people intend to incite enmity or violence then it is appropriate for the state to act. Our proposed amendment establishes a 'bright line' so both the state and individuals know what speech is prohibited: that bright line is intent to incite actual or threatened enmity or violence against people or their property.

Following from the previous point, in our proposed amendment violence is defined to mean to actual or threatened unlawful physical violence against persons or their property. As noted above, legislation prohibiting racial discrimination is protective and hence should be interpreted broadly and beneficially. While this approach is laudable, in this instance violence may be interpreted too broadly. For example, if 'violence' is interpreted to mean 'verbal violence' (or similar)[818] then this creates uncertainty as to the types of verbal violence prohibited. Verbal violence may be construed to include speech that is offensive or insulting but which does not involve threatened physical violence. Construing verbal violence this way would impermissibly infringe the implied freedom of political communication. However, prohibiting incitement to physical violence is a clear, understandable – and constitutionally permissible – function of state power.

B *Enforcing laws of equal application – time for a second look?*

One of the rationales for enacting legislation specifically directed to combatting racial hatred was the inadequacy of existing laws to deal with the problem. The Inquiry noted:

> Evidence to the Inquiry indicates that enforcement of existing laws by investigating, prosecuting and even judicial authorities has been inadequate and at times entirely lacking. There is also significant evidence to indicate involvement in violence against members of racial minorities by police officers. Where this has occurred or is even believed to occurred the victims of racist violence or harassment are unlikely to even report crimes committed against them.[819]

And later:

---

817 Whether civil society leaves them be, however, is another matter. Freedom of expression does not mean freedom from having that expression challenged.
818 We note here that the amended clause 28 would (quite properly) be considered protective human rights legislation and hence may be construed broadly: Part III.B.2.(c) (page 21).
819 Inquiry 275-6.

Failure to enforce criminal laws in relation to racist violence and abuse leaved aggrieved people without the support and assistance of the investigatory powers of the State in identifying the perpetrators and gathering other evidence. To bring a civil action, the victim of racist acts or statements requires an understanding of his or her legal rights; the psychological and financial resources for pursuing those rights through legal proceedings; and the sense that the judicial system can provide redress.[820]

The ALRC Report noted:

In public places, racist violence usually takes the form of unprovoked, 'one-off' incidents by strangers; on the other hand, neighbourhood incidents are more likely to be sustained campaigns by perpetrators known to the victim. Racist violence reported to HREOC included abusive and threatening letters and telephone calls, vandalism, burglary and arson, the desecration of sacred buildings and disruption of religious worship and attacks on religious schools.[821]

It appears that the problems outlined are not the laws per se, but the following:

1. Minorities being unaware of the relevant law;
2. Law enforcement being unwilling or unable to enforce the relevant law;
3. Law enforcement actually being involved in violence against racial minorities; and
4. The lack of financial and/or the psychological resources to press civil claims.

It is not clear how a law specifically targeting racial hatred would overcome these difficulties. Criminal laws prohibiting racial hatred would encounter the same difficulties with law enforcement as other laws. Laws providing a civil action for racial hatred would encounter the same difficulties as other civil claims regarding the lack of awareness of such laws, and lack of financial and/or other psychological resources to press such claims.

However, were existing laws of equal application enforced, they would have an effect on those who threaten or attack people or their property because

---

820 Inquiry 277.
821 ALRC Report [7.18].

of race, colour, ethnicity or nationality. This because, should a person's prejudice be such that they attack people or their property, then they would be penalised with fines or jail. People not displaying such prejudice would not be so penalised. Of course, the law would have a disparate impact against people whose prejudice leads them to threatened or actual violence, but this is the type of disparate impact that should be welcome: by operation of a law of equal application, violent bigotry is discouraged. The same dynamic would also apply for civil claims.

Further, since the Inquiry and the Royal Commission made their reports, another law of equal application has been added to the arsenal – laws pertaining to stalking. These laws prohibit someone pursuing another in a manner that could reasonably be expected to intimidate.[822] Such laws would assist overcoming the types of conduct noted above in the ALRC report concerning sustained campaigns in neighbourhoods, repeated abusive or threatening messages[823] or the like.

Finally, and practically, there are now more effective means for interested groups in civil society to monitor the performance of executive agencies in enforcing criminal law, and to apply pressure on these agencies for any perceived lack of action. Measures to increase the transparency of government, combined with the communications revolution brought on by the internet and the rise of social media, mean that groups can identify shortcomings in executive action and bring pressure to bear far more easily than previously.

The one reform we propose to existing laws of equal application would be to remove references to "offence" and "insult" in laws concerning disorderly conduct and similar offences and replace them with "abuse". For the reasons we have noted, scope of offence and insult is too wide. Provisions containing these words have already been subject to High Court challenge,[824] and more challenges are likely.

"Abuse" suggests language that is stronger and more personal. The *Macquarie Dictionary* defines 'abuse' as, relevantly:

> 2. to maltreat; act injuriously towards: *to abuse the dog.* 4. to speak insultingly

---

822 *Criminal Code* (WA) s 338E(2).
823 By "messages" we mean phone calls, letters, emails, text messages, posting to social media, and the like.
824 See, for example, *Coleman* [2004] HCA 25; (2004) 220 CLR 1; *Monis* [2013] HCA 4; (2013) 249 CLR 92.

to; revile... 7. insulting language.[825]

An earlier edition of the *Macquarie Dictionary* includes in its definition of abuse as 'to revile; malign'.[826]

The definition of 'abuse' encompasses a range of conduct, from that which is reviles, maligns and injures to that which insults. If "abuse" is taken to mean insult, then the term encounters the same problems as using the word "insult", noted above. However, in its more severe aspect, "abuse" suggests conduct that is at once hateful and personal: someone is specifically targeted using language that denigrates them. Hence, we suggest that "abuse" be defined within the legislation to restrict its operation to its severe aspect.

Further, the abuse needs to be directed at an identifiable person in a public place.[827] This would mean that people going about their business in public would be protected from abusive language. However, abusive language concerning people not present would not be so protected. Hence, the law would protect against someone yelling vile epithets (including racial epithets) at passers-by on the street. However, it could not be used against someone using strong language about (say) a public figure not present in a public place, or about a race, culture, ethnicity or nationality at a public gathering (unless that language was directed at a person or people present — protesters at a counter-rally, for example).

How would such a provision look? As an example, s 74A of the *Criminal Code 1913* (WA) presently reads, relevantly:

(1) In this section —

behave in a disorderly manner includes —

(a) to use insulting, offensive or threatening language; and

(b) to behave in an insulting, offensive or threatening manner.

(2) A person who behaves in a disorderly manner —

(a) in a public place or in the sight or hearing of any person who is in a public place...

is guilty of an offence and is liable to a fine of $6 000.

The reform would read, relevantly:

---

825 *Macquarie Dictionary* 6. The definition also includes 'insulting language': see ibid 769 (emphasis in original).
826 *Macquarie Concise Dictionary* (Macquarie Dictionary Publishers, 5th ed, 2009) 5.
827 This reform is based on comments of the majority judges in *Coleman*: see *Coleman* [2004] HCA 25; (2004) 220 CLR 1, 40-1 [64], [66] (McHugh J); 74 [183] (Gummow and Hayne JJ); 97-8 [253] (Kirby J).

(1) In this section —

abuse means using language that, in the view of a reasonable person, would revile, malign or denigrate.

behave in a disorderly manner means—
(a) to abuse or threaten a person who is in the public place; or
(b) to behave in a manner that is threatening, or that creates a reasonable apprehension of a breach of the peace.

reasonable person means a citizen of Australia who is aware that Australia has a constitutionally prescribed system of representative and responsible government and the need to communicate about matters related to politics and government fully, frankly and robustly.

(2) A person who behaves in a disorderly manner —
(a) in a public place or in the sight or hearing of any person who is in a public place…
is guilty of an offence and is liable to a fine of $6 000.

Abuse must be language that, in the view of a reasonable person, would revile, malign or denigrate. Thus we employ an objective test.

A criticism of using the 'reasonable person' test in legislation making unlawful expressions of racial hatred is that using such a test may entrench mainstream prejudicial attitudes.[828] However, such criticism is misconceived. The assumption that the reasonable person in Australia would be prejudiced itself appears to employ a stereotype of the 'typical Australian'. A criticism guilty of the very thing it criticises is hardly sustainable. Further, a universally applicable reasonable person test is not subject to the fatal defect that we identified earlier with the "reasonable representative" test – it does not violate the principle of equality before the law.[829]

In any event, we have made the reasonable person a citizen of Australia aware that Australia has a constitutionally-prescribed system of representative and responsible government. Further, the reasonable person is aware that the

---

828 See *Eatock* [2011] FCA 1103; (2011) 197 FCR 261, 321 [253] (Bromberg J). See also Adrienne Stone, 'The Ironic Aftermath of *Eatock v Bolt*' (2015) 38 *Melbourne University Law Review* 926, 931; Tim Soutphommasane, *I'm Not Racist, But… 40 Years of the Racial Discrimination Act* (University of New South Wales Press, 2015) Kindle Ebook Location 1494.
829 See Part IV.E.2 (pages 53-6).

exchange of ideas may be full, frank and robust.[830] Given these parameters, the reasonable person should be able to distinguish strongly expressed views about an issue or a public figure from the gratuitous use of vile epithets directed at passers-by.

However, the reasonable person test only applies to abuse. It does not apply to threats or threatening behaviour. Threats and threatening behaviour jeopardise the security of persons, and constitutes disorderly conduct.

We have used 'breach of the peace' as it is used in similar provisions of the *Criminal Code 1913* (WA).[831] It is worth noting that behaving in a manner that creates a reasonable apprehension of a breach of the peace would include conduct that advocated or encouraged people to attack others or their property. However, it would not include strong language concerning government or political matters.

C *More specific targeting of legislative and executive action*

Another problem identified by the Royal Commission, the Inquiry[832] and the ALRC Report[833] is the relationship between Aborigines and the police. The Royal Commission noted:

> What is at issue in the legislation... is the matter of balancing the individual's rights, in this case to freedom of speech with the rights of other individuals and groups and the legitimate interests of the state in the promotion of civil order. There is another issue, however, that is perhaps even more fundamental: that is the question of the rights of the individual that the basis of much of liberal western thought as distinct from the rights of the collective, the group that exists by virtue of its treatment in society as a whole. The Royal Commission hearings have demonstrated that Aboriginal people are such a group. They have also shown that, within the systemic discrimination that Aboriginal people receive from police, language is one of the forms of violence that has most impact on relations between the two. Indeed, one quarter of all complaints of racist

---

830 The reason we have drafted the reasonable person test with these parameters is out of concern about how a reasonable person test might function without them. If (without these parameters applying) a reasonable person test resulted in the view that a strongly-expressed opinion about a government or political matter violated a disorderly conduct law, then this may impermissibly infringe the implied freedom of political communication.
831 *Criminal Code 1913* (WA) ss 69, 70 and 74.
832 Inquiry 275-6.
833 ALRC Report [7.21].

statements lodged with the Human Rights Commission up to 1984 – by various groups – concerned statements made by officials such as public servants and members of the police…[834]

With the greatest of respect to the Royal Commission, the undoubted problems that the Aboriginal community have had with specific agencies, and in particular the police, do not justify a blanket prohibition on freedom of expression. Rather, solving the problems with government agencies generally, and the police in particular, requires appropriate, focused legislative and executive action, instead of a broad-brush approach.

Another common complaint is abuse on public transport. However, unless the victim knows (or can find out the identity of) the person using the abusive language, then s 18C is unlikely to be effective. Further, even if the person can be identified, conciliation takes place a time far removed from that of the hurt. A more practical solution may be for public transport providers to continue to refine "rapid response" measures so that a person using abusive language can be dealt with then and there by being fined, or (in more severe cases) arrested.[835]

Put another way, restricting freedom of expression by means of s 18C in order to overcome particular issues like police attitudes or abuse on public transport may well be using a sledgehammer to do a scalpel's work.[836] Tailored solutions may better address the problem while minimising the damage to

---

834 Royal Commission [28.3.35].
835 For example, in Western Australia, Transperth (which provides bus and rail services in the Perth metropolitan area) prohibits acts that cause a nuisance or annoyance: see *Public Transport Authority Regulations 2003* (WA) reg 13. Further, Transperth provides a range of countermeasures to antisocial behaviour (including racist taunts), such as security officers, emergency assistance buttons, and phone numbers for assistance. Finally, it has implemented a 'reward' system for reporting offensive behaviour. This type of diffused response – encouraging concerned citizens to respond to unacceptable behaviour – should be encouraged: see: Transperth, *Safety and Security* (online).
836 We have used the metaphor deliberately (that is, sledgehammer as opposed to axe). This is because not only will the sledgehammer inflict massive trauma, it also won't actually do the job of cutting.

freedom of expression.[837]

D *Avoiding approaches based on intersectionality or privilege*

In advocating for the legislative reform as stated above, we close by advocating what legislative reform should *avoid*. In particular, it should avoid general restrictions on freedom of expression based on concepts of "intersectionality" or "privilege". These concepts are becoming part of government discourses.[838] There is no universally accepted definition of intersectionality.[839] Patricia Hill Collins expressed the concept as follows:

> As opposed to examining gender, race, class, and nation, as separate systems of oppression, intersectionality explores how these systems mutually construct one another...[840]

In other words, examining the type of oppression that a person or group may experience requires examining issues pertaining to gender, race, class and

---

[837] What about places of education? Once again, our concern is with state-imposed limitations on freedom of expression. As we noted in Part II, private persons can agree to limit the range of their expression. That said, places of education occupy a position unlike those encountered in most workplaces and other organisations, in that places of education routinely deal with controversial ideas. We have the following comments to make. First, laws of equal application obviously also apply to those attending places of education. This means people cannot, for example, threaten, stalk, or harass others in places of education. By this measure, anti-bullying measures are also justified. Second, in places of education, restrictions on the discussion of controversial ideas are justified in primary and secondary education. This is because students attending these places are not adults but children. (We note here Mill's observation that the harm principle is 'meant to apply only to human beings in the maturity of their faculties': J S Mill, *On Liberty* (Penguin Classics, first published 1859, 1985 ed.) 69.) Given this, restrictions are more justified in primary education than secondary education. This is because children in primary education are far from adulthood. However, children in secondary education are approaching adulthood, and hence should be made ready to handle controversial ideas in their adulthood. Third, apart from restrictions based on laws of equal application as described above, there should be no restrictions on the discussion of controversial ideas in tertiary education. Save certain school-leavers and gifted children, the vast majority of those participating to tertiary education are adults. All those who participate in tertiary education should expect to encounter all manner of ideas ranging from the pleasant to the repellant. Further, they should be encouraged to respond to ideas in ways that challenge the idea, rather than shut down its expression.
[838] See, for example, Australian Human Rights Commission, 'Gender and Race Intersectionality', Australian Human Rights Commission ; see also Tim Soutphommosane, 'Empathy, Power and Privilege', Australian Human Rights Commission, 2 November 2014.
[839] Leslie McCall notes three categories of intersectionality: anticategorical; intracategorical and intercategorical: see Leslie McCall, 'The Complexity of Intersectionality' (2005) 30(3) *Signs* 1771, 1773-4. See also Anna Carastathis, 'The Invisibility of Privilege: A Critique of Intersectional Models of Identity' (2008) 3(2) *Les Ateliers De L'Éthique* 23, 24-6.
[840] Patricia Hill Collins, 'It's All in the Family: Intersections of Gender, Race, and Nation' (1998) 13(3) *Hypatia* 62, 63.

nationality, and how these categories overlap or reinforce each other. Further, the categories are not closed: in addition to gender, race, class and nationality there may be (for example) ethnicity, religion, sexuality and age.[841]

As to privilege, Tim Soutphommasane has noted:

> The concept of privilege refers to how some may enjoy unearned or unacknowledged advantages over others. The concept emerged in the 1980s through the feminist scholar Peggy McIntosh. In a celebrated essay, McIntosh wrote that 'as a white person', she had been taught not to see how social privilege place her at a certain advantage. Privilege was like an 'invisible package of unearned assets' a 'weightless backpack of special provisions, maps, passports, codebooks, visas, clothes, tools and blank cheques'.[842]

Soutphommasane went on to note:

> The beneficiaries of social privilege may not be aware of their privileged position. Part of this is because conversations about discrimination tend to focus on those who are disadvantaged by prejudice. We do not always consider the other side of the coin: what it says about those who do not experience discrimination.[843]

Peggy McIntosh noted with respect to privilege:

> Thinking through unacknowledged male privilege as a phenomenon, I realized that, since hierarchies in our society are interlocking, there are most likely a phenomenon of white privilege that was similarly denied and protected. As a white person, I realized I had been taught about racism as something that puts others at a disadvantage, but had been taught not to see one of its corollary aspects, white privilege, which puts me at an advantage.[844]

And later:

> To redesign social systems we need first to acknowledge their colossal unseen dimensions. The silences and denials surrounding privilege... are

---

841 Ibid 64. Disability is another frequently employed category: see Anna Carastathis, 'The Invisibility of Privilege: A Critique of Intersectional Models of Identity' (2008) 3(2) *Les Ateliers De L'Éthique* 23, 24.
842 Tim Soutphommasane, *I'm Not Racist, But... 40 Years of the Racial Discrimination Act* (University of New South Wales Press, 2015) Kindle Ebook Location 2327 (citations omitted).
843 Ibid Kindle Ebook Location 2337.
844 Peggy McIntosh, 'White Privilege and Male Privilege: A Personal Account of Coming To See Correspondences through Work in Women's Studies' (Working Paper 189, Wellesley College Center for Research on Women, 1988) 1.

the key political tool here. They keep the thinking about equality or equity incomplete, protecting unearned advantage and conferred dominance by making these subject[s] taboo. Most talk by whites about equal opportunity seems to me now to be about equal opportunity to try to get into a position of dominance while denying that systems of dominance exist.[845]

The esoteric nature of privilege and intersectionality is grist for the academic mill.[846] However, it is beyond the scope of this treatise to give a detailed critique of privilege and intersectionality from a theoretical standpoint.[847] Our concern is whether, ultimately, laws restricting freedom of expression should reflect these concepts. Our view is that such laws would have significant conceptual and practical problems.

1   Conceptual problems

Laws prohibiting racist hate speech on the basis of intersectionality or privilege would restrict freedom of expression on the basis of intersections of (amongst other things) race, culture, religion and ethnicity.[848] As noted above, culture, religion, ethnicity and even race are *concepts* comprised of *ideas*.[849] They are the products of the human capacity for conceptual thought. As also noted above, states should be slow to restrict the expression of the capacity for conceptual thought in order to protect a concept produced by such thought.

In addition, the concepts of intersectionality and privilege appear to use "hierarchies of oppression" which then influence a person's capacity to speak about certain matters. In short, the more oppressed a person is according to

---

845 Ibid 6. See also Kimberle Crenshaw, 'Demarginalizing the Intersection of Race and Sex: A Black Feminist Critique of Antidiscrimination Doctrine, Feminist Theory and Antiracist Politics' (1989) *University of Chicago Legal Forum* 139, 140.
846 Leslie McCall has noted with respect to research on intersectionality: 'The categorical space can become very complicated with the addition of any one analytical category to the analysis because it requires an investigation of the multiple groups that constitute the category. For example, the incorporation of gender as an analytical category into such an analysis assumes that two groups will be compared systematically – men and women. If the category of class is incorporated, then gender must be cross-classified with class, which is composed (for simplicity) of three categories (working, middle, and upper), thus creating six groups. If race-ethnicity is incorporated into the analysis, and it consists of only two groups, then the number of groups expands to twelve. And this example makes use of only the most simplistic definitions.': Leslie McCall, 'The Complexity of Intersectionality' (2005) 30(3) *Signs* 1771, 1786.
847 It would take another book to perform this task.
848 Hate speech laws of more general application could also extend to gender, sex, sexuality, disability and age.
849 The same can be said about other categories that are considered social constructs, like gender and class.

this hierarchy, the more free they are to speak about certain subjects concerning race, ethnicity, culture or nationality.[850] Wendy Brown viewed the creation of such hierarchies in terms of *ressentiment*. The concept of *ressentiment* (which can be considered the same as the more familiar term "resentment") was developed by Friedrich Nietzsche as a form of his infamous "will to power". Brown cited Nietzsche's concept as follows:

> For every sufferer instinctively seeks a cause for his suffering, more exactly, an agent; still more specifically, a *guilty* agent who is susceptible to suffering – in short, some living thing upon which he can, on some pretext or other, vent his affects, actually or in effigy. ... This ... constitutes the actual physiological cause of *ressentiment*, vengefulness, and the like: a desire to *deaden the pain by means of affects*, ... to *deaden*, by means of a more violent emotion of any kind, a tormenting, secret pain that is becoming unendurable, and to drive it out of consciousness at least for the moment: for that one requires an affect, as savage an affect as possible, and, in order to excite that, any pretext at all.[851]

Brown goes on to note the following with respect to "identity politics":

> *Ressentiment* in this context is a triple achievement: it produces an affect (rage, righteousness) that overwhelms the hurt; it produces a culprit responsible for the hurt; and it produces a site of revenge to displace the hurt (a place to inflict hurt as the sufferer has been hurt). Together these operations both ameliorate (in Nietzsche's term, "anaesthetize") and externalize what is otherwise "unendurable."[852]

And later:

> If the "cause" of *ressentiment* is suffering, its "creative deed" is the reworking of this pain into a negative form of action, the "imaginary revenge" of what Nietzsche terms "natures denied the true reaction, that of deeds." This revenge is achieved through the imposition of suffering "on whatever does not feel wrath and displeasure as *he* does" (accomplished especially through the production of guilt), through the establishment of suffering as the measure of social virtue, and through casting strength

---

850 The categories also extend to such things as sex, gender, sexuality, age and disability.
851 Friedrich Nietzsche, *On the Genealogy of Morals* (Vintage, 1969) 127 cited in Wendy Brown, *States of Injury: Power and Freedom in Late Modernity* (Princeton University Press, 1995) 68.
852 Wendy Brown, *States of Injury: Power and Freedom in Late Modernity* (Princeton University Press, 1995) 68 (emphasis in original).

and good fortune ("privilege," as we say today) as self-recriminating, as its own indictment in a culture of suffering: "it is disgraceful to be fortunate, there is too much misery."[853]

Brown goes on to note:

> In what could easily characterize the rancorous quality of many contemporary institutions and gatherings – academic, political, cultural – in which politicized identity is strongly and permissibly at play, Nietzsche offers an elaborate account of this replacement of pain with a "more violent emotion" that is the stock in trade of suffering:
>> The suffering are one and all dreadfully eager and inventive in discovering occasions for painful affects; they enjoy being mistrustful and dwelling on nasty deeds and imaginary slights; they scour the entrails of their past and present for obscure and questionable occurrences that offer them the opportunity to revel in tormenting suspicions and to intoxicate themselves with the poison of their own malice: they tear open their oldest wounds, they bleed from long-healed scars, they make evildoers out of their friends, wives, children, and whoever else stands closest to them. "I suffer: someone must be to blame for it" – thus thinks every sickly sheep.[854]

Brown was very much in favour of feminism and identity politics moving

---

853 Ibid 70 (citations omitted).
854 Wendy Brown, *States of Injury: Power and Freedom in Late Modernity* (Princeton University Press, 1995) 73 fn 40. To be clear, we do not subscribe to the philosophies of Nietzsche. However, the concept of *ressentiment* does appear to usefully describe an aspect of human pride where someone perceives that wrongs have been done to them. This then justifies either denigrating the perceived wrongdoer, feelings of superiority towards the perceived wrongdoer, or both. (Of course, there are instances where actual wrong is done, but it is useful to distinguish between perceived and actual wrong. This may not be an easy task at times, but it is a necessary one, and one that demands perspective and insight.)

beyond *ressentiment*,[855] a view[856] shared by others.[857] Unfortunately, beliefs and actions based on *ressentiment* appear to have exploded in the age of the internet.[858] Brendan O'Neill paints a rather bleak picture:

> At a time of great misanthropy, when individuals' capacity for autonomy is called into question and the idea of free will is ridiculed, Western society has come to value the easily harmed individual who demands therapy and recognition of his suffering over the self-motored, morally independent individual who believes that he can cut it by himself, with a little help from his friends, comrades, community. And in such a climate, those who lack victim status, who aren't actually suffering, must hunt down insults, exaggerate slights, and build a case for their being wounded creatures equally deserving of social sympathy and state resources. We are *incited* to play the victim. This explains everything from the obsession with microaggressions to feminists' obsessive logging of normal behaviour as 'everyday sexism' to Oxford students' depiction of a statue as violence: it's all an attempt to construct victimhood and thus win respect.[859]

We explore these issues further in the next section.

2 Practical problems

The use of intersectionality and privilege in civil society create grave concerns about how laws based on these concepts would operate. Further, and in any event, such laws would create issues concerning due process and the rule of law. We will examine each of these issues in turn.

---

855 Ibid 74-6. We must emphasise that Brown was *not* saying (and nor are we saying) that discrimination and harassment does not occur. Individuals who suffer discrimination or harassment should be able to seek and obtain redress.

856 The solutions to *ressentiment* that Brown proposed were based on postmodern theory – a theory (the reader will not be surprised to learn) with which we disagree.

857 Elspeth Probyn, 'Re: Generation. Women's Studies and the Disciplining of Ressentiment' (1998) 13(27) *Australian Feminist Studies* 129, 134. Unfortunately, Brown's argument has not caught on in the manner that she expected. For example, Brown's conception of *ressentiment* has been used to *justify* using degrees of injury in disadvantaged or underprivileged groups: see Fiona Probyn, 'Playing chicken at the intersection: the white critic of whiteness' (2004) 3(2) *Borderlands e-journal*.

858 See, for example, Jonah Goldberg, 'The Nietzschean Concept That Explains PC Culture', *National Review* (online), 19 June 2015.

859 Brendan O'Neill, 'Never mind Rhodes – it's the cult of the victim that must fall', *Spiked* (online), 29 December 2015 (emphasis in original). O'Neill did not mention *ressentiment* in his article, though his description matches *ressentiment* perfectly. (The statue O'Neill mentions is the statue of Cecil Rhodes at Oriel College, Oxford University. As O'Neill recounts in his article, certain students have describing walking past the statue as 'an act of violence'.)

As to how intersectionality and privilege are used in civil society, we note the use of "callouts", and the demand that others "check their privilege" when expressing views. "Callouts" are used to draw public attention to "problematic" behaviour.[860] Social media has vastly expanded the reach and impact of callouts. As David Auerbach noted:

> The callout focuses on *unintended* facets of one's behavior: accidental use of race-inflected language, unwitting assertions of privilege and power over members of less advantaged groups, and general lack of awareness. The internet is tailor-made for callouts and has provided a fertile and febrile ground for them.[861]

Auerbach continued:

> The callout is intrinsically an *ad hominem*... Where the Moralist [that is, the person deploying an intersectionality or privilege argument] departs from standard *ad hominem* practice... is in the insistence on false consciousness. In declaring that the stated, conscious intentions behind a target's behavior are subordinate to the social forces causing the target to promote oppression unknowingly, the Moralist makes an argument *about the target's character*, namely that she is the victim of false consciousness. False consciousness is not a costume one dons and discards at will; it is something that the target carries with her, and so an individual callout, while focused on a single bad act, is in fact an indictment of a person's entire character – a character that is founded upon, and must forever reckon with, the original sin of false consciousness. This is why the callout can never truly be answered in a single instance; the most one can do is promise to *try* to do better in fighting the system, knowing that eyes will be watching from that point on. Should the target *deny* the callout, the target will then lose the ability to claim ignorance as an excuse for her faulty behavior from that point on. Those who deploy callouts put themselves in the position of an anointed Moral elect, diagnosing false consciousness as a character flaw – though this does not exempt them

---

860 David Auerbach, '#JeNeSuisPasLiberal: Entering the Quagmire of Online Leftism', *The American Reader* (online) citing Lucy Uprichard, 'In Defence of Call-Out Culture', *The Huffington Post* (online), 27 December 2013.
861 David Auerbach, '#JeNeSuisPasLiberal: Entering the Quagmire of Online Leftism', *The American Reader* (online), (emphasis in original, citations omitted). To be clear, not every person subscribing to intersectionality and privilege believes in false consciousness. However, intersectionality and privilege are derived from Marxist theory, and false consciousness is part of Marxist theory.

from being targeted by other members of the elect.[862]

Auberbach noted the following about this notion of "the elect":

> As with any similarly conceived elect, from Plato's guardians to Calvinism's unconditional elect to Ayn Rand's creators, there is an ongoing need to identify and police the boundary of the elect from the non-elect: those of pure character and those of false, oppressive character. This process is particularly urgent to Moralist activists, as there is frequently a need to adjudicate competing callouts, sometimes by expelling one of the parties from the elect. Since expulsion amounts to a pronouncement of moral inferiority, the stakes are high. Two primary strategies exist to identify and police elect members: first, the hierarchical quantification of oppression described above, so that members of more oppressed groups carry greater Moral authority, alongside privileged "allies" who have had their awareness sufficiently raised; and second, what anthropologist Judith T. Irvine defines as "formal speech" (e.g., "privilege," "intersectionality," "ally," "structure") which rhetorician George Kennedy explains as an elite, regimented linguistic practice known primarily to a priestly caste. These two mechanisms ameliorate but do not prevent the frequent schisms in anti-oppression circles.[863]

Auberbach notes that 'the one rule that can be followed' is that 'the more marginalized an individual or group, the more they merit attention'.[864] He then notes 'Consequently, anti-oppression [intersection] discourse sometimes turns into an arms race (sometimes caricatured as "Oppression Olympics"), in which participants appear to compete for the label of who belongs to the most oppressed groups.'[865] Various commentators have given examples of the online

---

862 Ibid (emphasis in original, citations omitted). We should note that, in Auerbach's article, he charts various leftist positions using a Cartesian diagram. Each quadrant of the diagram is described as a cluster, and Auberbach notes the "Moralist", "Liberal", "Radical" and "Theory" clusters. (To avoid doubt, we used "idea clusters" earlier in our treatise, but our use of "cluster" is not the same as Auberbach's use of "cluster".)
863 Ibid n 11.
864 Ibid.
865 Ibid. Auerbach then notes 'But the cause is not just narcissism or ressentiment, but the prerequisite of some sort of comparative ranking (taking intersectionality into account) in order to do anti-oppression work.' : see ibid. With respect to Auerbach, and given Brown's observations on the subject, our view is that *ressentiment* appears to be the significant (if not the sole) factor in such competition.

battles prompted by such thinking in progressive circles,[866] leading Jonathan Chait to conclude '[t]he p.c. style of politics has one serious, possibly fatal drawback: It is exhausting.'

Laws prohibiting racist hate speech that are based on intersectionality risk making a person's range of speech dependent on various factors such as their race, colour, ethnicity or nationality. People who fall into a group considered more oppressed would have a wider range of speech, at least regarding certain issues. Such laws breach principles of equality before the law, including the Convention's guarantee of equality before the law.

Privilege encounters a further problem that (perhaps) intersectionality does not. Intersectionality appears primarily concerned with how various types of discrimination compound each other. However, privilege (at least superficially) does not rest on discrimination. Arguments concerning privilege tend to run thus: we have laws to combat discrimination, but structures perpetuating privilege remain. These structures must be recognised and addressed. The request to "check one's privilege" is a request to review and acknowledge the structural advantages one enjoys.

Assessing the privileges that a person does or does not enjoy involves them undertaking something like the following process:[867]

- Identifying themselves according to an attribute such as colour, race or ethnicity.[868]
- Identifying themselves with a group sharing that attribute.
- Identifying others according to an attribute such as colour, race or ethnicity.
- Identifying others with a group sharing that attribute.
- Making assumptions about how members of other groups think about the individual on the basis of the individual's attribute.
- Making assumptions about how members of other groups think about members of the group with which the person associates.

---

866 See, for example, the internecine dispute between feminist authors in the Facebook group Binders Full of Women Writers recounted in Jonathan Chait, 'Not a Very P.C. Thing to Say', *New York Magazine* (online), 27 January 2015; see also Julie Burchill, 'Don't you dare tell me to check my privilege', *The Spectator* (online), 22 February 2014; Helen Lewis, 'The uses and abuses of intersectionality', *New Statesman* (online) 20 February 2014.

867 We say "something like" because the process may not be as conscious or elaborate as what we describe.

868 As noted above, the range of attributes is much broader than this. We are confining the attributes to deal specifically with issues concerning privilege's application to law concerning racial discrimination and racial hatred.

- Making assumptions about how members of the group with which the person associates think about members of other groups.
- Making assumptions about how members of other groups treat members of other groups. (That is, groups who do not share particular attributes with the individual).

There are significant problems with arguments employing privilege. First, privilege makes an attribute the defining characteristic of an individual. The process of identifying privilege involves not just the person defining themselves by an attribute, but defining others by an attribute. Doing this overlooks tremendous differences between individuals. As noted above, each individual is unique in time and space, and each individual is possessed with a capacity for conceptual thought that brings a unique perspective.

Second, privilege is premised on making sweeping assumptions about what others think based on a given attribute. These assumptions are not relevantly different from employing stereotypes. Given that a legitimate concern with prejudiced attitudes is employing stereotypes, the apparent use of stereotypes in privilege is concerning. Further, such assumptions are often wrong as regards any particular individual.[869] Thus, there is a real risk that errors are incorporated into any analysis concerning groups (which, after all are comprised of individuals), leading to erroneous conclusions. In a situation that calls for multiple assumptions to be made about a particular individual's privilege (such as when someone assesses how an individual from one group is privileged in relation to an individual from another group) error will compound error.

Third, arguments stating that others are privileged because of certain attributes are no less prejudiced because the person making the argument comes from a less privileged background. Lack of wealth or status or power does not excuse thinking that a person or people has less (or more) inherent worth as humans because of their race, colour, ethnicity or nationality, even

---

869 For example, one of the privileges McIntosh claims about herself as a white person with respect to African-Americans is 'I can avoid spending time with people whom I was trained to mistrust and who have learned to mistrust my kind or me': Peggy McIntosh, 'White Privilege and Male Privilege: A Personal Account of Coming To See Correspondences through Work in Women's Studies' (Working Paper 189, Wellesley College Center for Research on Women, 1988) 2. McIntosh may herself have been trained to distrust African-Americans. However, thinking that other white people have been "trained" to distrust African-Americans is a sweeping (and erroneous) assumption. Further, thinking that (presumably all) African-Americans have learned to mistrust white people is also a sweeping (and erroneous) assumption. The assumptions underlying this claim of privilege are bad enough. However, McIntosh makes another 49 such claims, many of which contain similar flaws.

if those attributes are perceived to confer privileges.[870] Thinking this way may poison the spirit of any person. Indeed, thinking that lack of wealth or status or power may confer an immunity may mask or worsen the festering of such poison.[871]

Given these problems, it follows that laws restricting freedom of expression (or, indeed, any other right) on the basis of privilege would not be relevantly different from discriminatory laws. To restrict a person's freedom of expression on the basis of the privilege conferred by their race, colour, ethnicity or nationality would be racial discrimination. This is because the Convention, for good reason, makes no such distinctions regarding the enjoyment of freedom of expression. Under the Convention, every person is entitled to equal enjoyment of all rights, including freedom of expression.

Further, purporting to restrict freedom of expression on the basis of someone's privilege is antithetical to due process. Privilege is premised on "systems" or "structures" conferring unearned and unacknowledged advantages upon certain groups of people. However, when pressing a civil claim or criminal charge against a person, "systems" and "structures" are not on trial – *individuals are*.

Laws directed at racist hate speech that are premised on privilege presumably would to do the following:

- Take into account the race, colour, ethnicity or nationality of the speaker, including historic advantages or disadvantages associated with the relevant race, colour, ethnicity or nationality; and
- Take into account the race, colour, ethnicity or nationality of the audience, including historic advantages or disadvantages associated

---

870 Or other attributes like (for example) sex, gender, class, religion, sexuality, age or disability.
871 We note this problem in response to the contention that racism is not prejudice, but prejudice *plus power*. This is not the definition of racial discrimination in the Convention, for good reason. One's real or perceived lack of power is no excuse for dehumanising another person or people.

with the relevant race, colour, ethnicity or nationality.[872]

It is antithetical to due process to impose legal liability on someone partly or wholly because of the purported benefits that a system or structure confers on the group to which they belong. Doing so imposes a type of "collective punishment" on the person: holding them personally accountable for the real or perceived faults of the group to which they belong. Put another way, making a person's legal liability contingent on the invisible backpack that someone imagines they wear is as disturbing as it sounds.

On this point, we return to the benefits of enforcing laws of equal application. The rule of law is a powerful check to the caprice of others. As T R S Allan noted:

> The idea of the rule of law, in contradistinction to rule by men, is an ancient one. At its core is the conviction that law provides the most secure means of protecting each citizen from the arbitrary will of every other.[873]

An individual's legal liability should not influenced by their background. Nor should it depend on actual or imagined offence being taken by another person.

3   *Is s 18C a law based on intersectionality and/or privilege?*

Given our analysis thus far, readers may conclude that s 18C is a law based on intersectionality or privilege. Section 18C does bear hallmarks of such a law. It does not go so far as imposing legal liability on the basis of offence being taken by another person. Nor does s 18C include the full range of categories

---

[872] This is similar to Matsuda's proposal for hate speech laws. Matsuda noted: 'We can determine when subordination exists by looking at social indicators: wealth, mobility, comfort, health and survival tend to mark the rise to the top and fall to the depths': Mari Matsuda, 'Public Response to Racist Speech: Considering the Victim's Story' (1989) 87 *Michigan Law Review* 2320, 2362. Sandmann is rightly critical of this approach: 'The faith in social scientific research is questionable on at least two counts. As [Critical Legal Studies] adherents have reminded us, categories such as wealth, mobility, and comfort are discursive concepts we have invented. They do not reflect anything other than our own prepackaged conceptions. To use these categories as indications of subjugation is to reify both the categories and the concept of subjugation. The use of categories cannot verify the condition of group subjugation. Secondly, the existence of group categorization in itself is a byproduct of the belief that the simple product of aggregating individual attributes creates an accurate description of the group. The creation of a group through this process is once again a discursive process that fails to justify the either the acceptance or restriction of racial hate messages.': Warren Sandmann, 'Three Ifs and a Maybe: Mari Matsuda's Approach to Restricting Hate Speech Laws' (1994) 45 (3-4) *Communication Studies* 241, 253 (citations omitted).
[873] T R S Allan, 'Legislative Supremacy and the Rule of Law: Democracy and Constitutionalism' (1985) 44(1) *Cambridge Law Journal* 111, 112-3.

that intersectionality and privilege cover. However, s 18C does impose legal liability if a person's acts are such to offend, insult or humiliate a reasonable representative of a group based on their race, colour, ethnicity or nationality.

Of course, to some, that s 18C appears to embody an approach based on intersectionality and privilege is a welcome development. We disagree. One of the great achievements of modern philosophy is philosophical liberalism. It has influenced politics and society in Australia and elsewhere, and continues to do so. Pursuant to philosophical liberalism, individuals are to be judged *as individuals*, and not (as in earlier times) on account of their race, colour, sex or class. That intersectionality and privilege purport to do otherwise is, in fact, a retrograde step. Further, for the reasons stated in this treatise, s 18C encounters fundamental difficulties concerning its impact of freedom of expression and equality before the law. It is a law at odds with Australia's common law legal tradition and liberal democratic heritage.

VII

CONCLUSION

Without more, freedoms don't end where feelings begin. Clearly, racism must be combatted. However, states must take care to ensure that laws combatting racism do not unduly inhibit fundamental rights and freedoms. This is especially so in states with a common law legal tradition. Unfortunately, Part IIA generally, and s 18C in particular, unduly inhibit freedom of expression. This freedom is both a universally recognised human right in international law and a fundamental common law freedom.

Section 18C cannot be sustained under the external affairs power. There is no doubt that racism is a matter of international concern, and Australia entered into the Convention *bona fide*. However, s 18C's employment of offence, insult and humiliation greatly overreach the purpose of the Convention, which obliges States Parties to reconcile the prohibition of racial hatred with guarantees of freedom of expression. Section 18C's legislative overreach, if not legislative overkill, does not conform to Australia's obligations under the Convention, as it is not reasonably capable of being considered appropriate or adapted to the Convention's purpose.

Even if the external affairs power supported s 18C, then its operation impermissibly infringes the implied freedom of political communication. Section 18C burdens discussions about many matters that are the subject of Commonwealth and State legislative and executive action. Its aim, which on its terms is to prohibit racial hatred or promote racial tolerance by prohibiting offensive speech, is not an end compatible with Australia's system of representative and responsible government.

Section 18C is not reasonably appropriate or adapted to its purpose. Many of the terms that s 18C and s 18D employ are too broad and too vague. In any event, these terms directly affect discussions about government and political matters – discussions that are often robust and heated and result in offence, insult or humiliation. Section 18C's operation appears far wider than other protective legislation such as the SDA, the DDA and defamation law. The mechanism employed to resolve disputes imposes unacceptable burdens of its own. The uncertainties and burdens created by s 18C and s 18D affect not only on established news organisations, but individuals engaged in discussions concerning government and political matters.

As an alternative to the present Part IIA, we have proposed a provision modeled on clause 28 of the RDB. This provision prohibits speech that is intended to incite actual or threatened physical violence against people belonging to groups identifiable by race, colour, ethnicity or nationality, or property belonging to such people. This provision has a scope far narrower than s 18C. However, it would be sustained by the external affairs power, and not infringe the implied freedom of political communication. We have also proposed reforming existing offences against public order to better target abusive speech, as the present use of "offence" and "insult" may encounter similar problems to s 18C.

Ultimately, our proposal for legislative reform leaves much of the work of combating racism to Australia's civil society. However, given that Australia is a well-established democracy with a common law legal tradition, such work should not only be expected but welcomed.

BIBLIOGRAPHY

A Articles/Books/Reports

Allan T R S, 'Legislative Supremacy and the Rule of Law: Democracy and Constitutionalism' (1985) 44(1) *Cambridge Law Journal* 111

Anderson, Benedict, *Imagined Communities* (Verso, revised ed, 2006)

Balkin, R P and J L R Davis, *Law of Torts* (LexisNexis Butterworths, 4th ed, 2009)

Bower, Spencer, *A Code of the Law for Actionable Defamation* (Butterworth, 2nd ed, 1923)

Brown, Wendy, *States of Injury: Power and Freedom in Late Modernity* (Princeton University Press, 1995)

Butler, Susan (ed), *Macquarie Concise Dictionary* (Macquarie Dictionary Publishers, 5th ed, 2009)

Butler, Susan (ed), *Macquarie Concise Dictionary* (Macquarie Dictionary Publishers, 6th ed, 2013)

Carastathis, Anna, 'The Invisibility of Privilege: A Critique of Intersectional Models of Identity' (2008) 3(2) *Les Ateliers De L'Éthique* 23

Chesterman, Michael, *Freedom of Speech in Australian Law: A Delicate Plant* (Ashgate, 2000)

Clarke, David, 'The Icon of Liberty: The Status and Role of the Magna Carta in Australian and New Zealand Law' (2000) 24(3) *Melbourne University Law Review* 866

Collins, Patricia Hill, 'It's All in the Family: Intersections of Gender, Race, and Nation' (1998) 13(3) *Hypatia* 62

Conquest, Robert, *The Great Terror: A Reassessment* (Oxford University Press, 1990)

Crenshaw, Kimberle, 'Demarginalizing the Intersection of Race and Sex: A Black Feminist Critique of Antidiscrimination Doctrine, Feminist Theory and Antiracist Politics' (1989) *University of Chicago Legal Forum* 139

Dawkins, Richard, *The Selfish Gene* (Oxford University Press, 1989)

Dworkin, Ronald, *Taking Rights Seriously* (Duckworth, 1977)

Ekman, Paul and Daniel Cordaro, 'What is Meant by Calling Emotions Basic' (2011) 3(4) *Emotion Review* 364

Fleming, John G, *The Law of Torts* (Law Book Company, 5th ed, 1977)

Fuller, Lon, *The Morality of Law* (Yale University Press, 1964)

Glendon, Mary Ann, 'Foundations of Human Rights: The Unfinished Business' (1999) 44(1) *American Journal of Jurisprudence* 1

Guevara, Ernesto Che, *The Motorcycle Diaries: Notes on a Latin American Journey* (Ocean Press, 2003)

Havel, Vaclav, *The Power of the Powerless* (Huchinson, 1985)

Janssen, Esther, 'Limits to expression of religion in France' (2009) (1) *Agama & Religiusitas di Europa, Journal of European Studies* 22

Killenbeck, Mark R, 'Introduction: Prologues without Pasts, Answers without Questions' (1991) 44 *Arkansas Law Review* 915

Kristol, Irving, *Neoconservatism: The Autobiography of an Idea* (The Free Press, 1995)

Krygier, Martin, 'Virtuous Circles: Antipodean Reflections on Power, Institutions, and Civil Society' (1997) 11(1) *East European Politics and Societies* 36

Lee, Patrick and Robert P George, 'The Nature and Basis of Human Dignity' (2008) 21(2) *Ratio Juris* 173

Lerner, Natan, *The UN Convention on the Elimination of all Forms of Racial Discrimination* (Sijthoff & Nordhoof, 2nd ed, 1980)

Lichtenberg, Judith, 'Foundations and Limits of Freedom of the Press' (1987) 14(4) *Philosophy and Public Affairs* 329

Marx, Karl, *Capital: A Critique of Political Economy* (Penguin Classics, 1991)

Matsuda, Mari, 'Public Response to Racist Speech: Considering the Victim's Story' (1989) 87 *Michigan Law Review* 2320

McCall, Leslie, 'The Complexity of Intersectionality' (2005) 30(3) *Signs* 1771

McCrudden, Christopher, 'Human Dignity and Judicial Interpretation of Human Rights' (2008) 19(4) *European Journal of International Law* 655

McNamara, Luke *Regulating Racism: Racial Vilification Laws in Australia* (Sydney Institute of Criminology, 2002)

Meagher, Dan, 'So Far So Good?: A Critical Evaluation of Racial Vilification Laws in Australia' (2004) 32(2) *Federal Law Review* 225

Mégret, Frédéric, *The Relevance of international instruments on racial discrimination to racial discrimination policy in Ontario* (Ontario Human Rights Commission, December 2004)

Mill, J S, *On Liberty* (Penguin Classics, first published 1859, 1985 ed)

Milton, John, *Areopagitica* (The Legal Classics Library, 1992)

Moore, Harrison, *The Constitution of the Commonwealth of Australia* (John Murray, 1902)

Nietzsche, Friedrich, *On the Genealogy of Morals* (Vintage, 1969)

Note, 'The Voice for Vagueness Doctrine in the Supreme Court' (1960) *University of Pennsylvania Law Review* 67

Orwell, George, *Animal Farm* (Penguin Group (Australia), first published 1945, 2004 ed)

Orwell, George, 'Review of *Power: A New Social Analysis*', *The Adelphi* (January 1939)

Painter, Nell Irvin, *The History of White People* (WW Norton & Company, 2010)

Probyn, Elspeth, 'Re: Generation. Women's Studies and the Disciplining of Ressentiment' (1998) 13(27) *Australian Feminist Studies* 129

Robinson, David L, 'Brain function, emotional experience and personality' (2008) 64(4) *Netherlands Journal of Psychology* 152

Rose, Flemming, *The Tyranny of Silence: How One Cartoon Ignited a Global Debate on the Future of Free Speech* (Cato Institute, 2014)

Sandmann, Warren, 'Three Ifs and a Maybe: Mari Matsuda's Approach to Restricting Hate Speech Laws' (1994) 45 (3-4) *Communication Studies* 241

Schwelb, Egon, 'The International Convention on the Elimination of All Forms of Racial Discrimination' (1966) 15 *International and Comparative Law Quarterly* 996

Soutphommasane, Tim, *I'm Not Racist, But ... 40 Years of the Racial Discrimination Act* (University of New South Wales Press, 2015)

Stone, Adrienne, 'The Ironic Aftermath of *Eatock v Bolt*' (2015) 38 *Melbourne University Law Review* 926

Strauss, Leo, *Natural Right and History* (University of Chicago Press, first published 1953, 1965 ed)

Thampapillai, Dilan, 'Inconsistent at Best? An Analysis of Australia's Federal Racial Discrimination Laws' (2010) 1 *Canberra Law Review* 1

Thampapillai, Dilan, 'Managing Dissent under Part IIA of the *Racial Discrimination Act*' (2010) 17(1) *Murdoch University Electronic Journal of Law* 52

United Nations Educational, Social and Cultural Organisation (ed), *Human Rights: Comments and Introduction* (UNESCO, 1948)

Vonnegut, Kurt, 'Harrison Bergeron' (1991) 44 *Arkansas Law Review* 927

Waldron, Jeremy, 'Dignity and Defamation: The Visibility of Hate' (2010) 123 *Harvard Law Review* 1596

Waldron, Jeremy, 'How Law Protects Dignity' (2012) 71(1) *Cambridge Law Journal* 200

Waldron, Jeremy, *The Harm in Hate Speech* (Harvard University Press, 2012)

Wolfe, Tom, *Mauve Gloves & Madmen, Clutter & Vine* (Farrar, Straus and Giroux, 1976)

Woodcock, Andrew, 'Jacques Maritain, Natural Law and the Universal Declaration of Human Rights' (2006) 8 *Journal of the History of International Law* 245

Zimmermann, Augusto, 'The Constitutionality of Religious Vilification Laws in Australia: Why Religious Vilification Laws are Contrary to the Implied Freedom of Political Communication Affirmed in the Australian Constitution' (2013) *Brigham Young University Law Review* 457

Zimmermann, Augusto and Lorraine Finlay, 'A Forgotten Freedom: Protecting Freedom of Speech in an Age of Political Correctness' (2014) 14 *Macquarie Law Journal* 185

Zines, Leslie, *The High Court and the Constitution* (Butterworths, 3rd ed, 1992)

B Case Law

.au Domain Administration Ltd v Domain Names Australia Pty Ltd [2004] FCA 424; (2004) 207 ALR 521

A v Minister for Immigration and Ethnic Affairs [1997] HCA 4; (1997) 190 CLR 225

Aid/Watch Incorporated v Federal Commissioner of Taxation [2010] HCA 42; (2010) 241 CLR 539

Amalgamated Society of Engineers v Adelaide Steamship Co Ltd (1920) 28 CLR 129

BIBLIOGRAPHY

Attorney General (SA) v Corporation of the City of Adelaide [2013] HCA 3; (2013) 249 CLR 1

Australian Capital Television Pty Ltd v The Commonwealth [1992] HCA 45; (1992) 177 CLR 106

Australian Competition and Consumer Commission v C G Berbatis Holdings Pty Ltd [2000] FCA 2; (2000) 96 FCR 491

Bropho v Human Rights and Equal Opportunity Commission [2004] FCAFC 16; (2004) 135 FCR 105

Bropho v Western Australia [1990] HCA 24; (1990) 171 CLR 1

Bryant v Queensland Newspapers Pty Ltd [1997] HREOCA 23

Catch the Fire Ministries, Inc v Islamic Council of Victoria [2006] VSCA 284

Cheatle v The Queen [1993] HCA 44; (1993) 177 CLR 541

City of Chicago v Tribune Co (1923) 139 NE 86

Clarke v Nationwide News Pty Ltd trading as The Sunday Times [2012] FCA 307; (2012) 201 FCR 389

Coleman v Power [2004] HCA 25; (2004) 220 CLR 1

Combined Housing Organisation Limited v Hanson [1997] HREOCA 58

Commonwealth v Tasmania [1983] HCA 21; (1983) 158 CLR 1

Creek v Cairns Post Pty Ltd [2001] FCA 1007; (2001) 112 FCR 352

David Syme & Co v Canavan [1918] HCA 50; (1918) 25 CLR 234

David v Commonwealth [1988] HCA 63; (1988) 166 CLR 79

De La Mare v Special Broadcasting Service [1998] HREOCA 26

Derbyshire C.C. v Times Newspapers [1993] AC 534

Eatock v Bolt [2011] FCA 1103; (2011) 197 FCR 261

Eatock v Bolt (No 2) [2011] FCA 1180

Electrolux Home Products Pty Ltd v Australian Workers' Union [2004] HCA 40; (2004) 221 CLR 309

Evans v State of New South Wales [2008] FCAFC 130; (2008) 168 FCR 576

Ex parte Walsh; In re Yates (1925) 37 CLR 36

Harrison v Melham [2008] NSWCA 67; (2008) 72 NSWLR 380

Hogan v Hinch [2011] HCA 4; (2011) 243 CLR 506

Islamic Council of Victoria v Catch the Fire Ministries, Inc [2004] VCAT 2510

IW v City of Perth [1997] HCA 30; (1997) 191 CLR 1

James v Commonwealth (1936) AC 578

Jones v Scully [2002] FCA 1080; (2002) 120 FCR 243

Jones v Toben [2002] FCA 1150; (2002) 71 ALD 629

K-Generation Pty Ltd v Liquor Licensing Court [2009] HCA 4; (2009) 237 CLR 501

Kable v Director of Public Prosecutions (NSW) [1996] HCA 24; (1996) 189 CLR 51

King-Ansell v Police [1979] 2 NZLR 531

Kirmani v Captain Cook Cruises Pty Ltd (No 1) [1985] HCA 8; (1985) 159 CLR 351

Koowarta v Bjelke-Petersen [1982] HCA 27; (1982) 153 CLR 168

Lange v Australian Broadcasting Corporation [1997] HCA 25; (1997) 189 CLR 520

Langlands v Leng [1916] SC (HL) 102

Mandla v Dowell Lee [1983] 2 AC 548

McCloy v New South Wales [2015] HCA 34

Minister for Immigration & Citizenship v Haneef [2007] FCAFC 203; (2007) 243 ALR 606

Monis v The Queen [2013] HCA 4; (2013) 249 CLR 92

Nationwide News Pty Ltd v Wills [1992] HCA 46; (1992) 172 CLR 1

Nyungar Circle of Elders v West Australian Newspapers Ltd [2001] HREOCA 1

New York Times Co. v Sullivan (1964) 376 US 254

Pape v Federal Commissioner of Taxation [209] HCA 23; (2009) 238 CLR 1

Polyukhovich v Commonwealth [1991] HCA 32; (1991) 172 CLR 501

Povey v Qantas Airway Ltd [2005] HCA 33; (2005) 216 ALR 427

Prior v Queensland University of Technology & Ors, Federal Circuit Court of Australia Case no. BRG990/2015

Project Blue Sky Inc v Australian Broadcasting Authority [1998] HCA 28; (1998) 194 CLR 355

Purvis v New South Wales [2003] HCA 62; (2003) 217 CLR 92

R v Burgess; Ex parte Henry [1936] HCA 52; (1936) 55 CLR 608

R v Keegstra [1990] 3 SCR 697

R v Sharkey [1949] HCA 46; (1949) 79 CLR 121

R v Woollin [1999] 1 AC 82

Radio 2UE Sydney Pty Ltd v Chesterton [2009] HCA 16; (2009) 238 CLR 460

Re Bolton; Ex parte Beane [1987] HCA 12; (1987) 162 CLR 514

Re Alberta Statutes [1938] SCR 100

Saeed v Minister for Immigration & Citizenship [2010] HCA 23; (2010) 241 CLR 252

Shron v Telstra Corporation [1998] HREOCA 24

South Australia v Totani [2010] HCA 39; (2010) 242 CLR 1

Sunol v Collier (No 2) [2013] NSWCA 196; (2012) 260 FLR 414

Tajjour v New South Wales; Hawthorne v New South Wales; Forster v New South Wales [2014] HCA 35; (2014) 313 ALR 221

Taylor v Canadian Human Rights Commission [1990] 3 SCR 892

Theophanous v Herald & Weekly Times Ltd [1994] HCA 46; (1994) 182 CLR 104

Toben v Jones [2003] FCAFC 137; (2003) 129 FCR 505

Union Steamship Company of Australia Pty Ltd v King [1988] HCA 55; (1988) 166 CLR 1

Unions NSW v New South Wales [2013] HCA 58; (2013) 252 CLR 530

Victoria v Commonwealth [1996] HCA 56; (1996) 187 CLR 416

Wainohu v New South Wales [2011] HCA 24; (2011) 243 CLR 181

Western Australia v Commonwealth [1995] HCA 47; (1995) 183 CLR 373

Whitney v California 274 US 357 (1927)

Wotton v Queensland [2012] HCA 2; (2012) 246 CLR 1

XYZ v Commonwealth [2006] HCA 25; (2006) 227 CLR 532

C Legislation

28 Edward III (1354)
Acts Interpretation Act 1901 (Cth)
Australian Human Rights Commission Act 1986 (Cth)
Canada Act 1982 (UK) c 11, sch B pt I
Commonwealth of Australia Constitution Act (Cth)
Competition and Consumer Act 2010 (Cth)
Crimes Act 1914 (Cth)
Criminal Code 1995 (Cth)
Criminal Code, RSC 1985, c C-46 (Can)
Criminal Code 1913 (WA)
Defamation Act 1974 (NSW)
Defamation Act 2005 (WA)
Digital Millennium Copyright Act, Pub L No 105-304, 112 Stat 2860 (USA)
Disability Discrimination Act 1992 (Cth)
Fair Work (Registered Organisations) Act 2009 (Cth)
Human Rights and Equal Opportunity Act Commission 1986 (Cth)
Judiciary Act 1903 (Cth)
Magna Carta 25 Edward I (1297)
Parliamentary Privileges Act 1987 (Cth)
Parliamentary Privileges Act 1891 (WA)
Petition of Right 3 Charles I (1627)
Public Transport Authority Regulations 2003 (WA)

Racial Discrimination Act 1975 (Cth)
Racial Discrimination Bill 1974 (Cth)
Racial Hatred Bill 1994 (Cth)
Sex Discrimination Act 1984 (Cth)
Trade Practices Act 1974 (Cth)
Vagrants, Gaming and Other Offences Act 1931 (Qld)

D Treaties

Charter of the United Nations

International Convention on the Elimination of All Forms of Racial Discrimination, opened for signature 21 December 1965, 660 UNTS 195 (entered into force 4 January 1969)

International Covenant on Civil and Political Rights, opened for signature 16 December 1966, 999 UNTS 171 (entered into force 23 March 1976)

Universal Declaration of Human Rights

Vienna Convention on the Law of Treaties, opened for signature 23 May 1969, 1155 UNTS 331 (entered into force 27 January 1980)

E Other Sources

Abbott, Tony, George Brandis and Julie Bishop, 'Joint Press Conference' (Press Statement, 5 August 2014) <https://www.pm.gov.au/media/2014-08-05/joint-press-conference-canberra-0>

Abraham Lincoln Online, 'Annual Message to Congress – Concluding Remarks', 11 May 2015 <http://www.abrahamlincolnonline.org/lincoln/speeches/congress.htm>

Auerbach, David, '#JeNeSuisPasLiberal: Entering the Quagmire of Online Leftism', *The American Reader* (online) <http://theamericanreader.com/jenesuispasliberal-entering-the-quagmire-of-online-leftism/>

Australian Human Rights Commission, 'Gender and Race Intersectionality', Australian Human Rights Commission <https://www.humanrights.gov.au/hreoc-website-racial-discrimination-national-consultations-racism-and-civil-society-0>

Australian Human Rights Commission, *Freedom from Discrimination: Report on the 40th anniversary of the Racial Discrimination Act* (Australian Human Rights Commission, 2015)

Australian Law Reform Commission, *Multiculturalism and the Law* (Report No. 57) (1992)

Australian Law Reform Commission, *The Protection of Human Genetic Information* (Report No. 96) (2003)

Australian Law Reform Commission, *Unfair Publication: Defamation and Privacy* (Report No. 11) (1979)

BBC News, *Bardot fined over racial hatred*, BBC News (online), 3 June 2008 <http://news.bbc.co.uk/2/hi/entertainment/7434193.stm>

Berteaux, Anthony, 'An Open Letter to Jerry Seinfeld from a "Politically Correct" College Student', *The Huffington Post* (online), 10 June 2015 <http://www.huffingtonpost.com/anthony-berteaux/jerry-seinfeld-politcally-correct-college-student_b_7540878.html?ir=Australia>

Bolt, Andrew, 'I wish I could say more, but this is dangerous', *Herald Sun* (online), 4 April 2012 <http://blogs.news.com.au/heraldsun/andrewbolt/index.php/heraldsun/comments/i_wish_i_could_say_more_but_this_is_dangerous/>

Bolt, Andrew, 'No comments', *Herald Sun* (online), 8 April 2012 <http://blogs.news.com.au/heraldsun/andrewbolt/index.php/heraldsun/comments/no_comments/>

Bolt, Andrew, 'No comment', *Herald Sun* (online), 13 October 2012 <http://blogs.news.com.au/heraldsun/andrewbolt/index.php/heraldsun/comments/no_comment30/>

Bolt, Andrew 'My own words can be quoted, but not by me', *Herald Sun* (online), 25 February 2013 <http://blogs.news.com.au/heraldsun/andrewbolt/index.php/heraldsun/comments/my_own_words_can_be_quoted_but_not_by_me/>

Bolt, Andrew, 'No comment from me, but pray Dallas may discuss' *Herald Sun* (online), 26 March 2013 <http://blogs.news.com.au/heraldsun/andrewbolt/index.php/heraldsun/comments/no_comment_from_me_but_pray_that_dallas_may_discuss/>

Burchill, Julie, 'Don't you dare tell me to check my privilege', *The Spectator* (online), 22 February 2014 <http://www.spectator.co.uk/2014/02/dont-you-dare-tell-me-to-check-my-privilege/>

Chait, Jonathan, 'Not a Very P.C. Thing to Say', *New York Magazine* (online), 27 January 2015 <http://nymag.com/daily/intelligencer/2015/01/not-a-very-pc-thing-to-say.html#>

Cheng, Jacqui, 'Five examples of lame DMCA takedowns', *Ars Technica* (online), 17 May 2010 <http://arstechnica.com/tech-policy/2010/05/five-examples-of-lame-dmca-takedowns>

Cleese, John, 'Political Correctness Can Lead to an Orwellian Nightmare', *Big Think* (online), 31 January 2016 <https://www.youtube.com/watch?v=QAK0KXEpF8U>

BIBLIOGRAPHY

Committee on Defamation (New Zealand), *Recommendations on the Law of Defamation* (1977)

Committee on the Elimination of Racial Discrimination, *General Recommendation No 14: Definition of Racial Discrimination* (Forty-second session, 1993), UN Doc A/48/18 (1994)

Committee on the Elimination of Racial Discrimination, *General Recommendation No. 15: Measures to eradicate incitement to or acts of discrimination* (Forty-second session, 1993), UN Doc A/48/18 (1994)

Committee on the Elimination of Racial Discrimination, *General Recommendation No 32: The meaning and scope of special measures in the International Convention on the Elimination of All Forms of Racial Discrimination*, CERD/C/GC/32 (24 September 2009)

Committee on the Elimination of Racial Discrimination, *General Recommendation No 35: Combating racist hate speech*, CERD/C/GC/35 (26 September 2013)

Committee on the Elimination of Racial Discrimination, *Reports submitted by States parties under article 9 of the Convention (Combined fifteens, sixteenth and seventeenth periodic reports of States parties due in 2008, Australia)*, CERD/C/AUS/15-17, 7 January 2010

Commonwealth, *Parliamentary Debates*, House of Representatives, 15 November 1994

Commonwealth, *Parliamentary Debates*, Senate, 19 August 2003

Commonwealth, Royal Commission into Aboriginal Deaths in Custody, *National Report* (1991)

Crawley, William, '"Militant Atheist" found guilty of religious harassment', *BBC Will & Testament: William Crawley's Blog*, (online) 4 March 2010 <http://www.bbc.co.uk/blogs/legacy/ni/2010/03/militant_atheist_found-guilt-o.html>

Croatian Times, *Croats in France insist in a court case with Bob Dylan*, 25 November 2013 <http://www.croatiantimes.com/news/Panorama/2013-1125/34821/_Croats_in_France_insist_in_a_court_case_with_Bob_Dylan>

Declaration on the Granting of Independence to Colonial Countries and Peoples, GA Res 1514 (XV), UN GAOR, 15th sess, 947th plen mtg (14 December 1960)

Dylan, Bob, *Dignity* (1963)

EuropeNews, *President of Danish Free Press Society convicted for 'Racism'*, *EuropeNews* (online) 3 May 2011 <http://europenews.dk/en/node/42859>

Explanatory Memorandum, *Racial Discrimination Bill 1974* (Cth)

Flanagan, Caitlin, 'That's Not Funny! Today's college students can't seem to take a joke', *The Atlantic* (online), September 2015 <http://www.theatlantic.com/magazine/archive/2015/09/thats-not-funny/399335/>

Foster, Noel, 'Anti-Vilification Laws and Freedom of Religion in Australia – Is Defamation Enough?' Paper presented at the Conference 'Justice, Mercy and Conviction: Perspectives on Law, Religion and Ethics', University of Adelaide School of Law, 7-9 June 2013

France24, 'French court drops 'hate speech' case against Bob Dylan', *France24* (online) 15 April 2014 <http://www.france24.com/en/20140415-france-bob-dylan-charges-inciting-hatred-dismissed-paris-court/>

Goldberg, Jonah, 'The Nietzschean Concept That Explains PC Culture', *National Review* (online), 19 June 2015 <http://www.nationalreview.com/article/420010/nietzschean-concept-explains-todays-pc-culture-jonah-goldberg>

Goldberg, Rube, 'Rube Goldberg Biography' (20 December 2014), *Rube Goldberg: Home of the Official Rube Goldberg Machine Contests* <http://www.rubegoldberg.com/about>

Goldman, Devorah, 'The Closing of the Campus Mind', *The Weekly Standard* (online), 6 April 2015 <http://www.weeklystandard.com/articles/closing-campus-mind_89943>

Greer, Scott, 'The Left's Outrage At Jerry Seinfeld Proves His Point', *Daily Caller* (online), 13 June 2015 <http://dailycaller.com/2015/06/13/the-lefts-outrage-at-jerry-seinfeld-proves-his-point/>

Griffiths, Emma, 'Government Backtracks on Racial Discrimination Act 18C Changes; Pushes Ahead with Tough Security Laws', *ABC News* (online), 6 August 2014 <http://www.abc.net.au/news/2014-08-05/government-backtracks-on-racial-discrimination-act-changes/5650030>

Human Rights Committee, *General Comment 18: Non-discrimination,* 37th sess (10 November 1989)

Human Rights Committee, *General Comment 22 (art 18)* (27 November 1993)

Human Rights Committee, *General Comment 34: Article 19 (Freedom of opinion and expression),* CCPR/C/GC/34 (12 September 2011)

Human Rights Committee, *General Comment 35; Article 9 (Liberty and security of person),* CCPR/C/GC/35 (13 February 2014)

Human Rights and Equal Opportunity Commission, *National Enquiry into Racist Violence* (Australian Government Publishing Service, 1991)

Kern, Soeren, 'Free Speech on Trial in Europe', *Gatestone Institute* (online), 27 January 2011 <http://www.gatestoneinstitute.org/1829/free-speech-on-trial-in-europe>

Koukl, Gregory, 'The Intolerance of Tolerance', *Townhall* (online), 14 December 2006 <http://townhall.com/columnists/gregorykoukl/2006/12/14/the_intolerance_of_tolerance/page/full>

Kozlowska, Hannah, 'Has Ebola Exposed a Strain of Racism?', *New York Times* (online), 21 October 2014 <http://www.op-talk.blogs.nytimes.com/2014/10/21/has-ebola-exposed-a-strain-of-racism/?_r=1>

Legal Project, *European Hate Speech Laws* <http://www.legal-project.org/issues/european-hate-speech-laws>

Lewis, Helen, 'The uses and abuses of intersectionality', *New Statesman* (online) 20 February 2014 <http://www.newstatesman.com/helen-lewis/2014/02/uses-and-abuses-intersectionality>

Lukianoff, Greg and Jonathan Haidt, 'The Coddling of the American Mind', *The Atlantic* (online), September 2015 <http://www.theatlantic.com/magazine/archive/2015/09/the-coddling-of-the-american-mind>

Mad Men (Directed by Phil Abraham, AMC, 2010) episode 4.8 'The Summer Man'

Marsden, Rachel, 'Your Rights End Where Mine Begin' *Human Events* (online) 18 September 2011 <http://humanevents.com/2011/09/18/your-rights-end-where-mine-begin/>

McArdle, Megan, 'Ex-60 Minutes Producer Is No Hollywood Hero', *Bloomberg View*, (online) 24 July 2014 <http://www.bloombergview.com/articles/2014-07-24/ex-60-minutes-producer-is-no-hollywood-hero>

McIntosh, Peggy, 'White Privilege and Male Privilege: A Personal Account of Coming To See Correspondences through Work in Women's Studies' (Working Paper 189, Wellesley College Center for Research on Women, 1988)

Milli Gazette, 'Swiss Muslims File Suit Over 'Racist' Fallaci Book', *The Milli Gazette* (online), 1 July 2002 <http://www.milligazette.com/Archives/01072002/0107200263.htm>

O'Conner, Lydia, 'Bill Maher Calls College Student A "Little Sh*t" for Criticizing Jerry Seinfeld', *The Huffington Post* (online), 21 June 2015 <http://www.huffingtonpost.com.au/2015/06/20/bill-maher-pc-comedy_n_7628188.html?ir=Australia>

O'Neill, Brendan, 'Never mind Rhodes – it's the cult of the victim that must fall', *Spiked* (online), 29 December 2015 <http://www.spiked-online.com/newsite/article/never-mind-rhodes-its-

the-cult-of-the-victim-that-must-fall/17762#.VoxkLVJ4L9D>

Owens, Jared, 'Tony Abbott Dumps Planned Changes to Section 18C of Racial Discrimination Act', *The Australian* (online), 5 August 2014 <http://www.theaustralian.com.au/national-affairs/tony-abbott-dumps-planned-changes-to-section-18c-of-racial-discrimination-act/story-fn59niix-1227014479772>

Quote Investigator (online), 'Your Liberty to Swing Your Fist Ends Just Where My Nose Begins', *Quote Investigator* (online), 15 October 2011 <http://quoteinvestigator.com/2011/10/15/liberty-fist-nose/>

Parliamentary Research Service (Department of the Parliamentary Library), *Bills Digest: Racial Hatred Bill 1994*, 14 November 1994

Pearson, Allison, 'We must listen to Trevor Phillips and his inconvenient truths about race', *The Telegraph* (online), 19 March 2015 <http://www.telegraph.co.uk/news/uknews/immigration/11479761/We-must-listen-to-Trevor-Phillips-and-his-inconvenient-truths-about-race.html>

Phys Org, 'Earth survived near-miss from 2012 solar storm: NASA', *Phys Org* (online) 25 July 2014 <http://phys.org/news/2014-07-earth-survived-near-miss-solar-storm.html>

Probyn, Fiona 'Playing chicken at the intersection: the white critic of whiteness' (2004) 3(2) *Borderlands e-journal* <http://www.borderlands.net.au/vol3no2_2004/probyn_playing.htm>

Rich, Frank, 'In Conversation with Chris Rock', *Vulture* (online) 30 November 2014 <http://www.vulture.com/2014/11/chris-rock-frank-rich-in-conversation.html?mid=twitter_nymag#>

Sheehan, Paul, 'Spreading the Word of Intolerance', *Sydney Morning Herald* (online), 4 October 2004 <http://www.smh.com.au/articles/2004/10/03/1096741896292.html>

Sherman, Amy, 'Did Che Guevara write "extensively" about the superiority of white Europeans? Rubio says yes', *Politifact* (online), 17 April 2013 <http://www.politifact.com/florida/statements/2013/apr/17/marco-rubio/did-che-guevara-write-extensively-about-superiorit/>

Snyder, Ann, 'Danish Supreme Court Acquits Hedegaard', *The Legal Project*, (online) 21 April 2012 <http://www.legal-project.org/blog/2012/04/danish-supreme-court-acquits-hedegaard>

Soutphommasane, Tim, 'Empathy, Power and Privilege', Australian Human Rights Commission, 2 November 2014 <https://www.humanrights.gov.au/news/speeches/empathy-power-and-privilege-0>

Special Committee on Hate Propaganda in Canada, *Report of the Special Committee on Hate Propaganda in Canada* (Queen's Printer, 1966)

Spigelman, James, 'Free Speech Tripped up by Offensive Line', *The Australian*, 11 December 2002

Steyn, Mark, 'Lars Hedegaard, Defender of Freedom', *SteynOnline* (online), 16 December 2014 <http://www.steynoline.com/5420/lars-hedegaard-defender-of-freedom>

The Princess Bride (Directed by Rob Reiner, Act III Communications, 1987)

Thomas, Hedley, 'Racial stoush erupts over QUT computer lab', *The Australian* (online), 4 February 2016 <http://www.theaustralian.com.au/higher-education/racial-stoush-erupts-over-qut-computer-lab/news-story/b80de339339f2d5588839ac06f3c8909>

Thomas, Hedley, 'Offer to drop QUT race "slur" case for $5,000', *The Australian* (online), 5 February 2016, <http://www.theaustralian.com.au/higher-education/offer-to-drop-qut-race-slur-case-for-5000/news-story/2cd2f6b1598d776a49acd14ef2f9bcba>

Thomas, Hedley, 'Watchdog kept 18C respondent in dark about QUT complaint', *The Australian* (online), 8 February 2016 see: <http://www.theaustralian.com.au/national-affairs/indigenous/watchdog-kept-18c-respondent-in-the-dark-about-qut-complaint/news-story b5aa4706ba62548 bd20353bd1682f31b>.

Thomas, Hedley, 'QUT Oodgeroo Unit race row: staffer "aggressive, unpleasant"', *The Australian* (online), 23 February 2016 <http://www.theaustralian.com.au/higher-education/qut-oodgeroo-unit-race-row-staffer-aggressive-unpleasant/news-story/eb18db9c689a7d6e4215ca5264571552>

Transperth, *Safety and Security* <http://www.transperth.wa.gov.au/using-transperth/safety-security>

Universal Declaration of Human Rights, GA Res 217A (III), UN GAOR, 3rd sess, 183rd plen mtg, UN Doc A/810 (10 December 1948)

Uprichard, Lucy, 'In Defence of Call-Out Culture', *The Huffington Post* (online), 27 December 2013 <http://www.huffingtonpost.co.uk/lucy-uprichard/call-out-culture_b_4507889.html>

Urban Dictionary (online), 2 May 2003 <http://www.urbandictionary.com/define.php?term=itt>

Western Australian Law Reform Commission, *Defamation* (Project No 8 – Part II) (1979)

Wilson, Tim, 'Insidious Threats to Free Speech', *The Weekend Australian*, 5-6 April 2014

Yiannopoulos, Milo, 'Coming 2016: All-Out War on So-Called "Social Justice"' *Breitbart* (online), 31 December 2015 <http://www.breitbart.com/tech/2015/12/31/coming-2016-all-out-war-on-so-called-social-justice/>

INDEX

Abbott, Tony 7
Aboriginal 46, 96, 120, 131-2, 179, 225-6
Abuse 85, 219, 222-5
Academic, artistic or scientific purpose 16, 56-7, 162-3
Acts Interpretation Act 1901 (Cth) 20-1, 124
Adapted 35-6
Adelaide Preacher's Case 150-3
Advocacy 24, 92-3, 100, 102, 105
Affirmative action 57-8
Aides Haute-Garonne 218
Allan, T R S 150, 238
Amusement 46-7
Anger 47
Anxiety 139, 140, 141
Appropriate 35-6
Appropriate and adapted
    External affairs power 9, 22, 28, 35, 36, 44, 45, 51, 53, 59, 63, 87, 89-91, 92, 105-6, 113-5, 116
    Implied freedom of political communication 10, 118, 146, 148, 153, 154, 168, 197, 198-210

Artistic work 16, 56-7, 160, 162-3, 211-2
Assault 140, 212
Auerbach, David 233-4
Australian electors 10, 118, 121, 122, 130, 164-6
Australian Human Rights Commission 85, 133, 162, 174-6
    Conciliation process 88, 91, 107, 125, 174
    Lived experience of racism 85-6
Australian Human Rights Commission Act 1986 (Cth) 91, 174-6
Australian Law Reform Commission
    Multiculturalism and the Law 97, 98, 221-2, 225
    Protection of Human Genetic Information 131, 132
    Unfair Publication: Defamation and Privacy 171-2, 187, 190-1

Bad faith 27, 50, 93, 160, 162, 205
Balancing approach to rights and freedoms 97, 98, 99, 117, 147, 200, 202, 203, 206, 225
Bardot, Brigitte 217
Belief 16, 20, 40, 55, 83, 98, 134, 135, 143, 170, 183, 192, 211, 232

Biology 10, 131, 134
Body/idea distinction 11, 71, 76, 124, 136-45
Bolt, Andrew 179-80
Bona fide treaty 25, 27
Border protection 120, 121
Brandeis, Justice 86
Branson, Justice 17, 54
Brennan, Chief Justice 25
Brennan, Justice 79
Broad, too 49, 52, 60, 96, 194, 207, 211, 219, 241
Bromberg, Justice 53, 54, 62, 75, 76, 77, 79, 82, 153, 161, 170, 194
Bropho v Human Rights and Equal Opportunity Commission 17, 49-50, 159-61, 169, 171
Brown, Wendy 230-1

Canada 77, 83, 84, 87, 195, 196
Canada, Supreme Court of 78, 79, 80
Canadian Human Rights Act 195
Capacity for conceptual thought 67-71, 137, 143-4, 229, 236
Carr, Justice 18, 99-106, 114, 171
Chait, Jonathan 235
Charlie Hebdo 218
Charter of Rights and Freedoms 78, 79
Checking one's privilege 233-7
Child pornography 184, 190
Chilling effect 21, 41, 127, 155, 162, 177, 178, 179, 180, 193, 196, 209, 219
Civil society 8, 13-4, 154, 163, 204, 222, 228, 239
Civilisation 171, 197-8
Class 57, 116, 133, 163, 167, 187, 212, 227, 228, 239
Coded language 127
Cohen Committee 82-4
Coleman v Power 9, 117, 127, 129, 147
Collins, Patricia Hill 227
Colour 8, 10, 11, 13, 15, 18, 20, 29, 36, 42, 43, 44, 45, 46, 48, 49, 51, 53, 55, 56, 58, 59, 60, 63, 71, 73, 76, 77, 82, 89, 91, 94, 100, 101, 111, 112, 115, 116, 119, 120, 121, 122, 124, 125, 126, 131, 132, 133, 134, 136, 141, 143, 144, 145, 146, 155, 156, 157, 158, 160, 161, 168, 184, 186, 187, 191, 206, 207, 209, 214, 215, 222, 235, 236,

237, 238, 239
Committee on the Elimination of Racial Discrimination 27, 43, 44, 52, 57-8, 60, 107, 127
Common law 7, 13, 31, 84, 87, 140, 146, 147, 148-9, 150-1, 152, 153-4, 167, 187, 192, 195, 197, 203, 204, 210, 239, 241, 242
Commonwealth Constitution
External affairs power: see External Affairs Power
Heads of power 119-20
Implied equality of political communication: see Implied equality of political communication
Implied freedom of political communication: see Implied freedom of political communication

Commonwealth government
Executive government 10, 118, 119, 121, 122, 123, 126, 130, 131, 132, 145, 147, 156, 157, 164, 188, 189, 201, 206, 207, 241
Submissions in Toben v Jones 100-2

Communism 64, 74, 172-3
Complaint 27, 55, 99, 126, 174-5, 183, 225, 226
Complexity 146, 190-2, 194, 196, 197
Concern 46, 47
Conciliation 88, 91, 107, 125, 174
Conformity requirement 9, 25, 34, 35-91, 92-6, 105-6, 113-5, 213
Conscience, freedom of 40, 51, 64, 69, 72, 73, 109, 111, 139, 142, 143, 144
Constructs 227
Consumer protection legislation 153, 184, 190
Convention on the Elimination of All Forms of Racial Discrimination
Article 1 26, 63, 109, 111
Article 2 9, 26, 29, 30, 31, 32, 33, 34, 36, 57, 58-87, 88, 89, 90, 91, 99, 102, 103-4, 108, 110, 111, 112, 113, 114, 116
Article 4 9, 17, 26, 29, 30, 31, 33, 34, 36-51, 52, 53, 56, 57, 58, 59, 60, 87, 88, 89, 90, 91, 92, 93, 99, 102, 103, 106, 107, 108, 110, 111, 112, 113, 114, 115, 116, 214, 215
Article 5 9, 26, 36, 40, 42, 43, 49, 51, 53-8, 60, 61, 77, 87, 89, 90, 103-4, 107, 110, 111, 112, 114, 115, 116, 216
Article 6 9, 26, 27, 29, 32, 34, 36, 87-8, 90,

108, 110, 112, 114, 116
Article 7 9, 27, 29, 31, 32-4, 36, 88-9, 91, 99, 100, 102, 104, 108, 110, 112, 114, 116
Preamble 63, 109

Crimes Act 1914 (Cth) 125
Criminal Code 1913 (WA) 223, 225
Criminal defamation 186-9
Cuba 172-173
Culture 10, 26, 34, 54, 56, 58, 62, 64, 69, 70, 72, 78, 83, 89, 91, 98, 104, 131, 135, 136, 138, 139, 141, 143, 144, 145, 159, 197, 198, 208, 216, 223, 229, 230, 231
Cultural appropriation 139

Defamation 11, 80, 140, 167, 169, 170, 171, 176-8, 184, 186-9, 190, 205, 209-11, 242
Defamation Act 1974 (NSW) 209-11
Degradation 20, 74, 75, 76, 77
Dehumanise 20, 76, 77
Democracy 7, 11, 58, 78, 84, 98, 123, 126, 129, 140, 141, 145, 150, 156, 162, 163, 167, 171, 192, 208, 216, 239, 242
Demosthenes 127
Denigrate 224
Depression 140, 141
Dickson, Chief Justice 78-84
Dignity 12, 19, 20, 61, 62, 63-71, 73, 74, 75, 76, 78, 84, 87, 90, 98, 109, 110, 188, 189, 217
Disability discrimination 186, 190, 213, 242
Disorderly conduct 222, 223, 225
Dissemination 29, 31, 36, 37-8, 40, 42, 43, 44, 63, 83, 107
Dog whistling 127
Due process 193, 195, 232, 237-8
Dworkin, Ronald 73, 74, 129-30, 193
Dylan, Bob 217

Eatock, Pat 179
Eatock v Bolt 53, 62, 75, 76, 77, 134, 153, 161, 170, 179-80
Education 13, 26, 33, 34, 72, 83, 87, 89, 91, 121, 171, 174, 185, 186, 198, 227
Emotions 84, 85, 86, 89, 128, 129, 140, 230, 231
Categorising 45
Creating 39, 44, 45, 47, 48, 49, 101, 208
Motivation by 45, 46, 101
Manifesting 39, 45, 46, 47, 49, 101, 208
Strong 42, 44, 47
Visceral nature of 39

INDEX

Empathy 142
Enmity 8, 11, 214-6, 220
Equality 61, 62, 71, 73, 76, 79, 87
  Definition 62, 63
  Equality before the law 51, 53, 56, 75, 90, 94, 96, 116, 224, 235, 238, 239
  Equality in range of rights 71-2
  Of political communication: see Implied equality of political communication

Ethnicity 10, 11, 13, 20, 42, 45, 46, 48, 49, 53, 55, 56, 58, 71, 89, 101, 115, 116, 119, 120, 121, 122, 123, 126, 131, 132, 133, 134, 135, 136, 138, 139, 145, 156, 157, 158, 161, 168, 191, 206, 207, 214, 215, 222, 223, 228, 229, 230, 235, 236, 237, 238, 239

Executive 10, 11, 118, 119, 121, 122, 123, 126, 130, 131, 132, 145, 147, 150, 156, 157, 164, 188, 189, 201, 206, 207, 222, 226, 241
Expression, freedom of 8, 9, 11, 13, 14, 21, 31, 42, 44, 49, 51, 52, 53, 60, 61, 62, 63, 64, 65, 66, 67, 69, 70, 71, 72, 73, 75, 76, 77, 78, 79, 80, 81, 84, 85, 87, 89, 90, 94, 95, 96, 98, 103, 104, 107, 109, 111, 115, 129, 130, 137, 143, 144, 145, 149, 150, 151, 152, 153, 154, 155, 161, 169, 184, 189, 194, 204, 207, 216, 226, 227, 229, 237, 241
External Affairs Power 8, 23, 24, 25, 27, 28, 29, 35, 37, 63, 91, 93, 97, 99, 116, 117, 146, 213, 241, 242

Fair and accurate report 16, 169, 171
Fair comment 16, 75, 170-1, 173, 177, 178, 187, 189, 192, 205
Fallaci, Oriana 217-8
Fallacious methods of argument 42, 85, 139
Fascism 84, 87
Fear 19, 47, 73, 82, 85, 115, 156, 178, 187, 191, 211
Federal Circuit Court 174, 175, 176, 180
Federal Court 24, 150, 174, 175, 176, 179
Foster, Noel 150
Freedom of expression: see Expression, freedom of
Freedoms don't end where feelings begin 144, 241
Free speech (see also Expression, freedom of) 52, 59, 73, 74, 75, 82, 97, 129, 130, 137, 150, 153, 154, 171-2, 176, 177, 186, 187, 188, 190, 193, 194, 204, 208, 214, 219, 225
French, Chief Justice 150, 153, 198
French, Justice 17, 159, 160, 161, 163, 169, 171
Fulller, Lon 193-4

Gageler, Justice 198, 200-1, 201
Gaudron, Justice 176-7
Genuine 16, 162-3, 170, 191, 192, 205, 206, 208, 211, 212
George, Robert P 67, 69, 137
Goldberg, Rube 191
Good faith 16, 27, 50, 92, 159-62, 163, 169, 170, 173, 191, 192, 193, 205, 208, 210, 212
Gordon, Justice 198, 203-3
Group 10, 15, 21, 29, 32, 36, 39, 42, 43, 44, 46, 47, 48, 49, 51, 53, 54, 55, 56, 57, 58, 59, 60, 61, 67, 75, 76, 78, 82, 83, 84, 86, 94, 97, 98, 99, 107, 108, 110, 112, 119, 121-2, 124, 128, 129, 130, 131, 134, 135, 141, 144, 146, 155, 156, 157, 158, 173, 181, 182, 183, 186-9, 190, 191, 197, 207, 208, 211, 214, 222, 225, 227, 233, 234, 235, 236, 237, 238, 239
Group libel 186-9
Guevara, Ernesto Che 172-3
Gummow, Justice 127

Haidt, Jonathan 141
Harm 20, 49, 50, 62, 69, 70, 77, 85, 86, 89, 92, 145, 157, 160, 161, 162, 169, 171, 173, 187, 190, 191, 192, 200, 205, 206, 207, 209, 232
Harm minimisation 161-3, 169, 171, 173, 191, 192, 205
Harm threshold 50, 62, 77, 89, 92, 145
Hate 35, 42, 45, 46, 47, 48, 49, 78, 82, 83, 84, 85, 86, 101, 208, 213, 215
  Definition 38
  Emotion 45, 47, 48, 101, 208, 213
  Racial hatred: see Racial Hatred
Hate speech 29, 33, 36, 42, 59, 66, 86, 188, 217, 219, 229, 235, 237, 238
Havel, Vaclav 74-5
Hayne, Justice 127, 128, 147
Hedegaard, Lars 217
Hely, Justice 17, 18
Herald and Weekly Times Pty Ltd 176, 179

Heydon, Justice 28, 30, 127
High Court 8, 15, 17, 18, 19, 24, 28, 117, 118, 133, 146, 148, 149, 157, 165, 166, 198, 209, 210, 211, 222
History 10, 25, 26, 56, 64, 75, 87, 103, 106, 114, 123, 128, 129, 135, 138, 145, 149, 160, 161, 177, 188, 198, 208
Human Rights and Equal Opportunity Act 1986 (Cth) 91
Human Rights and Equal Opportunity Commission 96, 125
Human Rights Committee 40, 61-2, 95-6
Humiliation: see Offend, insult or humiliate and Offend, insult, humiliate or intimidate
   Definition 19, 20
   Scope 15, 16, 17-8, 20, 22
Hurt feelings 98, 139, 140, 141, 194

Idea
   Body/idea distinction: see Body/idea distinction
   Concept as 137
   Dissemination of: see Dissemination
   Involuntarily adopted 143, 144
   Involuntarily generated 143, 144
   Manifestation of capacity for conceptual thought 137
   Voluntarily adopted 143, 144
   Voluntarily generated 143, 144

Idea clusters 138-9
Immigration 101, 120, 121, 207, 218
Implied equality of political communication 11, 56, 164-9
Implied freedom of political communication 9, 9-10, 11, 12, 22, 79, 97, 116, 117, 118, 119, 123, 146, 147, 148, 153, 156, 164, 165, 166, 167, 168, 169, 171, 173, 177, 178, 180, 185, 186, 188, 190, 194, 195, 200, 201, 202, 203, 204, 205, 206, 207, 209, 211, 213, 216, 220, 241, 242
   Burden on 118-23
   Nature of 146-8
   Relationship of common law with 153-4

Incitement
   To racial discrimination 18, 24, 29, 36, 37, 42, 43, 44, 49, 52, 56, 57, 92, 93, 100, 101, 102, 103, 104, 105, 106, 108, 110, 112
   To racial hatred 26, 36, 43, 44, 45, 51, 59, 89, 92, 93, 97, 98, 99, 100, 101, 102, 103, 104, 105, 106, 108, 110, 125, 216, 220
   To racial violence 8, 29, 36, 37, 42, 43, 44, 49, 61, 92, 105, 145, 214, 215, 216, 220, 242

Individual 14, 27, 31, 39, 51, 54, 57, 58, 61, 62, 64, 66, 68, 69, 70, 71, 72, 73, 76, 78, 80, 83, 86, 88, 94, 97, 99, 121, 124, 130, 134, 135, 138, 139, 140, 141, 142, 143, 144, 146, 151, 154, 157, 158, 167, 169, 171, 172, 177, 179, 185, 186, 187, 188, 189, 191, 195, 196, 203, 211, 219, 220, 225, 232, 233, 234, 235, 236, 237, 239, 242
Industrial Relations Act Case 28
Insult: see Offend, insult or humiliate and Offend, insult, humiliate or intimidate
   Definition 19
   Scope 15, 16, 17-8, 20, 22

International concern or character 23, 25, 27-8, 92, 241
International Convention on Civil and Political Rights 9, 18, 40, 97, 101, 106
   Article 2(1) 94
   Article 3 94
   Article 5(1) 94
   Article 9(1) 61
   Article 19 62, 94, 95, 151
   Article 20(2) 9, 91, 92, 93, 95, 96, 99, 100, 102, 105
   Article 26 94

Intersectionality 213, 227-9, 232-5, 238-9
Intimidation see: Offend, insult or humiliate and Offend, insult, humiliate or intimidate
   Definition 19
   Scope 15, 16, 17-8, 20, 22

Isaacs, Justice 151
Islam 133, 183, 216, 217, 218
Islamic Council of Victoria v Catch the Fire Ministries Inc 182-3
Israel 56

Jew 54, 143, 217

Keegstra, R v 77-8, 81-4, 193, 195-6
Kiefel, Justice 17, 99, 198
King-Ansell v Police 132, 133, 134, 215
Kirby, Justice 127-8

INDEX

Koowarta v Bjelke-Petersen 24
Krygier, Martin 154

Lange v Australian Broadcasting Corporation 9, 10, 11, 117-8, 124, 126, 131, 145-6, 148, 149, 164, 166, 167, 194, 196, 198, 201, 202, 209-11
Laws of equal application 220-7, 238
Lee, Justice 160, 161, 169
Lee, Patrick 67, 69, 137
Legislature/legislative action 10, 11, 19, 28, 30, 35, 56, 118, 119-21, 121-2, 122, 126, 145, 147, 156, 157, 188, 189, 204, 206, 207, 226, 241
Legitimate purpose 10, 117, 123-6, 126-31, 131-6, 145, 146, 158, 168, 199, 202, 203, 211
Lerner, Natan 26, 27, 30, 31, 32, 33, 43, 52, 88, 108, 109
Liberal democracy 7, 64, 239
Lived experience 85-6
Lukianoff, Greg 141

Magna Carta 151, 195
Mandla v Dowell-Lee 132, 134-5, 215
Maritain, Jacques 64-5
Marketplace of ideas 77, 80-1, 171
Matsuda, Mari 85-6
McArdle, Megan 101
McCloy v New South Wales 9, 117-8, 146, 198-204
McCrudden, Christopher 65-6, 67, 68
McHugh, Justice 127, 147-8
McIntosh, Peggy 228-9
McLachlin, Justice 81, 193, 195-6
Meagher, Dan 49
Mégret, Frédéric 60
Mental harm 140
Mere slights 17, 18
Microaggressions 137, 232
Mill, John Stuart 14, 137, 227
Milton, John 7, 83, 84
Mischief 25, 26, 49-50, 103, 106, 109, 125
Modified Lange test 9, 10, 117-8, 119, 124, 126, 131, 145, 146, 194, 196, 198, 211
Monis v The Queen 128, 147
Multiculturalism 79, 97, 98, 206-7
Muslim 134, 183, 217, 218

National Inquiry into Racist Violence 96-7, 98-9, 220-1, 222, 225

Nationality 8, 10, 11, 13, 15, 18, 20, 44, 45, 46, 48, 49, 51, 53, 55, 56, 58, 59, 60, 63, 71, 73, 77, 82, 89, 91, 92, 93, 94, 95, 100, 101, 105, 111, 115, 116, 119, 120, 121, 122, 123, 124, 125, 126, 131, 132, 133, 134, 135, 136, 138, 139, 141, 144, 145, 146, 155, 156, 157, 158, 160, 161, 168, 186, 191, 195, 206, 209, 214, 215, 216, 222, 223, 227, 228, 230, 235, 236, 237, 238, 239
Necessity 95, 199, 203-6
Negligence 139-40
Nettle, Justice 198, 201-2, 204
Nietzsche, Friedrich 230-1

Offence: see Offend, insult or humiliate and Offend, insult, humiliate or intimidate
  Definition 19
  No right not to be offended 60-1, 61-87
  Scope 15, 16, 17-8, 20, 22

Offend, insult or humiliate 9, 10, 11, 13, 20, 21, 22, 36, 43, 45, 46, 47, 48, 49, 50, 53, 60, 61, 62, 63, 65, 66, 70, 71, 73, 75, 76, 77, 82, 87, 89, 90, 92, 93, 98, 101, 102, 110, 115, 116, 126, 127, 131, 136, 145, 156, 157, 158, 159, 161, 186, 196, 197, 203, 205, 208, 209, 239, 241, 242
Offend, insult, humiliate or intimidate 8, 15, 16, 17, 18, 19, 20, 21, 53, 100, 101, 104, 105, 106, 115, 116, 119, 122, 124, 126, 155, 156, 160, 161, 163, 185, 190, 191, 209
O'Neill, Brendan 232
Orwell, George 154, 155, 159

Painter, Nell Irvin 131
Palestine 55-6
Parliament 8, 10, 17, 21, 24, 35, 80, 97, 112, 114, 122, 128, 130, 131, 132, 133, 134, 165, 167, 184, 202, 209, 213, 214
Parliamentary Research Service 24, 132-3
Philosophical liberalism 239
Plenary power 122
Police 75, 225-6
Popular sovereignty 10, 119, 122-3, 130, 145, 167
Pride 19, 20, 46, 127, 144, 231
Principle of freedom 149-52
Prior v Queensland University of Technology 180-2
Privilege 227-39
Progress 198

Public interest 16, 129, 140, 150, 161, 162, 169-71, 177, 178, 191-2, 200, 209, 211
Public order 80, 95, 153, 188-9, 242
Public place 15, 16, 155, 214, 221, 223-4
Public transport 226
Pyrrhus 183

Qualified privilege 167, 187, 189, 210

Race 8, 10, 11, 13, 15, 18, 20, 44, 45, 46, 48, 49, 51, 53, 55, 56, 58, 59, 60, 63, 71, 73, 77, 82, 85, 89, 91, 93, 94, 97, 99, 100, 101, 108, 110, 111, 112, 115, 116, 119, 120, 121, 122, 124, 125, 126, 131, 133, 134, 135, 136, 138, 139, 144, 145, 146, 155, 156, 157, 158, 160, 161, 168, 180, 186, 187, 191, 195, 205, 206, 207, 209, 214, 215, 216, 219, 222, 223, 227, 228, 229, 230, 235, 236, 237, 238, 239
  Definition, lack of 132-6
  Hatred see: Racial hatred
  Idea of 131-2

Racial discrimination 7, 8, 18, 23, 24, 26, 27, 29, 30, 31, 32, 33, 34, 36, 37, 40, 42, 43, 44, 49, 51, 52, 55, 56, 57, 58, 59, 60, 77, 84, 87, 88, 89, 90, 91, 92, 93, 94, 98, 99, 100, 101, 102, 103, 104, 105, 106, 107, 108, 109, 110, 111, 112, 113, 114, 174, 175, 176, 184, 220, 237
Racial Discrimination Act 1975 (Cth) 7, 9, 10, 13, 17, 18, 21, 23, 24, 124, 125, 158, 159, 160, 163, 174, 176, 213
  Section 9 24
  Section 12 24
  Section 18C: see Section 18C
  Section 18D: see Section 18D

Racial Discrimination Bill 1974 (Cth) 8, 125, 213, 214, 242
  Clause 28 8, 11, 213, 214, 216, 242

Racial hatred 10, 17, 18, 20, 21, 24, 26, 34, 36, 37, 38, 39, 40, 41, 42, 43, 44, 49, 51, 53, 56, 59, 62, 82, 87, 89, 90, 91, 93, 96, 97, 98, 100, 101, 102, 103, 104, 105, 106, 108, 109, 110, 112, 114, 115, 123, 125, 126, 140, 145, 146, 158, 188, 203, 205, 206, 207, 208, 209, 213, 218, 220, 224, 241
Racial Hatred Bill 1994 (Cth) 24, 91, 96, 97, 125, 184

Bills Digest 24, 133
Explanatory Memorandum 112, 125
Second Reading Speech 112, 125, 126

Racial identity 214-5
Racial superiority 24, 29, 31, 36, 37, 38, 39, 40, 41, 42, 43, 44, 46, 86, 107, 112, 142, 214
Racial tolerance 10, 21, 123, 126, 145, 146, 208, 241
Racism 8, 13, 14, 66, 85, 86, 173, 181, 213, 228, 237, 241, 242
Realm of freedom 11, 152-3
Reasonable person test 41, 128, 162, 185, 189, 224, 225
Reasonable proportionality 35, 53, 92, 93, 98, 154
Reasonable representative test 47, 48, 53, 54, 55, 57, 82, 89, 115, 157, 158, 173, 191, 205, 239
Reasonably likely 11, 15, 18, 19, 49, 54, 55, 56, 77, 82, 89, 93, 115, 119, 155, 156, 157, 158, 161, 191, 196, 205, 209
Religion 10, 51, 67, 69-70, 72, 93, 94, 111, 133, 135, 136, 138, 139, 143, 144, 159, 197, 228, 229
Remedies 26, 27, 32, 34, 87, 88, 90, 108, 110, 114, 162, 175-6, 178, 187, 212
Representative government 9, 10, 11, 12, 79, 118, 122, 123, 124, 126, 128, 131, 145, 148, 150, 163, 164, 167, 168, 173, 188, 189, 201, 203, 208, 211, 224, 241
Reputation 95, 140, 177, 187-9, 190-1, 210
Responsible government 9, 10, 12, 79, 118, 122, 123, 124, 131, 145, 148, 173, 188, 189, 201, 203, 211, 224, 241
Ressentiment 230-2, 234
Royal Commission into Aboriginal Deaths in Custody 96, 97-8, 222, 225, 226
Russell, Bertrand 155

Saeed v Minister for Immigration & Citizenship 19, 124
Schwelb, Egon 26, 27, 30, 31, 32, 33, 51, 52, 88, 108, 109, 111
Section 18C
  Bills digest 24, 133
  Explanatory memorandum 112, 125
  Insult see: Insult
  Humiliation see: Humiliation
  Intimidation see: Intimidation
  Legislative overkill 50, 93, 96, 241

INDEX 265

Legislative overreach 9, 50, 85, 86, 93, 96, 241
Offence: see Offence
Offend, insult or humiliate: see Offend, insult or humiliate
Offend, insult, humiliate or intimidate: see Offend, insult, humiliate or intimidate
Purpose: see Legitimate purpose
Second reading speech 112, 125, 126
Text 15-6
Too broad see Broad, too
Too vague: see Vague

Section 18D
Academic, artistic or scientific purpose see Academic, artistic or scientific purpose
Fair comment: see Fair comment
Good faith: see Good faith
Public interest see Public interest
Text 16
Truth: see Truth
Vague: see Vague

Security of person 61-2, 72, 90, 116, 225
Separation of powers 133-4, 193
Sexual harassment 185-6, 190
Sheehan, Paul 182-3
Sikh 134
Soutphommasane, Tim 66, 142, 184, 186, 228
Specificity requirement 8, 9, 24, 28-34
Stalking 222
State (nation-state) 8, 14, 18, 25, 26, 27, 29, 30, 31, 32, 33, 34, 36, 37, 38, 39, 41, 42, 43, 44, 51, 52, 57, 58, 59, 61, 62, 66, 70, 71, 72, 73, 77, 80, 87, 88, 90, 91, 92, 94, 95, 97, 99, 100, 102, 104, 107, 110, 111, 112, 113, 114, 133, 136, 137, 138, 139, 141, 151, 152, 154, 163, 192, 204, 216, 219, 220, 221, 225, 227, 229, 232, 241
State (of Australia) 10, 119, 120, 121, 122, 131, 145, 147, 149, 154, 157, 195, 206, 207, 210
States Parties 25, 26, 27, 29, 30, 31, 32, 33, 34, 36, 37, 38, 39, 41, 42, 43, 44, 51, 52, 57, 58, 61, 62, 87, 88, 90, 91, 94, 95, 99, 102, 104, 112, 113, 114, 241
Statutory interpretation
Broad and beneficial interpretation of protective statutes 21
Conformity to Commonwealth Constitution 21-2

Principle of legality 21, 154
Principles of interpretation 15, 18, 19, 20, 21

Steyn, Mark 178
Stone, Adrienne 179-80
Suitable 199, 203
Superiority 24, 29, 31, 36, 37, 38, 39, 40, 41, 43, 44, 46, 86, 107, 112, 142, 173, 214, 231
Taboo 136, 229
Tasmanian Dam Case 28, 30
Taylor, Harry 216
Taylor v Canadian Human Rights Commission 195-6

Teaching, education, culture and information 26, 33, 34, 89, 91
Theophanous v Herald & Weekly Times Ltd 176-8
Theoretical harm 49, 156-7, 190, 192, 205, 209
Threat 44, 51, 61, 70, 71, 84, 85, 90, 115, 116, 137, 138, 139, 144, 145, 177, 187, 211, 212, 215, 220, 221, 222, 223, 224, 225, 227, 242
Toben v Jones 18, 24, 25, 36, 96, 99-115
Justice Allsop's reasons 106-115
Justice Carr's reasons 99-106

Toohey, Justice 176-7
Torres Strait Islander 132
Treaties 15-6, 28, 60, 87, 91, 92, 96, 102, 109, 115, 117
Tribe, Laurence 193
Truth 7, 11, 77, 78, 79, 80, 81, 82, 83, 142, 169, 170, 171, 172, 177, 178, 192, 206, 209, 219

Unions NSW v New South Wales 9, 117, 146-7, 166
Unique
Human uniqueness 67, 68, 69, 70, 137
Individual uniqueness 68, 69, 71, 73, 80, 137, 138, 139, 142, 143, 144, 236

United Nations 27, 32, 43, 63, 109
United Nations General Assembly 27, 109
Universal Declaration of Human Rights 32, 34, 36, 43, 51, 52, 61, 63, 64, 65, 66, 71, 72, 73, 88, 90, 111, 142
Unreasonable 50, 93, 162, 205, 212

Vague 10, 31, 52, 60, 63, 64, 73, 85, 90, 192-7, 205, 207, 211, 219, 241
Violence 8, 11, 24, 29, 36, 37, 42, 43, 44, 49, 51, 61, 72, 84, 92, 93, 97, 98, 100, 102, 105, 109, 139, 140, 188, 214, 215, 216, 220, 221, 222, 225, 232, 242

Waldron, Jeremy 66, 188-9
Wilson, Tim 75
Woodcock, Andrew 65

www.ingramcontent.com/pod-product-compliance
Ingram Content Group UK Ltd.
Pitfield, Milton Keynes, MK11 3LW, UK
UKHW041302180426
11947UKWH00009B/631